The Beauty Trade

Oxford Studies in Gender and International Relations

Series editors: J. Ann Tickner, University of Southern California, and Laura Sjoberg, University of Florida

Enlisting Masculinity: The Construction of Gender in U.S. Military Recruiting Advertising during the All-Volunteer Force
Melissa T. Brown

Cosmopolitan Sex Workers: Women and Migration in a Global City
Christine B. N. Chin

Intelligent Compassion: Feminist Critical Methodology in the Women's International League for Peace and Freedom
Catia Cecilia Confortini

Gender, Sex, and the Postnational Defence: Militarism and Peacekeeping
Annica Kronsell

From Global To Grassroots: The European Union, Transnational Advocacy, and Combating Violence against Women
Celeste Montoya

The Political Economy of Violence against Women
Jacqui True

THE BEAUTY TRADE

Youth, Gender, and Fashion Globalization

By Angela B. V. McCracken

OXFORD
UNIVERSITY PRESS

OXFORD
UNIVERSITY PRESS

Oxford University Press is a department of the University of Oxford.
It furthers the University's objective of excellence in research, scholarship,
and education by publishing worldwide.

Oxford   New York
Auckland   Cape Town   Dar es Salaam   Hong Kong   Karachi
Kuala Lumpur   Madrid   Melbourne   Mexico City   Nairobi
New Delhi   Shanghai   Taipei   Toronto

With offices in
Argentina   Austria   Brazil   Chile   Czech Republic   France   Greece
Guatemala   Hungary   Italy   Japan   Poland   Portugal   Singapore
South Korea   Switzerland   Thailand   Turkey   Ukraine   Vietnam

Oxford is a registered trademark of Oxford University Press
in the UK and certain other countries.

Published in the United States of America by
Oxford University Press
198 Madison Avenue, New York, NY 10016

© Oxford University Press 2014

All rights reserved. No part of this publication may be reproduced, stored in a
retrieval system, or transmitted, in any form or by any means, without the prior
permission in writing of Oxford University Press, or as expressly permitted by law,
by license, or under terms agreed with the appropriate reproduction rights organization.
Inquiries concerning reproduction outside the scope of the above should be sent to the
Rights Department, Oxford University Press, at the address above.

You must not circulate this work in any other form
and you must impose this same condition on any acquirer.

Library of Congress Cataloging-in-Publication Data
McCracken, Angela B. V.
The Beauty Trade: Youth, Gender, and Fashion Globalization /
by Angela B. V. McCracken.
pages cm
Includes bibliographical references and index.
ISBN 978-0-19-990806-6 (hardback : alk. paper)   1. Beauty, Personal—Social aspects.
2. Beauty, Personal—Economic aspects.   3. Cosmetics industry—Social aspects.
4. Feminine beauty (Aesthetics)   5. Teenage girls.   6. Women—Identity.   I. Title.
HQ1219.M33 2014
306.4'613—dc23
2013022814

TABLE OF CONTENTS

List of Tables vii
List of Figures ix

Introduction: The Beauty Trade 1
1. Seeing the Global Economy of Beauty Through Gender Lenses 12
2. Here Comes the *Quinceañera*: Isn't She Beautiful? 36
3. Princess Dresses, Sexy Dances, and Eye Shadow: The Construction of a Global Political Economy of Beauty Through a Makeover 78
4. Beauty and the *Quince*: A Reproductive Economy View 93
5. Beauty Has a Price: The Global Productive Economy of Beauty 116
6. Different Brands of Beauty: Subcultures and the Global Virtual Economy 136
Conclusion: Youth, Gender and Fashion Globalization 156

Acknowledgments 171
Notes 175
Appendix A: A Note about Methods 179
Appendix B: Youth Interview Questions 183
Appendix C: Adult Interview Questions 187
Bibliography 189
Index 201

LIST OF TABLES

4.1	Summary of highly valued identities, ideologies, and institutions in the reproductive economy of beauty in the quince	106
5.1	Highly valued identities, ideologies, and institutions in the global cosmetics and toiletries industry	125
5.2	Less valued identities, ideologies, and institutions in the global cosmetics and toiletries industry	125
7.1	Highly valued identities, ideologies, and institutions in the global political economy of beauty	163
7.2	Less valued identities, ideologies, and institutions in the global political economy of beauty	163
7.3	Highly valued identities, ideologies, and institutions in the global political economy	164
7.4	Less valued identities, ideologies, and institutions in the global political economy	164

LIST OF FIGURES

2.1 A plaza in the downtown *quinceañera* and bridal shopping district   40

3.1 A *quinceañera* or a bride used in a flower shop advertisement   80

3.2 An alien-esque hairstyle advertisement at a home-based salon   91

4.1 The *Instituto Internacional de Belleza y Moda Paris* is an example of European or United States references common in the beauty industry   110

5.1 Top company shares, cosmetics, and toiletries   120

5.2 Relative employment patterns in Mexican cosmetics and toiletries industry   123

5.3 A home-based beauty salon   124

5.4 Distribution channels   126

5.5 Direct sales by product category   127

5.6 Global distribution channels—cosmetics and toiletries 2006   128

6.1 An "ethnically ambiguous" advertisement in the Medrano district, the most popular fashion district among the aspiring middle class in Guadalajara   143

The Beauty Trade

Introduction: The Beauty Trade

Everybody line up! The show is about to start.
Places! The show is about to start.
You have to show a look, have a look, or give a look.

Faces.
Beautiful.
No one *ugly* allowed (laughing)...

Fashion is the art, designers are the gods.
Models play the part of angels in the dark.
Which one of you would ever dare to go against that beauty is a trade and everyone is paid?

Fashionista, how do you look? (refrain)

New York, London, Paris, Milan, Tokyo, I think it's in Japan, Asia, Malaysia, Las Vegas to play, LA, if you pay my way... (refrain)

Who are you wearing?

Sean John, Calvin Klein, Donna Karan's fashion line.
Valentino, YSL, Ferragamo and Chanel.
Halston, Gucci, Fiorucci, don't forget my Pucci.
Fendi and Armani, God, I miss Gianni.
Kenneth Cole, Michael Kors, Mr. Ford I can't afford.
D&G and BCBG, looking good is never easy.
Alexandre Herchcovitch, Naomi Campbell—such a bitch!
I wanna be *delgada* [tr: thin] to fit into my Prada.
Oscar de la Renta.
Louis Vuitton.
Imitation of Christ, beauty has a price...

—Jimmy James, *Fashionista*, 2006

Jimmy James's single *Fashionista* is a club hit in 2006 and 2007 in Mexico's second-largest metropolitan area, Guadalajara, Jalisco, and while it makes my feminist red flags go up, a crowd of youth move rhythmically to its repetitive beat at almost every nightclub I visit, sweat to it in exercise classes, shop as it plays in fashion stores, blast it out of their car stereos, and dance to it at disc-jockeyed celebrations such as weddings, first communions, and *fiestas de quince años*. There is a small set, maybe ten, of electronic pop hits that show up on almost every disc jockey's list, and this is one of them.

Similar in beat and style to all the rest, one might question whether it has any social significance at all in this Spanish-speaking country. Except for two words—*fashionista* meaning fashionable woman or girl in several languages, and *delgada*, meaning "thin" in Spanish—James's call to his audience to make itself fashionably beautiful in face, clothing, body shape, and poise, and at a hefty price, is sung in English. The song is one of a long series of global pop hits that are played repeatedly one year and infrequently thereafter. The tune and its lyrics might reasonably be considered inconsequential, social-scientifically-speaking, in urban Mexico.

On the other hand, some would include *Fashionista* among a list of cultural forms, like Miss Universe beauty pageants and *Baywatch*, that illustrate how the fashion and pop industries replicate manufactured, commercial aesthetic ideals globally, contributing to the dispersion, or even imperialism, of a global, universal, Eurocentric beauty ideal (Moskalenko 1996; Li 1998; Altman 2002; Cudd 2005). In this view, globalization is creating a universal beauty ideal based on Western ideals of thinness, Whiteness, Anglo-American facial features, and consumption that erodes local culture to the detriment of women. A new global beauty ideal enslaves women to consumption, poor self-image, and dangerous dieting. Both beauty and globalization are categories of analysis that are often attributed powers of relentless domination and imperialism over women's bodies (Wolf 1991), and non-Western cultures (Moskalenko 1996). Local discussions of Western beauty imperialism are often used to decry globalization for corrupting women, and lead to a backlash of discourses of control and religious piety for women (Ong 2010: 183-199).

In actuality, the social significance of *Fashionista*, as well as the industry and fashionistas that populate its verse, is more complicated. Discourses on fashion and beauty like *Fashionista*, and the institutions and images that it cites, are neither irrelevant nor omnipotent to cultural globalization. Rather, the song is part of a global political economy of beauty wherein production, marketing, distribution, and consumption are intertwined with the construction of gendered bodies, youth cultures, social identification, the blurring of distinction between public and private spheres, and the generation of fashion entrepreneurialism. Perhaps most surprisingly, the global political economy of beauty is responsible for the spread of diversity, not uniformity, in beauty cultures. The global political economy of beauty is not defined or even significantly characterized by the monolithic spread of Anglo-American beauty ideals corrupting youth's innocence. To the contrary, the globalization of beauty is a phenomenon propelled by youth, eager for belonging and originality, using every mechanism at their disposal to connect with something bigger. The global economy of beauty is not a monolithic imposition on women and young people, but a phenomenon generated by young people, mostly women, laboring in, teaching, and consuming beauty. At its heart, the global economy of beauty is both shaped by and shaping intimate practices and imaginations, leading to unexpected outcomes and transformations, as opposed to an externally imposed globalization of Western commercial beauty ideals and practices.

Fashionista itself hints at the global economy to which I refer, as it reveals a complex beauty industry: beauty as a trade, fashion cosmopolitanism, global branding, the imperatives to be considered beautiful, fashionable, and thin, and historically new forms of sexual dancing. The song hints at a global economy of beauty that includes the highly valued: designers, models, celebrities, art, originality, brands, consumers, cities, thinness, and investment in beauty with the exhortations that "Looking good is never easy" and "beauty has a price." Ugliness is also present, though the "ugly" are explicitly excluded from the song's fantastic images of club dancing, shopping, modeling, designing, traveling, and selling; the ugly are not allowed. So, too, are the lesser-valued aspects of the global industry of beauty excluded from the song: manufacturing, copying, brand piracy, direct-selling, second-hand reselling, the out-of-fashion, the counter-cultural, the fat. Yet together both the highly valued and the lesser valued participants and processes in the beauty and fashion industries make up the *politics*[1] of the global beauty industry.

The politics of the global beauty economy, however, are not defined by straightforward winners and losers. To the contrary, innovative youth, women entrepreneurs, and multinational companies all enter into the trade with something to gain: social identification or differentiation, extra income, and even fun. For example, young women seek a sense of confidence, belonging, and advantage in finding employment and romantic partners by learning to put on cosmetics in accordance with fashion trends. This point of view on the global economy and globalization is therefore an antidote to the widespread assumptions about inexorable globalization causing cultural obliteration and the corruption of femininity, in the tradition of several feminist critiques of globalization studies (Ong 2010; Freeman 2000, 2001, 2010; Bergeron 2001; True 2003).

And yet, the benefits of participation in the global economy of beauty are highly uneven. The power relations evident in its construction are not defined by those with power and those without, but rather in the privileges associated with the identities, institutions, and ideologies that it rewards. Thus the global economy of beauty, through its intimate involvement in the production of gendered subjects, social belonging and differentiation, and capitalist entrepreneurialism, is primarily political because it is a product of, and reproduces, gender, race, class, and national power. Gender[2] is particularly relevant to the global political economy of beauty because beautification and fashion are central to the construction of gendered bodies, so the global beauty industries are playing an important role in constructing gender difference and, by extension, gendered[3] power. As a popular method of social identification and differentiation, youth participation in the global beauty economy creates both fashion trends and their globalization, reproducing gendered and racial divisions.

At the same time, as it is a product of youth cultural practices and highly fluid across geographic boundaries, the global economy of beauty is susceptible to disruptions of hierarchies of privilege. For example, rather than spreading a Western Anglo-American ideal of thinness and beauty that wipes out local beauty cultures, the global beauty economy is actually responsible for more colorful, multicultural ideals of beauty in Mexico than have been known in recent history. Additionally, the scope and forms of commercialization of beauty products and services has facilitated the widespread involvement of women in capitalist entrepreneurialism. Finally, the enormity of beauty commercialization and women's participation in it is contributing to large-scale blurring of boundaries between public and private spheres, especially for women.

The developments in the global economy of the twentieth and twenty-first centuries that are commonly referred to as globalization[4] or global restructuring provide several reasons to inquire into how global flows of goods, information, and ideas about beauty circulate and how gendered bodies are constructed under transforming social, cultural, economic, and technological conditions. Beauty products, images, and ideas have become a significant part of the global economy; beauty product distribution is global, reaching even regions with little infrastructure; mass media and product advertising are increasingly translated and broadcast across languages; migrants increasingly cross borders. News media frequently report the global dispersion of skin lighteners, plastic surgery procedures, and body ideals. In academic scholarship, the global spread of beauty products, media, and Anglo-American standards of beauty in non-Western countries are frequently cited as examples of cultural globalization and cosmopolitanism.[5] And yet, despite repeated reference, the globalization of beauty products, practices, and ideas is rarely explored as an issue of global political and economic importance. An area of intense media coverage, and a frequent point of reference for the argument that the world is shrinking, culturally speaking, the global beauty economy is fascinating to many, but remains little understood.

Why should the globalization of fashion be taken seriously for its political economy? Because understanding the political economy of the global beauty industry can inform us both about privilege and power in the beauty industries, and about gender and intimacy in the global political economy. Feminist scholarship on beauty practices has long argued that beauty products, ideals, and practices are fraught with the politics of gender, race, and social hierarchy. A political economy perspective adds to the understanding of material and ideological patterns of privilege within the beauty industries. This is important because women historically are the principal consumers, tastemakers, producers, and often-time entrepreneurs in the beauty trade (Jones 2010; Peiss 1998), but are frequently seen as exploited ideologically (Bartky 1990) and materially through their participation in beautification and its related industry (Wolf 1991). This presents an interesting question: are women or men benefiting from or being exploited by the beauty industry? Is it empowering or undermining women's agency? A political economy perspective, by focusing on power in the industry, can help to unravel the apparent paradox between women's high-volume participation in and supposed exploitation by the beauty economies.

In addition, a political economy perspective is useful for understanding how privilege in the beauty industries is tied up with the global political economy. Due to the importance of beauty products, images and ideas to the global political economy, there is now a need to understand the politics of beauty in the context of a process of economic, political, and cultural globalization. As beauty ideals and practices are contextually dependent on cultural norms and expectations, globalization has changed the context within which beauty cultures and politics operate. The globalization of fashion has introduced foreign practices and products into local beauty cultures. The arguments about Western beauty imperialism generally come from observations of this globalization. The consideration of a global political economy of beauty is therefore an opportunity to explore the feminist argument that the politics of the market economy cannot be understood in isolation from reproductive work (Bernería 1982; Mies 1986; Elson 1991; Bakker 1994; Barker 2005) and cultural economies (Ong 2010; Peterson 2003, 2009), as well as the claims that there is a new beauty imperialism. By taking a global political perspective on the beauty trade, this book exposes how the process of beautification and youth social identification through fashion are driving forces of globalization, and how beauty globalization is shaping and transforming gender norms, consumption, and labor in Mexico.

Feminist scholars have already begun to explore the political economy of globalizing beauty industries. Feminist scholarship on labor in the fashion and apparel industries exposes how Northern women's increased fashion consumption contributes to demand for Southern women's labor in the apparel industry (Collins 2003; Enloe 2004). Shop-floor analyses explore how export-oriented fashion industries exploit existing and create new gender and racial hierarchies (Salzinger 2003; Elias 2004). Seager (2003) illustrates the heavy concentration of fashion and cosmetics consumption in the North, even as it proliferates in less developed regions. True (2000) argues that the spread of Western beauty media to Eastern Europe has had contradictory consequences, introducing both Western gendered notions of beauty consumption and feminist discourses of empowerment. Others have begun to explore how the changing context of globalization intersects with historical beauty ideals and practices, creating new ideals of beauty tied up with nationalism, cosmopolitan ideals, and gendered hierarchies (Cohen et al. 1996; Niessen and Brydon 1998; Adrian 2003). These insights into the globalizing beauty industries reveal that beauty production and consumption are closely tied to intersections of global, national, local, gendered, and other axes of privilege and power.

Not only is political economy important to the study of power in the beauty industry; the beauty industries are also key to understanding the global political economy. Grasping how power and privilege operate in the beauty industry is especially helpful in understanding and illustrating how gender, race, and identity are integral to the global political economy. Consider the potential consequences to factories, advertising, chemical laboratories, chemical plants, regulators, lobbyers, television, public relations, magazines, publishing, salons, beauty schools, beauty services, distributors, retail sales, and direct sales if the $274.8 billion US dollar global cosmetics and toiletries industry were to collapse. Or consider the collapse of the $1.1 trillion USD clothing and footwear industry (Euromonitor 2008, data reflects 2006). A shock of this magnitude would ripple throughout the global economy, with unknowable consequences. But, one might say, so would the collapse of the untold-billions global industry in illegal narcotics, or the multibillion dollar economy in soft drinks. What distinguishes a hypothetical collapse in the beauty industry, however, is its unique set of politics that are distinctly shaped by gender, race, nation, competing identities, and visions of modernity. Without things like hair gel and eye shadow and butt-lifting, the embodied expressions of gender dichotomies, and the almost all-female workforce, the beauty industries would be substantially deflated. The global cosmetics industry is unique due to the unique politics of the global political economy of beauty. That is, the configurations of gender, race, and national power in the global economy of beauty necessitate attention to the gender, race, social, and national politics implicated in its success.

In order to understand the political economy of beauty in relation to global flows, this book asks how beauty images, products, and ideals circulate in the industry. It also asks: Who benefits from the beauty industry? How do adolescents experience and act on the globalizing beauty industry? Are youths' norms of beauty and gender shifting in ways that signify changes in gender, race, or national identity constructions?

Furthermore, in focusing on beauty images, products, and ideals, the book addresses the widespread but virtually unexplored assumption that the global beauty industry is a monolithic, Western-centric trade that is eliminating local beauty cultures. In order to evaluate this popular assumption, the book traces beauty product and image consumption, inquiring as to how products and images come into use. Tracing the circulation of beauty products, images, and ideas in Guadalajara begins with the popular practice of the *quince años*, a coming-of-age celebration for fifteen-year-old girls, within which the process of beautification and the presentation of the beautiful Mexican *señorita* are the most important features.

From the vantage point of urban Mexico, I further ask: Do beauty products and images enter local markets from Anglo-American centers of power, creating a homogenous global beauty culture? How do beauty products come to be adopted into people's intimate beautification practices? Does beauty product consumption include an explicit or implicit consumption of "global beauty?"

By posing the classic feminist question of who benefits from the beauty industry, I begin to explore privilege and power, again interrogating the assumption that local cultures or local gender norms are obliterated by global beauty industries. In this spirit, I ask whether global beauty norms and practices reinscribe colonial race and gender relations, for example through image and consumption, instead of force and occupation? Is the beauty industry empowering or exploitative? Is agency exercised in beauty? At the same time, these questions address beauty industry claims that women benefit from their involvement in the beauty trade. These questions address marketing claims that beauty makes life better, the Mexican government-mandated disclaimer on all cosmetic and hygiene ads that "health is beauty" (*Salud es Belleza*), or claims by direct-selling cosmetics firms that they offer women a path to economic empowerment.

The questions of how beauty products come to be adopted into people's intimate beautification practices and whether their consumption includes an explicit or implicit consumption of "global beauty" are guided by the puzzle of how local consumption relates to globalized production, marketing, and distribution in the beauty industries. Of additional interest is whether and how the use of beauty products, images, and ideas are linked to ideas of global beauty, and whether that has identifiable significance for the construction of subjects, gender norms, social hierarchies, and ultimately the global political economy of beauty.

PLAN OF THE BOOK

Chapter one provides a framework for exploring the global political economy of beauty through gender lenses.[6] Weaving together the concept of beautification as a social and identity-forming process; feminist global political economy; methods of ethnographic inquiry; and the popular practice of the *quince años*, it establishes both the empirical and theoretical tools that readers will need to begin to understand the global political economy of beauty and how it is shaped by and shapes beautification on the ground.

Chapter two explores in more depth the *quince años* and the beautiful *quinceañera*. Commonly compared to a Western-style wedding without a groom, the *quince años* is a Latin American coming-of-age tradition that marks a girl's passage to adolescence. It bears resemblance to commercial weddings in many ways, and also includes a growing list of symbolic rituals, exchanges, and theater that establish social relations within and among the church, families, social networks, and generations.

Chapter two argues that the process of beautification leading up to the *quince* and the presentation of the *quinceañera* to her audience have replaced the church service and meal as the most important part of the tradition. By means of the beautification process and entering into heterosexual relationships, formalized in the *quince años* pageant, girls become *señoritas*, or "misses." Through a months-long beautification process, the girl's beauty makeover has become the most significant coming-of-age ritual. While the *quince* is not universally practiced in Mexico, the makeover is. As a result, the *quince* as practiced at the beginning of the twenty-first century, more than a religious rite of passage, is a special case of a now-universal rite of passage: the beauty makeover.

Chapter three develops the argument that the production of feminine beauty is intimately linked to globalization, both shaping and being shaped by the global political economy of beauty. Using the beautification rituals of the *quinceañera* as a window on the economy of beauty in Guadalajara, the chapter explores how that process is tied to the global economy through reproductive, productive, and virtual economies. Through the specific lenses of the *quinceañera* ball gown, dance performance in the celebration, and employment of cosmetics, this chapter explores how the politics of the global economy of feminine beauty is articulated on the ground, and how beautification on the ground is shaped by global economies. The reproductive, productive, and virtual categories demonstrate the diversity of dimensions to the *quince*, as well as the usefulness of the categories themselves. The global political economy of beauty has both diversifying and reinforcing effects on traditional gendered norms in the *quince años*. Increasing individualization and commercialization of the tradition enables and encourages varied approaches to the celebration of the fifteen- year milestone. And yet the channels of production and reproduction in the celebration continue to reinforce religious and patriarchal family-based norms of hierarchy. The beautification of the *quinceañera* also sheds light on the gendered processes of globalization. The globalization of the beautifying industries is successful in large part due to gendered production, reproduction, and consumption.

Chapter four further builds on the argument that beauty economies are global, extending out into the role the reproductive economy plays in the circulation of beauty products and in the construction of youth's beauty practices and norms. The chapter further asks which identities, ideologies, and institutions are privileged in the production of the beautiful *quinceañera*, and how youth respond to the reproductive economy of beauty.

The key role of the reproductive economy in the *quince años* is as a major conduit for the social reproduction of gendered beauty norms. It contributes to the reproduction of social hierarchies that privilege masculinities; institutions such as family, culture, and religion; and ideologies of patriarchy, racism, capital commercialization, and individual consumption.

Families, particularly mothers and close female relatives, play an important role in guiding *quinceañeras* in the production of the *quince años*. The families attempt to imbue the tradition with cultural, social, and religious meaning and values. Celebrants contest and negotiate with their families in an attempt to make their *quince* special and unique. Youths' pursuit of originality propels commercialization, individualization, and changes in beautification norms in the *quince* market. Negotiations among families lead to the reproduction of some norms and values, and to the transformation of others. Notably, both male and female youth are adopting increasingly varied and personalized tastes and diverging from norms of modesty and circumspection.

Building on the argument that local beautification is shaped by and shaping the global economy of beauty, chapter five extends out from the site of the *quinceañera* and into the global productive economy of beauty. Using the heuristic device of the "productive economy," this chapter focuses on a slice of the global productive economy of beauty that is of particular importance to the production of the beautiful *quinceañera* and illustrative of the politics of the productive economy of beauty: the global cosmetics industry. Cosmetic modification is an important part of the beautification process in the makeover, and this chapter looks at the cosmetic products used by *quinceañeras* in the context of a global political economy of beauty. The chapter addresses two questions that are central to this book: How do cosmetic beauty products circulate between the global economy and *quinceañeras* in Guadalajara, Mexico? Is the beauty industry in Guadalajara privileging groups by race, class, gender, and nation?

The analysis finds that beauty commercialization and the spread of entrepreneurialism is very strong in the beauty economy, particularly driven by expansion in direct sales marketing and distribution of beauty products, as well as a surge in the commercialization of personal beauty services. The rapidly expanding direct sales industry in beauty products is an overwhelming player in the global cosmetics industry, evident among *quinceañeras* as well as regional and global data on cosmetic sales. The service industry, from branding and marketing to consultation and makeup application, also plays an increasingly important role in the global productive economy of beauty and in how products circulate.

The global productive economy of cosmetics is gendered in a way that provides opportunities to some women, but at the expense of recreating social hierarchies. Everyone gets paid, but gendered social hierarchies still shape the industry and the extent to which each participant benefits. On the other hand, the cosmetics industry also shapes gender. From beautification to paid work to semi-informal direct sales, to the home, the market, and the body, gender is being shaped in the cosmetics industry.

Finally, chapter six extends out into the global virtual economy of beauty. The chapter focuses on the experiences and expressions of non-*quinceañera* beautification, as seen through the globalization of youth subcultures. Several study participants did not practice the *quince* themselves because *quince* ideas of beauty are considered conventional, and these youth rejected conventional beauty culture, instead creating and participating in subcultures of beauty. Following these youth, this chapter explores how the diversity of youth subcultures is contesting the globalization of hegemonic images of beauty. It shifts the focus away from the globalization of the mainstream "beauty pageant" variety of beauty to subculture or counter-cultural globalizations. While these youth do not subscribe to mainstream beauty standards and practices, their images of fashion are equally, if not more, globalized. These subcultures show how the global political economy of beauty and fashion actually facilitates increasing diversity on the ground, which in turn facilitates increased contestation of social norms. Still, even among subcultural groups, many hegemonic ideas about feminine appearances persist.

CHAPTER 1
Seeing the Global Economy of Beauty Through Gender Lenses

In order to gain insight into the global political economy of beauty in Mexico, this book uses four main analytical entry points: the *quince años*, or "sweet fifteen" celebration for female adolescents; youth beautification practices; feminist global political economy; and ethnographic inquiry. Woven together, the result is an analysis of the global political economy of beauty as seen through the beauty practices, ideas, and products employed on the ground by youth in urban Mexico.

THE *QUINCE AÑOS*

The *quince años* is among the modern Mexican traditions recorded by the national press since at least the 1940s. This is a ritual coming-of-age celebration that includes a religious service, a party (the *fiesta de quince años*) with dancing and a meal, and a growing number of symbolic rituals that signify the passage from girlhood. Beginning with preparation up to a year in advance, the tradition includes an elaborate production of youthful feminine beauty and dancing, where gendered performance of beauty is staged front and center. Indeed, hand-in-hand with the widespread commercialization of beauty products and services observable in Guadalajara, the makeover and presentation of feminine beauty has far surpassed the religious service and meal as the most time-consuming, expensive, and consequential part of the *quince años*.

The *quince* serves as a useful vantage point for studying beauty ideas, practices, and products because it is a popular and public expression of modern Mexican womanhood, and of feminine beauty in particular. A celebration exclusive to the privileged few in the 1940s, the *quince años* was popularized in the 1980s, and it has now become accessible to and practiced by families of all social classes, although particularly by the aspiring middle class. While believed to have originated in Mexico, the *quince*, as it is most commonly referred to in Guadalajara, is growing in popularity not only in Mexico, but also in the United States and other Latin American countries.

Frequently compared to conventional weddings in the United States, the occasion has become an opportunity for intense consumption. During field research, I had the opportunity to learn about *fiestas* that cost as little as a home-cooked meal for friends, to as much as 13,000 USD, and everywhere in between. Parties among the highly privileged cost significantly more, as can be seen in photography and announcements in the social columns of local newspapers. As the tradition has become commercialized and popularized, the role of beautification in every stage of the event's consideration, preparation, and execution has become more central and clearly observable. Due to its importance in Mexican society, relevance to youth as a social marker, and focus on gendered transitions through beautification, the *quince* is an exceptional occasion for exploring the ideals, practices, and processes of beautification among youth in Mexico. In addition, the *quince*'s association with Mexican tradition makes it an ideal opportunity for studying "traditional" beauty ideals and practices of girls, as well as how these traditions are changing and being contested.

The fact that the *quince* is a youth-centered practice is especially relevant to the study of beauty industry globalization. Neither at the historic centers of fashion industries nor on the outskirts, youth in urban Mexico are nonetheless at the forefront of beauty industry globalization. At the crossroads of trade, political, familial, and cultural globalization in the Western Hemisphere, urban Mexico is experiencing a process of intense globalization. Youth, especially girls, are the prospectors of beauty globalization, continually seeking information and products and new ways of being beautiful. By exploring the frontiers of information and cultural exchange, and as the inventors of new beauty traditions, youth in Mexico play an important role in propelling beauty globalization. By foregrounding youths' perspective and participation in the beauty industries, this book starts its analysis with the construction of beauty on the ground, among its most active, inquisitive, and demanding proponents.

BEAUTIFICATION

The second analytical entry point to the global political economy of beauty is the process of beautification itself. The process of beautification includes the use of beauty products, ideas, and practices by individuals in a manner that is both designed to meet social aspirations (Entwistle 2000) and affective on the body (Mahmood 2001). That is, the book asks how *quinceañeras* dress up for their *quince años*, and what meaning that dressing has for their social aspirations and for their identity. The book also asks how youth conceive of beauty in general, and how they adorn and modify themselves in everyday situations, encompassing a broad range of beautification practices. In this way, the process of beautification is examined in the slightly rarified presentation of Mexican womanhood in the *quince*, as well as everyday and countercultural beautification.

Beautification includes dress, but also other types of adornment and bodily modification. Adornments range from clothing to accessories to cosmetics to perfumes. Modifications range from haircuts to weight loss to cosmetic surgery. Beautification is therefore not only material and ideological fashion that is shaped by social context, but also includes bodily practices, such as diet and exercise, that are affective on the body and the lived experience. Through shaping the appearance of the body, beautification not only reflects social belonging and differentiation (Cannon 1998), but actively shapes social and intimate practices and values (Mahmood 2001). Given both the social and identity-forming dimensions of beautification, the changing context of social belonging and differentiation—globalization—is all the more relevant to bodily practices and the construction of identities, making beautification an interesting and important lens on globalization.

The process of beautification is particularly closely tied to gender identification and differentiation. Beautification practices help create bodies and comportment that are "recognizably feminine" (Bartky 1990: 65; Chapkis 1986; Young 2005) or masculine. That is, beautification practices contribute to the creation and communication of gendered differences and belonging. Since gender differences are historically and almost universally associated with heterosexual masculine privilege, beautification is a useful entry point for seeing how one significant dimension of gender is constructed, and how these constructions may be changing.

This conceptualization of beautification as is part of social belonging and identity formation, is distinct from arguments that beautification is universally oppressive of women. Feminist theorists and activists have long argued that body modification and fashion are evidence and tools of gendered power, and that they are oppressive. Feminist activism against culturally dominant beauty standards and practices date back at least to nineteenth-century fights against restrictive and heavy skirts (Banner 1983). Feminist activists in the early twentieth century used lipstick (Peiss 1998) and bloomers (Cunningham 2003) as ways to contest feminine docility and confinement. During the feminist movement that began in the 1960s, activists argued extensively that beautification is part of a body politics defined by patriarchal oppression. Liberal, socialist, and radical feminist activists and scholars of the "second wave" (Alcoff 1997) critiqued feminine beautification. They saw social norms for women's dress and makeup as physically limiting, visually marking women as "other" than men, sexually objectifying, and oppressive. These popular feminist arguments led to widespread feminist rejection of mainstream standards of feminine beautification (de Beauvoir cited in Wilson 2003, Morgan 1970).[1] A liberal feminist stance toward beauty ideals as oppressive was famously expressed in *The Beauty Myth* (Wolf 1991), which argued that unattainable ideals of feminine beauty keep women from achieving equality with men by undermining women's self-confidence, wasting their time and money, and encouraging debilitating practices such as eating disorders and cosmetic surgery.

As tempting as these arguments are for their clear vision, they are based on the assumption that all women experience conventional beauty standards as oppressive. This position neglects to consider that women in different subject positions, for example poor women, women of color, or women of different nationalities, may experience beautification differently from one another. The argument that beautification is oppressive also assumes that women are victims, not agents, of beauty and beautification. Feminist scholars and activists have extensively criticized the association between womanhood and victimhood for being both inaccurate and disempowering to women.

A second body of feminist scholarship on beautification takes different subject positions and women's agency seriously, arguing that beautification is not universally oppressive of women. This literature is shaped by the argument that "woman" is not a universal category, and that categorizing women universally as victims of patriarchal oppression is neither accurate nor useful (e.g., Hull et al. 1982; Moraga and Anzaldúa 1983; Mohanty 1988). Considering non-Anglo-American viewpoints, beautification could be seen as itself an expression of privilege of white women (Chapkis 1986; Leeds-Craig 2002). For example, Maxine Leeds-Craig questioned universal feminist abhorrence of beauty contests, pointing out that in 1968, the same year that (mostly white) feminists protested the Miss America contest by throwing their bras into a garbage can (hence garnering the moniker "bra-burners"), African American women held their own protest to contest their exclusion from the pageant (2002).

Some women may find pleasure or agency in beautification (Cahill 2003; Davis 1995). Etcoff (2000) goes so far as to argue that beauty standards are based on universal, biological imperatives, which makes beauty, and the pursuit of beauty (Etcoff et al. 2011), empowering in labor markets and romantic endeavors. According to this theory of the "beauty premium," there are quantifiable gains to be made through approximating social standards of beauty (Mobius and Rosenblat 2006; Hamermesh and Biddle 1994), and losses and discrimination for not doing so (Rhode 2011; Hamermesh 2011).

This book takes an ambivalent stance toward the argument that beauty standards are based on biological universals, since, despite any supposed universals, there is abundant evidence that beauty standards vary substantially by culture (Cassidy 1991; Cohen et al. 1996; Gremillion 2005) and that those culturally defined standards are intimately tied to power—be it representative or material power in the labor market, the marriage market, the sex industry, or the beauty and fashion industry. There are gains to be made and agency to be exercised in the process of beautification. Participants in the beauty economy in Guadalajara certainly see the possibility for reward through beautification, the commercialization of beauty, and the public presentation of beauty. In addition, participants in the study for this book understood that there were losses associated with not partaking in the beauty economy, making their involvement virtually obligatory.

And yet, not everyone exercises agency in the process of beautification equally. Individuals' agency and power in beautification are shaped by social relations of power and privilege. This leads to the question of what the process of beautification means *in the social context of Guadalajara*. Who gains, and what, through beauty economy participation? Who loses, and what, by not participating? Neither all women nor all men benefit from the beauty premium; a few benefit more than others. A universal theory of beautification as the manifestation or exercise of patriarchal oppression is therefore untenable. In remedy, this book conceptualizes beautification as a process that is shaped by and shapes both social context and individual identities.

The lens of beautification is useful for understanding the social relations within the beauty industries in Mexico because it does not assume universal notions of "woman," "man," and beauty, but rather asks how beautification is practiced on the ground. It is especially useful in that it foregrounds youths' actual practices and perspective. An on-the-ground perspective is important when considering whether and how the globalization of conventional Anglo-American beauty ideals has meaning for youth in Mexico. The lens of beautification, as it focuses on the use of beauty products, ideas, and practices in their social context, provides such an entry point.

In addition, the lens of beautification makes the body, rather than patriarchy, a central focus of study. In this sense, the lens of beautification makes more explicit the centrality of bodies in the global political economy. Feminist International Relations (IR)[2] scholars have called attention to how feminized bodies are central to the workings of the global political economy through their gendered work in the labor market, in the reproductive sphere, and in the informal market. For example, the feminized and racialized body itself, and its representation as being compliant and with nimble fingers, has been crucial to the successful feminization of export-processing labor (Elson and Pearson 1981; Salzinger 2003; Enloe 2004). Likewise, the sexualized and racialized body is central to the operations of the international sex industry (Pettman 1996; Agathangelou 2004). The feminine body is a key site for the construction and contestation of competing nationalisms (Grewal and Kaplan 1994; Yuval-Davis 1997; Tickner 1996; Enloe 2004). Women experience particular forms of violence due to the gendered nature of militaries and war (Moon 1997; Tickner 2001), as in the case of sexual violence when rape is used as a tool of war. Contests over women's bodies are a consistent source of NGO and social movement interest, as was the case of the anti-footbinding movement (Keck and Sikkink 1998) and, more recently, in campaigns against female genital mutilation. Furthermore, women shape globalization through fashion entrepreneurialism and fashion magazines (Freeman 2000; True 2003). This feminist scholarship of global politics has established that war, political economy, social movements, globalization, nationalism, and many of the foundational concepts of the discipline of International Relations are shaped by assumptions about what is masculine and feminine. That is, both international relations and the discipline of International Relations (IR) are gendered.

In addition to revealing how international relations and IR are shaped by gender, feminist IR is a body of literature that can further be used to understand how the gendering of the body itself, for instance through beautification, shapes international relations and IR. For example, rape in war, motherhood in service of the nation, and the feminization of the export-processing development model are instances of how gendered bodies shape the practices of international relations and the study of them as a discipline.

This book highlights and extends the feminist project of making the politics of gender and bodies visible in international relations by looking at the very gendering of the body through beautification and how that gendering is influenced by and influences processes of globalization. Drawing on the practices, ideas, and production of beautification, this research takes the project of linking bodies to international relations further, by making explicit that the production of gendered bodies and the working of the global political economy of beauty are interdependent.

FEMINIST GLOBAL POLITICAL ECONOMY

The third entry point on the global beauty industry is that of feminist global political economy (GPE).[3] As discussed above, a political economy approach is useful for understanding privilege and power in the global beauty industry. For analytical purposes this text draws on Peterson's (2003) framing of the global political economy as interdependent reproductive, productive, and virtual economies. This "RPV" framework is useful because it links production, consumption, and cultural signs; it weaves together analysis of identities, social institutions, and ideologies; and it is explicitly feminist.

The RPV framing posits that reproductive, productive, and virtual economies are "intertwining and inextricable" despite having been historically categorized and studied separately. Conventional IPE has focused on exchange in the public sphere of markets, or the productive economy. The reproductive economy, exchange that is responsible for biological and social reproduction, and the virtual economy, exchange of cultural symbols and signs, conventionally have not been considered part of economic activity. To illustrate, the productive economy of beautification in the *quince* would be the market exchange of cosmetics, fashion, and beauty services. The reproductive economy of *quinceañera* beautification would be the unpaid care labor invested in teaching beautification. The virtual economy of beauty in the *quince* would be the exchange of images and ideas about beauty through media of communication. Scholarship on IPE typically focuses on the productive economy. Scholarship on beauty typically focuses either on the role of media in dissemination of images of beauty or on the profits to be made in the productive economy of beauty. The RPV framework weaves these two economies with the reproductive economy, giving much more weight to the agency of women in building and driving the beauty economy through social reproduction.

In order to bridge the productive with reproductive and virtual economies, the RPV framework draws on several generations of feminist political economy that has tried to expose the false distinction between reproductive and productive economies. This scholarship has argued that the division between private and public spheres in the economy (Youngs 2000), between paid employment and unpaid reproductive labor in the household (Waring 1988), and between formal and informal employment (Prügl 1999) is a false distinction that solely credits the formal, paid sector for contributing to wealth. As a result, household, informal, and unpaid work has historically been treated as unimportant and infinite. By categorizing reproductive labor as both unimportant and infinite, the work that women are mostly responsible for has been both uncounted and overextended.

The RPV framing further bridges the reproductive and productive economies with virtual exchange by drawing on scholarship that argues that, due to technological innovations in communication, production, exchange, and consumption of information are now central to the functioning of the global economy. In addition, there is a marked unevenness in access to the benefits and contributions to the virtual economy (Castells 2000). The RPV framework bridges these two literatures with conventional IPE, arguing that the market, reproductive, and virtual economies are practically inseparable dimensions to the global economy, and therefore must be studied together in order to understand the global economy.

The reproductive, productive, and virtual economies are treated as separate categories for the purpose of analysis of the global beauty economy, although the categories are interdependent and mutually constitutive. This treatment may appear as contradictory given the argument that these categories are so intertwining as to be inextricable. Elisabeth Prügl (2010) raises this concern, suggesting that by separating reproductive, productive, and virtual economies conceptually, the RPV framework actually preserves the separation between the categories, and thereby potentially reinforces the historical placement of "women's work" in the unpaid "reproductive sphere," as a separate, nonproductive category. This "othering" of women's work is what has made it unimportant to economists and political science, and undervalued in general. While Prügl raises an important consideration, it does not obviate the use of the RPV framework for analytical purposes. The RPV framework employs historically relevant categorizations of exchange; virtually all scholarship in each category of exchange—paid, unpaid, cultural—draws on substantially different literatures, and very little such scholarship stretches across all three categories, much less at the level of the global economy. Therefore, the RPV framework and this book use the RPV categories in a way that is informed by historical conceptions about women's work, and at the same time makes visible the limits that the categories impose on understanding the global economy. For instance, it is difficult to categorize dressmaking at home for a *quince* as solely based in productive, reproductive, or cultural exchange. It is, indeed, the product of all three together. It is through failing to successfully delineate activity in the beauty industry between productive, reproductive, and virtual exchange in this book that I have come to agree with both Peterson and Prügl. The categories are, in fact, inextricable, and their separation is based on a pre-information revolution understanding of global economics as well as a myth that women's work exists in a private sphere in which such work is not economic, political, public, or valuable.

The RPV framework is especially convenient for the analysis of the beauty and fashion industries because beauty product manufacture, marketing, distribution, and consumption are intimately connected to social and cultural reproduction. The RPV approach is particularly appropriate for the study of global beauty politics because the beauty and fashion industries are so deeply cultural and social that a purely productive economy approach could not capture the degree of the industry's embeddedness in social and virtual life. Indeed, the beauty and fashion industries may illustrate better than any the deep and intimate connections between reproductive, productive, and virtual economies. By linking the beauty industry to reproductive, productive, and virtual economies, the framework also advances the goal of defining a global political economy of beauty beyond arguments that the political economy of fashion is primarily defined by production by "Southerners" for "Northern" consumers (Skoggard 1998; Enloe 2004).

An important feature of the RPV lens is feminism. Despite the heterogeneity of gender constructions in different social contexts, feminist scholarship has shown some remarkable generalizations about gendered inequalities. While women are expected to behave in a feminine way, and men are expected to behave in a masculine way, globally, those characteristics associated with femininity are less valued and less rewarded in general than those characteristics associated with masculinity. Therefore, gender is a near-universal hierarchy that values *masculinities* over *femininities*, and this gender inequality is reflected in diverse social norms in geographically dispersed locations (Peterson and Runyan 1999: 7-8; Hooper 2000).

Feminist scholarship in IR and IPE has made substantial progress toward understanding gendered inequalities between actors, particularly income and welfare inequalities between men and women. By exposing patterns of privilege based on gender, feminist scholarship brings us closer to unsettling historical inequalities that have excluded women from full political citizenship and made women the primary subjects of transnational gender-based violence, poverty, and insecurity. But there is still a way to go. Even in countries where women have had the right to vote for decades and do not suffer from high rates of poverty, women's legal equality has not led to equal political representation, women's property rights have not protected them from gender-based violence, and women's paid employment has not led to equal earnings or an equivalent reduction in household labor. Feminism, broadly defined as an academic and an activist movement to understand gendered inequality and to improve the prospects for women and other feminized actors and acts, is unpopular and commonly disparaged worldwide. Gendered inequality continues to be a basis on which women and racial and sexual minorities are marginalized. It is therefore as important as ever to try to understand gendered inequality and what we might do to overcome it. Given these general feminist commitments, this book takes a deliberately feminist approach to interpreting the role of gender in the global political economy of beauty. For this reason, the explicitly feminist approach of the RPV framework makes it all the more appropriate as an analytical tool.

An additional useful dimension of the RPV framework is its inclusion of identities, social institutions, and ideologies as categories of analysis. This is what Peterson dubs "triad analytics." Hierarchies of identities, institutions, and ideologies intersect with each other and shape who benefits and who loses in the global economy. Intersections occur between identity categories such as race and class, social categories such as family and nation, and ideological categories such as patriarchy, neoliberalism, or feminism. Triad analytics is therefore a useful tool of inquiry into how these hierarchies shape and are shaped by the global economy. This approach is useful because it is compatible with the sociological approach to beautification used in this book, and because it builds on intersectional feminist analysis.

Triad analytics draws from the insights of intersectional feminist analysis while also advancing it by going beyond the categories of identity or structure to include the intersections of identities, institutions, *and* ideologies. Intersectional feminist scholarship has been invaluable to understanding that gender is not a universal category resulting in a universal structure of gender bias and necessitating a universal solidarity movement on behalf of women. Black and Latina feminists in the United States (Hull et al. 1982; Moraga and Anzaldúa 1983) and Third World feminists (Mohanty 1988) seriously challenged the idea that gender, race, and class are universal categories of advantage or disadvantage, as was commonly put forward by feminist activists. To the contrary, women of color and Third World feminists argued that feminist theory and activism had eclipsed and excluded the experiences of women of color and women in developing countries, and therefore claimed a universal experience of patriarchal oppression of women. This supposed universal is in actuality based on a narrow range of white, upper-class women's experience and concerns, which biases feminist agendas toward white upper-class women's interests. This *essentializing* of women's experience and interests based on biological universals has been much criticized for being empirically inaccurate, furthering the aims of the most privileged women, excluding women of color and other women at the margins from political discourse, perpetuating the myth of women as lacking agency, and maintaining that essential gender difference is based on biologically grounded gender dichotomies.

Out of the critiques made by women of color and Third World feminists, an intersectional feminist approach was born. In an intersectional framework, gender intersects with other social categories such as race, class, ethnicity, and nationality. That is, gendered experience shapes and is shaped by other categories of analysis, explaining why women's experiences of gender are not universal (Collins 1990; Crenshaw 1991). In other words, some women have substantially more privilege than others. The recognition that "women" is not a universal has shaped how feminist inquiry and claims to knowledge about gender discrimination are made. Consider, for example, the economic, cultural, and political differences between women immigrant domestic workers in Los Angeles and the women who employ them (Hondagneu-Sotelo 2001).

Triad analytics is particularly useful for understanding the politics of the global economy as it looks at institutions and ideologies in addition to identities. Identity categories, such as gender and race, are the basis for intersectional critiques of feminism. Yet systems of "social norms, laws, practices and institutions" can also exhibit structural inequality (Weldon 2006: 236). Whereas Weldon argues that it is the "intersection of social *structures*, not identities" (author's emphasis) to which intersectional analysis applies, this book takes the position that both identities and social institutions, mutually constituting, must be analyzed for the hierarchies that they perpetuate. Furthermore, triad analytics includes the intersections of ideologies with institutions and identities. Hierarchies of ideologies favor capitalism over feminism, for example, except perhaps in a few institutions or among certain identity groups. Triad analytics is thus an analytical tool for understanding how identities, institutions, and ideologies intersect and shape the political economy of beauty.

Using triad analytics, this book addresses gender hierarchy in the global beauty industries in three dimensions: ideology, social relations, and in the construction of bodies and identities (see also Marchand and Runyan 2000: 8). On the level of ideology, this book asks whether the global political economy of beauty privileges masculinity and masculine-associated representations. On the level of social relations, it explores how men and women experience and participate in the global beauty industries. On the level of body and identity, it looks at how men and women's beauty are constructed differently through the use of beauty products and practices. Gender is an important category of analysis in every sphere of social and economic life, but feminist scholarship on beauty and fashion has illustrated that the politics of beauty industries is especially salient to reproducing gendered inequalities. Therefore, gender is especially relevant in the global political economy of beauty, and the global political economy of beauty is especially relevant to gender politics.

Further, the global beauty industries highlight the ways that the politics of gender are central to the global political economy. One of the central axes of gendered power in global political economy and GPE has been the valorization of and concentration on the public sphere over or at the expense of the private sphere (Tickner 1992; Youngs 1996). Feminists fault the public-private division with obscuring violence against women, the personal politics of war, and women's work in the global economy, among other things. They have also consistently challenged the historical divisions that make Political Science, IR, and IPE concerned with the politics of war and political economy exclusively in the public sphere, while leaving the private sphere to other disciplines. Feminist economics has consistently challenged the division of paid labor and free labor in the economy and the reproductive sphere. This book extends this feminist project of making visible the ways in which, to paraphrase Cynthia Enloe (1989), the personal, or the private sphere, is also political and economic and international. Therefore, this book extends the feminist project of undermining the public-private divide in politics, arguing that personal beautification is intimately tied to the global political economy.

ETHNOGRAPHIC INQUIRY

This book's fourth entry point on the global economy of beauty is ethnographic inquiry. Utilizing the extended case method (Burawoy 1991), this book uses an ethnographic lens to tease out the relationship between local consumption and production and its global and historical context, as seen from the ground-up. It does this by asking what beauty ideals and practices exist among youth in Guadalajara, what the global and historical context of beauty economies[4] are, and whether and how a global political economy of beauty and fashion may shape and transform local body politics.

The extended case method places the local, individual experience and production of beauty among *quinceañeras*[5] within its global and historical context by tracing the products, practices, and networks involved in the enactment of the *quince*, as well as the generational differences that have emerged in the staging of the celebration. My employment of this approach is therefore based on ethnographic methods for data collection and analysis, but also extends into other sources of data on the global beauty economy. The production of the beautiful *quinceañera* serves as an entry point to understanding the production of Mexican ideals of beauty among youth in Guadalajara, and the extended case study serves as a method for teasing out how those ideals are being produced, and possibly transformed, in relation to global flows of information, production, and consumption.

A ground-up view is important for two main reasons. First, research about body politics must pay close attention to local cultural context. This is particularly important because most theories of beauty politics have been articulated in a developed-world context. To simply extend these theories to other local contexts risks making the theoretical error of ethnocentric universalization (Mohanty 1988). Western feminism has long fallen victim to universalizing its theories to "Third World" women, thereby objectifying Third World women and undermining their agency while at the same time making the intellectual error of false universalization.

Second, it is important to take a ground-up view in order to foreground the practices and ideas about beauty in their lived context. This is a helpful way to bring marginalized subjectivities to bear on globalization. Tomlinson (1999) argues that the effects of globalization must be studied as they are articulated in specific localities because there is no literally "global" space to focus on; cultural and political effects are experienced through their local manifestations. Chang and Ling (2000) also strongly argue for shifting the focus of globalization away from "god's-eye-view" analyses of "macro-corporate entities" with privileged subjectivities, and toward analyses that center ground-up views, marginalized subjectivities, and bodies (see also Enloe 1996). Following these authors, this research focuses on how the politics of the globalization of beauty practices and ideals is experienced through youths' words and everyday lives. Even, or especially, when studying the globalization of beauty products, practices, and ideas, it is necessary to view them from a situated, personal perspective. Therefore, the empirical focus of this research is global body politics as they are experienced locally because this captures the lived politics of globalization, emphasizes marginalized subjectivities, and foregrounds bodies.

These four analytical entry points—*quinceañeras*, the process of beautification, feminist global political economy, and ethnography—are by definition and necessarily incomplete, but together they have something important to tell us about the globalization of beauty products, images, and ideas; the dilemma of women's participation in the beauty economy;

youth and the global economy; and gender in the global economy. And, vice versa, gender, the globalization of beauty, and women's participation in the beauty economy can tell us something interesting about *quinceañeras*, beautification, and the global economy.

RESEARCH SETTING AND HISTORICAL CONTEXT

The city of Guadalajara is the center of a metropolitan zone, with 4.1 million inhabitants recorded in 2005. Guadalajara is renowned in Mexico for its central role in Mexican national history, its enduring political and social conservatism, and its beautiful women. The area was a colonial center for Spanish and French colonists, and has been a stronghold for Catholic and social conservatives ever since. The zone also figures centrally in Mexico's integration into and restructuring within the global economy, having received a high degree of internal migration from central and western rural zones, contributed to out-migration to the United States, and restructured its industrial base in response to shifts in the global economy and Mexico's policies toward it.

As the second-largest metropolitan zone in Mexico, Guadalajara is representative of medium-size urban environments. In 2005, fifty-six metropolitan zones in Mexico counted 57.9 million people, or 56 percent of the country's population. The largest metropolitan zones, with over a million inhabitants, include the Valley of Mexico, Guadalajara, Monterrey, Puebla-Tlaxcala, Toluca, Tijuana, León, Juarez, and La Laguna. These nine metropolitan zones account for 36.6 million, or 35.4 percent of the national population (Secretaría de Desarollo Social et al. 2007: 31). The next eighteen largest metropolitan zones, with between 500,000 and 1 million inhabitants, account for 13.5 million, or 13 percent of national population, and are the zones where the most population growth is occurring (Secretaría de Desarollo Social et al. 2007: 31-32).

Guadalajara also reflects Mexico's integration into regional and global economies. The Guadalajara Metropolitan Zone (ZMG) has been an important part of the regional, national, and increasingly global economy. Guadalajara has been the economic hub for central-western Mexico since its foundation. In the twentieth century, Guadalajara and its surrounding region played a key role in the national economy during the period of time that the Mexican economy was relatively closed to the global economy. With the liberalization of the Mexican economy in the 1980s, the central-western region has played an important role in attracting foreign investment and engaging in international trade. Since the turn of the twentieth century, the city has attracted increasingly high levels of rural-to-urban migration, particularly from the surrounding region but also nationally. Up until 1930, and once again after World War II, the region has been deeply integrated into transnational flows of labor migration and return from the United States. The city and the region, therefore, have followed the national trajectory toward global economic integration and have been central to the transnational flows of people that link Mexico with the United States.

After World War II and through the mid-1970s, Guadalajara was central to Mexico's rapid industrialization and relatively closed economy. During this period, Mexico nationalized the oil industry and initiated the import substitution industrialization (ISI) model. ISI is a state-led model of economic growth based on substituting imported manufactured goods with locally manufactured ones. Policies aimed at protecting national industries and reducing imports included two currency devaluations and three tariff increases between 1949 and 1968 (Chant 1991: 32). National policies also included price supports and subsidies to manufacturers. Due to ISI, until the end of the 1970s, Guadalajara industrial activity was based in the manufacture of basic and consumer goods for local and national consumption. Likewise, consumption was filled by national production. Clothing, shoes, and processed foods were the industry's staples. Production was fed by primary goods produced in the central-western region, which in turn served as a market for the manufactured goods (Pozos 2004: 152).

Export-oriented growth was a second development initiative. Beginning in the 1960s, Mexico promoted export-oriented industrialization and agriculture. The institution of the Frontier Industrialization Program in 1965 established an export-processing zone along the US-Mexico border, where *maquiladora*, or in-bond factories, assembled manufactured inputs and exported them back to the US market. In agriculture, cash crop development was promoted over subsistence farming.

Through the mid-1970s, ISI was still successful at propelling economic growth, although income polarization remained problematic. In the end, however, ISI as a model for economic growth was unsustainable. The industries were not efficient or competitive enough, and they did not generate sufficient employment (Chant 1991). At the same time, modern and export-oriented agriculture also employed fewer workers.

In order to prop up economic growth, Mexican leadership began to borrow heavily from international financial institutions in the late 1970s to make up the difference, banking on the discovery of new oil reserves to guarantee industrial progress. What was called "indebted industrialization" (Frieden 1981) became equally unsustainable. Particularly because of successive drops in world oil prices in the early 1980s, oil was not the economic guarantee that was hoped for and needed.

No longer able to pay back over $80 billion in loans, Mexico sought refinancing from the International Monetary Fund (IMF) in 1981. The IMF refinanced loans and applied conditions on the new loan terms: structural adjustments. The Mexican structural adjustment program (SAP) called for general reductions in state expenditures, which included ending subsidies to industrialists and effectively ending ISI, and cutting public sector employment. The social impacts of the SAP have been extensively documented, and were particularly difficult on women's livelihoods (Benería and Roldán 1987; Chant 1991; Benería 1991).

The Miguel de la Madrid and Carlos Salinas de Gortari governments (1982–1994) implemented the IMF SAP and pushed the neoliberal agenda forward. In 1986, Mexico became a member of General Agreement on Tariffs and Trade (GATT). In 1991, the North American Free Trade Agreement (NAFTA) with the United States and Canada passed, and it went into effect in 1994. Together, the IMF structural adjustment plan and the market-minded Madrid and Salinas de Gortari governments started the country on its path toward neoliberal economic policy and integration into the global economy on a large scale.

Throughout the 1980s and 1990s, due to structural adjustments and the 1994–1995 monetary devaluations, small- and medium-sized businesses suffered tremendously (Durán and Pozos 1995). As the Mexican economy entered into crisis, informal work increased in importance (Escobar Latapí 1988). Women's participation in paid employment picked up beginning in the 1970s (Durán and Pozos 1995: 89) and increased though the 1980s (Pedrero 1990; Chant and Craske 2003). Women's wage labor could not make up the difference in lost male wages and government subsidies, and so women pursued other household strategies and informal market activity in order to make up the gaps. The adjustments made in households, largely by women, are credited with increasing reproductive labor. Public employment and social services were also curtailed, increasing household insecurity (Anastasakos 2002). Many of the burdens of adjustment fell on households, where mostly women picked up the extra work (Benería and Roldan 1987; Chant 1991; Gonzalez de la Rocha 1994). Despite women's increased participation in paid and unpaid labor, however, there was a concomitant increase in income polarization according to class and gender, meaning that women made fewer relative gains during the 1980s and 1990s (Chant and Craske 2003: 214).

The shift from ISI to neoliberal development entailed a high level of openness to foreign competition and foreign investment. Foreign competitiveness meant that the local economy shifted from locally owned manufacture of consumer goods to importation and distribution of consumer goods and an increase in foreign-owned manufacturing (Pozos 2004). Foreign investment in manufacturing has increased in particular the role of Guadalajara in manufacturing and service support for technology companies, leading many to hope that Guadalajara will become the Silicon Valley of Mexico (Barba and Pozos 2001; Gallagher and Zarsky 2007).

The transition from manufacturing to distribution and sales has been felt very strongly in the clothing and shoe sectors. The fashion clothing industry is illustrative of these changes. Due to the shifts in the manufacturing sector and increases in imports, the 1980s and 1990s saw an increase in commercial sector activity, especially in retail sales and distribution through *tianguis* (street markets) and in *plazas* (commercial malls and plazas). Between 1980 and 1992, sixty new *plazas* were built in the city. The street shopping districts of Álvaro Obregon, Medrano, and Esteban Alatorre were developed as commercial clothing districts (Duran and Pozos 1995: 88). In the 1990s, another forty plazas were built (Pozos 2004). In addition to the plazas and clothing districts, the growth of supermarkets and hypermarkets in the 1990s—Walmart, Aurrora, Soriana, Gigante, Comercial Mexicana, and Chedraui—added to an increase in overall commercial activity and a decrease in small and medium-sized businesses (Pozos 2004: 144).

At the same time, informal commercial activity, especially in *tianguis*, continued to proliferate. *Tianguis* vendors sold more and more imported products, especially in the clothing market. Many vendors import clothes themselves, from Los Angeles, and sell them in the East side of the city, in Medrano and Álvaro Obregon. These clothing zones have since become central to regional distribution, as wholesalers came to buy and resell in their cities (Mendoza, Pozos, Spener 2002). Guadalajara is now a regional hub for imports and distribution of clothing. On the other hand, manufacturing, especially small manufacturers and workshops in shoes and clothing, decreased significantly throughout the 1980s and 1990s, leaving many people unemployed, working in the informal economy, or moving to the retail and distribution sector (Escobar Latapí 1988; Hernández 2006).

In sum, post–World War II economic development in Mexico has seen two phases. From 1940 to the mid-1970s, state-led modernization, nationalization, and ISI created a relatively hermetic national economy. From the late 1970s onward, Mexico has lurched into the global economy, becoming a major borrower of international finance, undergoing neoliberal policy transformation, and entering into free trade agreements. The open economy has transformed the employment, production, and consumption landscape in Guadalajara, making it a local and regional hub for distribution of locally, nationally, and internationally produced and marketed consumer goods.

Mexico's integration into the global economy cannot be understood without at least cursory reference to its colonization and formation as a nation-state.[6] Colonization brought the future territory of Mexico definitively into the global economy for the first time, a process that only intensified in the last half of the twentieth century. The conquest of the Aztec and Maya empires in the territory of what is now called Mexico began in 1519, and established a three-century colonial system of forced labor and tribute to Spanish conquerors and settlers (*peninsulares*, being from the Spanish peninsula) and their descendants (*criollos* or Creoles, the term used to identify people of Spanish descent born in the Americas).

The Catholic Church was also central to the colonization process, as Catholic missionaries were charged with the conversion and civilization of the supposedly barbaric peoples of the territory, beginning centuries of Catholic Church patronage of the indigenous and later *mestizo* and *mulatto* (ethnically or racially mixed) populations. Spanish *peninsulares*, Mexican-born Spanish *criollos* and later *mestizos*, their numbers growing, took possession of more and more agricultural land, resulting in a feudal system of landlords and forced laborers and tribute-payers that, by the end of the eighteenth century, had created a sizeable landed and wealthy class. The monopoly of land by the wealthy led to a system of vast income polarization between Spanish or European descendants and indigenous and African descendants.

Mexican political development in the twentieth century was both revolutionary and status quo. The revolution was the establishment of a strong state party and presidential system that took political succession out of the battlefield and established long-term stability. This provided the context necessary for the postwar statist development model, its eventual demise (see Rubio and Newell 1984), and the subsequent liberalization of the economy. On the other hand, the status quo of elite-run politics, corruption, and the concomitant income polarization were not overcome, either during the more populist or more liberal years. Many argue that liberalization in the 1980s actually deepened income and social inequalities (Huntington 1968; Hellman 1988).

National identity, ethnicity, and race in the ZMG is complex and does not lend itself to brief summaries, but some general comments can lend context to the present study. Carrillo (2002) identifies two currents of national identity[7] construction in the twentieth century: leftist romanticism toward pre-Columbian roots and conservative exaltation of European roots. Romanticism toward pre-Columbian cultures was promoted by the PRI government and leftist intellectuals (Carrillo 2002: 21) as well as youth countercultures beginning in the 1960s (Zolov 1999). This current of nationalism was used to construct a new, popular, sense of national identity based on authentic Mexicanness defined as indigenous heritage and the rejection of colonial powers, including Europe and the United States. Intellectuals and politicians at the turn of the twentieth century expressed these ideals by rejecting earlier Social Darwinism and invoking *mestizaje*, or ethnic and racial mixing, as central to the creation of a national identity.

During the rule of Porfirio Díaz (1876–1910), Social Darwinists "promoted the whitening of the [Mexican] population through European immigration and colonization and uplifting Indians through civic assimilation and education" (Stern 2003: 189). They considered Indian populations to be backwards, and "interracial" mixing between Indians and Spanish descendants to lead to the degeneration of the Mexican population. They therefore sought to whiten the population by encouraging immigration from Europe.

Revolutionary intellectuals after the 1910 revolution turned Social Darwinism on its head and proclaimed the *mestizo* as the future of Mexico, and even the future of the world as the "cosmic race" (Vasconcelos 2002). Vasconcelos and his contemporaries used a biological concept of race[8] to argue that a new race of *mestizos* would supersede all previous races by combining all of their strengths. The idea of an ideal *mestizo* used a biological concept of racial mixing as the basis for ethnic cohesion and to promote a new basis for national identity. Vasconcelos hoped that the *mestizaje* would amalgamate racial phenotypes and bring together "a happy synthesis, the elements of beauty, that are today scattered in distinct peoples" (Vasconcelos, 1925 cited in Stern 2003: 191). The concept of *mestizaje* also made it possible for Indians to "pass" out of their ethnic identity and into a larger national *mestizo* identity by changing the way they dressed to match emerging national and transnational sartorial codes (Wilson 2007). Still, as has been widely noted, the concept of racial mixing as a way to construct and improve a Mexican race, ethnicity, and national identity, was a thinly veiled and sometimes explicit attempt to whiten the Mexican population (Wade 1997; Stern 2003; Rénique 2003). Therefore, *mestizaje* did not undo Darwinist notions of racial uniqueness, superiority, and biological improvement. Racism, for example anti-Chinese sentiment, remained a strong political force in postrevolutionary nation-building (Rénique 2003).

Guadalajara has also historically fostered and maintained a strong sense of conservative Mexican national identity. Conservative nationalism has promulgated the idea that true Mexicanness is based on the Catholic values of the distinguished European oligarchy. Historically, and reinforced by the rush of rural migrants during the Cristero Wars, Guadalajara has been a stronghold of religious conservatism. During the Cristero Wars, religious rural migrants from nearby villages in the region known as Los Altos escaped to the city for protection (Martínez Casas y de la Peña 2004: 233). Guadalajara has remained a bastion for cultural and political conservativism. The center-right opposition party, the PAN, grew in popularity in Guadalajara and Jalisco years before it did nationally (Alonso 2003). Guadalajara and the central-western region have also been the most resistant to conversion to Protestant denominations, falling significantly behind national averages (Dow 2005).

And, of course, Guadalajara is popularly known as the city with the most beautiful women because of their association with European phenotypical inheritance. Many in Guadalajara will say that there are even more beautiful women in the villages of Los Altos, where the French inheritance is even stronger. The women of Los Altos are commonly discussed for their beauty. But the general stereotype is that the women of Guadalajara are beautiful because they share European-Mexican phenotypes for pale skin, lighter hair, large and light eyes, and European figures.

INFORMANT DEMOGRAPHICS

Explaining the sociodemographic characteristics of the study population is complicated. In terms of race and nationality, all participants identified as Mexican, although one was born in the United States and raised in Mexico and two had spent half or more of their childhood in the United States. All participants had some relatives in the United States, but these three families and three others had immediate family ties to the US, with one or more of their immediate family members living there. With the exception of two, all participants were born in the city (*tapatío*), although many of their parents moved to the city through internal migration. If their parents were not migrants, their grandparents were.

The simple socioeconomic description of the study population is middle class. All youth participants reported themselves to be middle class, although a couple suggested that they are lower middle class and one suggested upper middle class. The most illustrative comment, however, was the oft-repeated refrain, and variations of it, that stated simply "we are neither very rich, nor very poor." Participants regularly assured me that they had everything they needed, but also usually included that they did not have money for everything they wanted. Participants came from all areas of the city except the wealthiest. No participants had servants at the time, although one had previously had a live-in childcare provider.

The difficult part of this description is explaining what middle class means, and what it means to these participants and their families. The self-identified Mexican middle class, having undergone economic hardships and increasing economic polarization in the last forty years, is not well-off. Indeed, the great majority of these families would be considered poor by US standards. Twelve adolescents worked in paid employment, mostly in family businesses. Two of these participants worked specifically in order to be able to afford luxuries such as fashionable clothing and cosmetics. Others worked in order to support their families and to help pay family expenses. Many spent considerable time in unpaid reproductive labor, caring for younger siblings, nieces, and nephews, and thereby supporting other family members who worked in paid employment.

School enrollment among my study population was average to high. In my population of forty fourteen- to seventeen-year-olds, thirty-three were attending school (82.5 percent). National statistics assess that 93.3 percent of kids aged five through fourteen attend school. High rates of school enrollment begin to drop off around the age of twelve, with nationwide school enrollment estimated at 84.7 percent for fourteen-year-olds and 52.9 percent for fifteen- through nineteen-year-olds. In Jalisco, 47.7 percent of those aged fifteen through nineteen attend school (INEGI 2007). I attribute the average-to-high rate of school enrollment among my study population to the fact that families familiar with field research and thesis writing, a normal part of both high school and university-level education, were more likely to encourage and approve of participation. Participants often counted teachers and university students among their family members. Parents' education levels varied between some primary school and advanced degrees (two parents in different families).

All of the participants lived in cement homes and received public services such as water and electricity, but their living conditions varied considerably. The more well-off families had new homes with individual bedrooms and driveways, as well as late-model cars. Two of these middle class families divided their time and/or their family members between the United States and Mexico, an arrangement that has given them considerably more economic advantage in Guadalajara but has not moved them into the class of the truly privileged in Mexico. I estimated that six participant families were comfortably middle class.

The majority of the participants' families, however, could not count on the privileges of middle class life. Having family members living and working in the US is not always an economic boon. One participant lived with extended family members because her mother could not care for her and her father was a recent labor migrant to the US. Her economic security was low compared to that of her peers. One family of nine people in a two-bedroom apartment in a government-financed housing complex identified as middle class. The one participant who identified herself as upper middle class did not appear to be so, because signs of her family's material wealth, including their large run-down house, poor neighborhood, untreated health problems, and lack of personal transportation, indicated that she was in the middle in terms of privilege among other participants. Her calculation captures best that, rather than typically middle class, this study population is more accurately described as aspiring middle class. The *quince*, particularly the *fiesta*, is a central social activity and feature of life among the aspiring middle class.

FINDINGS

Through analysis of beautification within the *quince años*, and its global and historical context, this book argues that the global political economy of beauty, from production to marketing and consumption, entails a gendered global body politics that incorporates women into the global political economy; employs gendered channels of operation; transforms norms of femininity; and privileges hegemonic masculinities and momentarily, if at all, achievable ideals of womanhood. Surprisingly, this global economy of beauty is primarily the product of the labor, commercialization, and consumption of women and youth in the beauty industries. There are gendered inequalities, but they are generated by initiatives primarily led by women and youth seeking benefits in labor, commercial, and social situations. Thus, women and youth exercise substantial agency in the construction of the global economy of beauty, and the beautifying industries do provide women with some opportunities to get ahead in labor and marriage markets, but through traditional channels that funnel their efforts into highly hierarchical structures of gender, race, and class inequality.

This book establishes empirically that personal beautification is intimately tied to the global political economy, and vice versa. Women and youth are the principal participants in the global economy of beauty though beauty production, marketing, distribution, and consumption. Through women's and youths' activities, the global economy is deeply intertwined with the production of gendered bodies, youth cultures, the spread of diverse beauty cultures, and the generation of global capitalist beauty entrepreneurialism. Through this ground-up perspective on the global economy of beauty, we can see the limits to the distinction between public and private spheres of economic activity; commercialization in the beauty industries has made the public/private divide more obviously mythical, if not obsolete in practice.

The RPV framing of the global economy is useful for understanding how the intimate is linked to the global, and how the public, private, and virtual spheres are inextricable from each other in the global economy of beauty. For example, the reproductive, productive, and virtual economies play central, mutually reinforcing roles in the production of the beautiful *quinceañera*, and by extension the global political economy of beauty. The politics of reproductive, productive, and virtual exchanges are not easily distinguished, even for heuristic purposes, suggesting that the categories are indeed closely intertwined.

The global political economy of beauty is not, as many assert, the process and result of the unidirectional globalization of Anglo-American beauty ideals. Nor is it a process by which women and youth are enslaved to consumption or lax morals or triviality. Quite the opposite, the globalization of beauty is generated by youth and women who are generally seeking social identification and differentiation, extra income, and connection with something bigger. Through their labor, expertise, commercialization, and consumption of beauty, young people and women are largely responsible for creating the global beauty economy. This global economy of beauty is both shaped by and shapes young people's and women's intimate lives. It results in small, multilateral, transformations in gender norms, rather than the inexorable globalization of Western commercial beauty and gender ideals and practices.

The success of the global beauty industry rests on producing and reproducing ideals of femininity that include ever-increasing amounts of makeup, hair products, dieting, beauty services, and incessant youth preservation. Through this process of beautification and gendering of bodies, the global economy of beauty contributes to the production of gender all over the world; the feminine, subordinate body; some transformations in gendered expectations; and many manifestations of gendered inequality.

The global productive economy of beauty and fashion plays a tremendous role in incorporating women, on unequal terms, into that economy as producers, distributors, service providers, images, and consumers. For example, most of the labor of producing the beautiful *quinceañera* is performed in the reproductive economy, playing a key role in reproducing social norms of gender appropriateness, and also leading to the commercialization of beauty services, beauty products, and images of *quinceañeras*.

Through youth's intergenerational contestation, the reproductive economy of beauty in the *quince* facilitates the changing gendered norms of beauty and comportment. The global virtual economy of beauty is a conduit for hegemonic norms that privilege thin, Anglo-American, global-beauty-pageant-style ideals, but also enables alternative globalizations that contest hegemonic standards. As youth use beautification to seek social identification, differentiation, and extra income, they employ global media channels for inspiration, commercialization, and dissemination of their subcultures of beauty. The increasing diversity of beauty ideals and practices among youth in Guadalajara illustrate trends toward individualization, celebration of difference, and social change. Presently, beauty globalization contributes to a more multicultural local Mexican culture in comparison with ideals fifty years ago. This indicates, in general, a multicultural shift in beautification that undercuts the idea of a dominant Anglo-American beauty, although gender hierarchies persist even among diverse youth subcultures.

The globalizing beauty and fashion industries also illustrate some areas of hope: the centrality of women to the construction and persistence of gendered inequality means that women are not passive victims, but rather that women will be central to unsettling inequality. Men's increasing use of beauty products indicates that masculinity is also becoming more obviously artificial, and that the use of cosmetics is no longer exclusively a sign of the gender dichotomy.

Through the lens of youth beautification practices in the *quince*, and subcultural resistance to the conventional norms of beauty that the *quince* represents, this book foregrounds a local, embodied perspective on globalization. By focusing on the experiences and ideas of youth, the book highlights their important role in propelling and shaping globalization. The story of beauty globalization also draws attention to the important role that women play in the economy. While not among the highest paid or globally mobile, young women's production, consumption, and reproduction in the beauty industries are paramount to their success.

CHAPTER 2

Here Comes the *Quinceañera*: Isn't She Beautiful?

A *quince* is, simply put, a religious service followed by a celebration of a girl's fifteenth birthday. It is also referred to as a *"quince años"* (fifteenth year), or, when personalized, *"sus quince"* (her/one's fifteenth). *Quinceañera* refers to the celebrant herself, or any fifteen-year-old girl, but with the added social significance that this year is an important one in the girl's life.[1] The basic elements of the event include the ceremony with a religious service and a *fiesta* afterward where the *quinceañera* dances a waltz with her father, dances a waltz with a male escort, opens the floor for dancing for the whole party, and celebrants share a meal and cake. Guides to celebrating the *quince* offer myriad more ways to commemorate the *quinceañera*, although still based around this format of church service, meal, and dancing (e.g., Salcedo 1997). One of the most important details, for *quinceañeras* at least, is the makeover into a celebrity-for-a-day, including princess ball gown, wardrobe changes, professional hairstyles, professional makeup, choreographed courtly dances, choreographed popular dance exhibitions, photographer, and videographer.

The 2006 movie *Quinceañera* provides a useful depiction of a typical, if there were one, Mexican American *quince años* in Los Angeles, California. In the film's opening sequence, Eileen celebrates her *quince años* in a full-length, full-skirt, strapless bodice pink gown with lace and corset details. She is accompanied, in a rented limousine, by a court of six *damas* (maids-in-waiting), six *chambelanes* (chamberlains), and one *chambelan-de-honor* in matching gowns and tuxedos. After an implied church service that the audience does not see, *la festejada* (celebrated girl) and her court of friends and young family members travel to a park to take pictures with each other and her family. They then proceed in a limousine to a rented dance hall for the food, *mariachi* music, a disc jockey, and dancing.

The main character Magdalena's desire for an even-more spectacular *quince*, one with a stretch-Hummer limousine, plays the backdrop to the rest of the movie as she struggles with her parents over money, the dress, and virginity. In the end, her honor salvaged, Magdalena is granted her dream and celebrates her *quince* as a virgin and with her parents' smiling approval. After her religious service, Magdalena's party is started with a waltz with her father, who then passes her to her male escort, her *chambelan-de-honor*, in this case her dear cousin, for a second waltz. This second waltz is choreographed to include her court of *damas* and *chambelanes*, or maids-in-waiting and male escorts. After the dance show, we see the *brindis* (toast) to the *festejada*. The details of these *fiestas de quince años* are also typical in Guadalajara, Chicago, and the rest of the Mexican diaspora. These and other symbols may or may not be employed in a single celebration, depending on family and *quinceañera* interpretations of the tradition, economic circumstances, and individual taste. Variations on the practice include different color preferences and varying symbols and rituals of religious maturity, female adulthood, and promised virginity.[2]

Despite the similarities, the history, details, and meaning of this celebration are contextual. The format for the *quince años* is not fixed, but rather changes depending on social context and social change, family circumstances, economic resources, and individual tastes. The historical origins and authenticity of the tradition are in doubt. Its status as a coming-of-age rite of passage is in question. These uncertainties are intelligible, however, with the understanding that the *quince* is a "living tradition" whose practices and meanings are the product of its context, and therefore are neither fixed nor eternal (Davalos 1996; Cantú 1999).

THE *QUINCE* IN GUADALAJARA

A rough format for contemporary *quinceañeras* in Guadalajara begins with attendance by family and other invitees at a religious service, most often a Catholic Mass, which is dedicated to the *quinceañera*. The Mass dedication may simply be a mention of the *quinceañera* in the Mass, but often it includes special flower decorations, musical accompaniment, a grand entrance down the aisle by the *quinceañera* escorted by her parents or by up to fourteen *damas* (ladies-in-waiting) and/or fifteen *chambelanes* (chamberlains). In the more formal *quince* Mass, the *quinceañera* kneels in front of the altar on a special pillow as in a typical marriage Mass but alone, receives a blessing at the end of Mass, and lays her bouquet at the feet of a statue of the Virgin Mary. After this wedding-like ceremony, the *quinceañera* often lingers at the altar or the steps of the church taking photos with family and friends.

After Mass, between one hundred and three hundred family members and friends congregate for a meal and a party at a rented dance hall or a large estate. Once family and guests are seated at the party, the *quinceañera* makes a grand entrance, is warmly applauded, performs a choreographed waltz, leads a toast (through another choreographed dance), and performs a "surprise" dance number. She might also perform any number of rituals to symbolize her passage to adolescence. Additional rituals may include a symbolic changing of shoes from flats to high heels by a *quinceañera's* father, the presentation of *la última muñeca* (the girl's last doll) signifying a farewell to childhood, and the presentation of other gifts such as: a gold medal with the image of *La Virgen de Guadalupe*, a missal, a ring promising commitment to the church and virginity until marriage, and earrings representing the ability to listen to god. She may perform a special dance while making and receiving a toast. After the dance performances and during the party, the *quinceañera* takes pictures with guests at every table, dances to popular music with her friends and family, and receives gifts at her table of honor. The event, from Mass to meal to the party's end in the mid- to late morning, is video recorded.

A *fiesta de quince años* may also diverge substantially from this prototype depending on economic resources and the desires of the *quinceañera*. A simple plan might skip the Mass and schedule the party at home rather than in a rented or borrowed venue. On the other hand, a more extravagant *fiesta* might include a chocolate fountain, a variety show, a lighted stage, and professional dance accompaniment for the waltz, toast, and surprise dances. Creative alternative *quince años* celebrations that were recounted to me by interviewees included a costume party, a home-disco, and a club outing with girlfriends. Paid social announcements in the newspapers and marketing materials show even more variety, including the not-entirely-mythical dance-club-*quince*, often talked about but seldom seen by the middle classes. These much larger parties have a higher ratio of youth or may even exclude adults, and closely imitate a club environment. For example, bartenders may be hired to serve the underage revelers non-alcoholic, brightly colored martini drinks.[3]

To give the reader an idea of the extensive preparations for a *quince años*, let me run through a list of things that need to be done by various parties. Find a place to have the party, and make reservations for the place if it is a rental (a *casino* or *salon*). Choose the temple where your religious service will be held, and reserve your date. Rent tables, chairs, and other utilities if they are not part of the location rental. Hire musical group(s) for party and Mass. Choose a color and/or a theme. Look at magazines, tv shows, or go to the Expo Quinceañera for ideas. Plan and contract food service. Look for sponsors to help with paying for parts of the party and to participate in the ceremony. Shop for a dress design in the downtown or Chapultepec bridal districts (see figure 2.1). Buy a dress, or find a dress maker to copy or create your design. Choose and ask friends, family members, and friends of family members to be *damas* and *chambelanes*. Select and reserve dresses and tuxedos for the court members. Find and hire a choreographer. Take dance lessons. Practice group choreographies. Pick out decorations. Make decorations. Diet and exercise. Contract a photographer for *quinceañera* portraits, and one for the night of the party. Contract a videographer to make a video documentary of the *quinceañera's* life to be shown at the party, and a video documentary of the party to be edited for later viewing. Find a hair stylist, cosmetician, and nail decorator. Choose a park or other beautiful place for photo and video shoots. Get a facial. Have nail extensions attached and decorated. Have hair and makeup done for a professional photo and/or video shoot to display portraits and videos at the party. Put on a ball gown and spend half a day taking pictures in the park. Hire or find volunteers to help set up and clean up at the party. Rent or borrow a special car for transportation. Get hair and makeup styled. Get dressed.

The above list hints at how considerable in time and size, and potentially expensive, an affair preparing for the *Misa* (Mass) and *fiesta de quince años* is. It is often, and quite fairly, compared to a wedding. This inventory of activities also suggests how major a part beautification plays in the process of becoming a *quinceañera*.

HISTORY OF THE *QUINCE*

The *quince años* is arguably a quintessential Mexican tradition: its "authentic," "traditional" roots are not clear, but are rather obscured by centuries of cultural mixing, including colonization as well as cultural exchange with the US (Cantú 1999) and other Latin American countries (Salcedo 1997; Alvarez 2007).

There is a recognizable European influence on the event, from the historically Catholic service to the Viennese waltz with a court of maids and chamberlains, but there is insufficient evidence to merit an exact historical account of the tradition (Cantú 1999, Alvarez 2007). It is unclear when

Figure 2.1: A plaza in the downtown *quinceañera* and bridal shopping district.

the ritual became popularized, to what degree, and what its "original" form was. Popular myth, speculative scholars, and some *quince* handbooks suggest that the *quince* originated in Mexico. Regardless of its provenance, the *quince* is considered a Mexican tradition in Mexico, and the practice of the *quince años* celebration became a public phenomenon in Guadalajara beginning in the 1940s (Napolitano 1997), and widespread in Mexico, other Latin American countries, and the Latino diaspora beginning in the 1980s (Davalos 1996; Cantú 1999; Alvarez 2007). Wherever it is practiced, including Mexico, the ritual reflects the facts of cultural and ethnic mixing, forced and voluntary, that characterizes Mexican history.

MEANING IN QUESTION

Due to the religious ceremony, it is no wonder that, in a discussion of the importance of food and drink in ritual celebrations in Mexico, Brandes (1990) refers to the *quince* as "religious in origin and meaning" (174). No academic study of the *quince años*, however, offers a certain or explicit answer to where the tradition comes from or even what its historical form was. The ceremony's supposed religious history and meaning is especially contentious, but so are other elements of the ritual's supposed meanings.

Individuals on the street and English-language how-to guides for celebrating the *quince* are much more confident. Study participants of different ages informed me of traditional facts that often contradicted each other, for example rules dictating zero *chambelanes*, one *chambelan*, seven *chambelanes*, and zero, six, or seven *damas*. Erevia (1996), a Sister in the order of the Missionary Catechists of Divine Providence in Texas, writes in a guide for parishes on the religious aspects of the ceremony that the tradition is inherited from Mayan and Aztec indigenous rites of passage. Napolitano (1997) reports that a catechism class for *quinceañeras* in Guadalajara, required in their parish, invokes the *quince años* as a tradition that has reinvented Toltec and Aztec initiation rites, European debutante balls, and Jewish coming-of-age ceremonies (282).

One event planning guide for celebrants (Salcedo 1997) writes that the ritual can be traced to various indigenous peoples of Latin America as well as the European court customs practiced by the Duchess of Alba and the Austrian empress of Mexico, Carlota. Street myths often recounted the idea that the Empress Carlota either started the tradition or had a party for her *damas* to be presented to society that was then reinterpreted as a *quince*. These stories, however, are best read as competing discourses about the meaning and traditionality of the celebration, instead of historical fact (Davalos 1997). Indeed, in the first half of the twentieth century, the tradition was exclusively celebrated by the wealthy classes, and was then gradually popularized over the last half of that century; the tradition was by no means widespread prior to 1950. In Guadalajara, the first public notices of *quince años* being celebrated were announced in the 1940s in the social pages of local newspapers (Napolitano 1997).

One of the most contentious historical claims, then, is the religious nature of the tradition. Religious institutions themselves are skeptical of the religious nature of the *quince* service. It is not a recognized Catholic sacrament, although the religious service before the *fiesta de quince años* has historically been practiced in Catholic churches in Mexico. Parishes therefore provide the religious service at their discretion. Although widely accepted in Mexico, several parishes in the United States have refused to provide the *quince* service. Even some parishes in Mexico refuse or put stringent requirements on participants (Napolitano 1997). The tie to Catholicism has been further destabilized in recent years with the spread of evangelical Christianity. The multiplication of Christian denominations in Latin American communities and the Latin American diaspora, instead of undermining the practice of celebrating the *quince*, has helped untie the practice from Catholicism, because the *quince* religious service has been adopted as a practice in some Protestant Christian churches in Mexico, as it has in Chicago (Stewart 2004).

Young women themselves usually do not articulate deep religious or even cultural meaning for the tradition. To "give thanks to God" for having reached fifteen years of age is virtually the extent of the reasoning offered to me by youth as to why there is a religious service for a *quince*. Some parents expressed a religious dimension to the ceremony, beyond giving thanks for having reached fifteen years of age. As a result of contention over religion in the *quince*, its widespread practice, and the youth's lack of concern over religious meaning, religious leaders and parents have used the *fiesta* as a strategy to guide the celebrants to find deeper religious or social meaning in the ceremony (Napolitano 1997; Davalos 1997; Alvarez 2007).

Several parishes choose to practice the ceremony in exchange for shaping the rituals in accordance with religious objectives. For example, Catholic ecclesial base communities (CEBs) in Guadalajara disapprove of the increasing luxury and expense of the *quince*, and therefore either discourage it or require celebrants to attend religious classes and make commitments to community service in order to share a *quince* Mass (Napolitano 1997). A similar adaptation made by church leaders in the US is to require preparation classes for girls, girls and parents, or girls, parents, and *padrinos* (godparents). For example, a handbook for parish teams in the parish of San Antonio prescribes ten different teaching points about womanhood and scripture for preparation of the girls approaching their *quince* (Erevia 1996). Sister Erevia's guides to the *quince años* are widely used in Chicago's Catholic parishes (Stewart 2004). Other parishes choose several days a year to perform group *quince* blessings, or will even refuse to hold special religious services for a *quinceañera*. In these cases, a celebrant can attend a Mass as any churchgoer, or she can schedule a special *quince* Mass outside of her parish. In 2008, The United States Conference of Catholic Bishops published the first Vatican-approved prayer book, the "Order for the Blessing on the Fifteenth Birthday," to help standardize and guide parishes to make the religious service and commitment to Catholic faith an important part of the *quince*.

An alternative interpretation of the historical origins and meaning of the *quince* is based on the legend that a girl's fifteenth birthday was important because she became legally and socially eligible for marriage in Mexico (Alvarez 2007). On the basis of this history, the ritual is said to have performed a coming-out like a debutante ball, and a path toward heterosexual courtship and marriage. This story is frequently and convincingly repeated by people today as an historical basis for the practice, but has little resonance with the reasons that youth and their parents give to explain why they practice the *quince* and what it means to them. To the contrary, the narrative of the *quince* as a debut, beginning of courtship, and path to marriage is frequently used to explain the original meaning of the tradition, but always as an historical reference, in contradistinction to current practice.

The theory that the *quince* marked the beginning of the path toward finding a heterosexual mate and marriage is as contentious as the assertion that it is a religious rite. Clergy, like parents, are apprehensive of the *quince* marking a passage into womanhood before marriage, particularly when the Church is asked to participate in the ritual. Those who agree to perform some type of religious service, considering it an observance of a ceremony of popular religiosity, make efforts to define the ritual as a thanksgiving, or a recommitment to God, the church, and the Virgin of Guadalupe (Davalos 1996; Erevia 1996; Napolitano 1997) rather than as a path toward marriage. Likewise, parents reject the definition of the *quince* as a path toward marriage, because they plan for their daughters to delay marriage for several years at least. *Quinceañeras* themselves and young men universally expressed that fifteen years old is too young to find a permanent partner or become an adult. *Quinceañeras* seemed the most convinced that the *quince* is no longer a path toward marriage, and cited many things they intend to do during their teen years, none of which include plans of marriage.

Contention over the religious or heterosexual meaning of the *quince* does not mean that the practice does not have elements of only one or the other. To the contrary, contentious discourse about the meaning of the *quince* creates a space for competition of ideas, the creation of meaning, and the transformation of the *quince* over time (Davalos 1996, Cantú 1999). The *quince* is an arena for contesting the very social, cultural, or religious norms that it purportedly supports. The competition over the significance of the practice to religious and/or sexual maturity is an example of how competing visions coincide and coexist within the same *quince*.

A third related contention revolves around whether the *quince* is a rite of passage (Van Gennep 2004). Van Gennep's *The Rites of Passage* first argued in 1909 that special acts mark the transition from one stage of life to another, and these acts universally include rituals of separation, transition, and incorporation that cultivate the sacred dimensions to these passages of life. Rituals of separation remove the person from their previous world. Cleansing is a common theme in rites of separation. Rites of transition usually occur on sacred thresholds during which the relationship to divinity is nurtured, such as at an altar. Rituals of incorporation ceremonialize a person's reincorporation into a new role or stage in life, and often include a meal. The universal structure of rites of passage make life transitions like birth, marriage, and death look surprisingly similar across cultures.

Several authors have interpreted the *quince* as a life-cycle ritual that inducts women into both religious and marital womanhood (Cantú 1999; Napolitano 1997; 2002). These scholars interpret the symbolic relationship between *quinceañera* and *chambelan-de-honor* as a rite of initiation into marital maturity, and the religious ceremony and symbols as rites of induction into a female role of religious responsibility akin to *marianismo*.[4] While acknowledging the diversity and constantly changing nature of the *quince años*, Cantú argues that the religious service and the waltz are the two essential elements that define a *quinceañera* and the two realms of life into which she is being inducted: responsibility for religious education and morality and the world of wifedom.

More faithful to Van Gennep's formulation of rites of passage, Napolitano uses the stages of the rites of passage to explain the *quince*. According to this interpretation, the ritual of separation is performed as a *quinceañera* is taken to the altar by her godparents and "left alone to receive the Mass" on the day of her celebration (283). The Mass then serves as the transitional, or liminal, stage, and the *quinceañera* begins reincorporation as she is "handed over" to her *chambelan-de-honor* (283). In this interpretation, the *quince* is a ritual of incorporation into heterosexual courtship, with variations depending on family and *quinceañera* interests. Napolitano also notes, however, that the *quince* does not exactly fit the criteria for a true rite of passage because it is not obligatory, it is not universally practiced, and girls become women with or without having celebrated a *quince* (Napolitano 1997).

A LIVING TRADITION

The uncertain history, contention, and varied format of the *quince* are understandable when the *quince* is conceived of as a "living tradition." In her study of the meanings and changing practices of the *quince años* celebration in Laredo, Texas, and Nuevo Laredo, Tamaulipas, Mexico, between the mid-1960s and the mid-1990s, Norma Cantú explains the historical uncertainty about and change within the *quince* by defining it as a living tradition. As such, the *quince* speaks to the persistence of tradition as well as the existence of social change (Cantú 1999). Because it is a living tradition, the *quince* can be understood as a tradition to the extent that it is constructed in society as a tradition; it is a tradition because it is called one, not because of a documented historical authenticity. The ritual's tradition and authenticity are derived from the tradition and authenticity ascribed to it by its participants. Girls, their family, and clergy contest, negotiate, and define what is "traditional" for a Mexican woman's coming-of-age ritual, and tradition and meaning is constantly constructed through the dialogue between the parties (Davalos 1996). The *quince* is a living socially constructed tradition that is in flux due to competing personal, familial, and social forces.

The very idea of "tradition" is potentially problematic as it evokes twentieth-century ideas about primitive tradition giving way to modernity through a linear, evolutionary pattern of progress. This type of modernization thinking inspires criticism of tradition as being backwards and exalts modernity as a superior, scientific, and moral way of life. The notion of a "living tradition," by contrast, does not imply that there is or will be any type of linear development from tradition into modernity. To the contrary, tradition is a concept that is socially constructed and contextually dependent. Tradition can be defined by the colloquial use of the term as "what was in the past" and what we learned about the past (Carrillo 2002: 16). A tradition is a tradition because we call it that and because we treat it like one, and aside from whether we treat it with reverence, criticism, or ambivalence.

Understood as a living tradition, it is no surprise that the *quince*'s status as a religious and marital coming-of-age ritual is not stable. It is also easier to understand how, at the beginning of the twenty-first century in Mexico, the supposed birthplace of the tradition as a coming-out and religious ceremony, the religious and matrimonial elements have been substantially displaced as the most important elements of the *quince*. Today, the tradition performs a much more significant role as a marker of transition into a gendered adolescence, and as an instrument for learning, practicing, and presenting the results of an intense process of beautification. The *quince* is a special case of a now-universal rite of passage: the beauty makeover.

One basic norm that is reproduced through the *quince* is the idea of adolescence itself. The *quince* is a medium for the communication of values between parents, *padrinos*, and extended family to their daughters (Stewart 2004; Alvarez 2007) as well as sons as adolescents. It is also an arena for contestation and redefinition of family roles and norms on the part of adolescents and adults (Davalos 1997; Stewart 2004), a way to deal with fears and hopes surrounding the struggles of adolescence, and adolescent psychological development (Stewart 2004). The *quince* is constructed through personal, familial, and public discourses as a way for a girl to "become" a Mexican, Catholic, adolescent woman (Davalos 1996). The *quince años* also provides a context or an opportunity to connect with family history, and cultural customs (Stewart 2004; Alvarez 2007). The *quince*, therefore, plays an important role for individuals, families, and society, in constructing ideals of womanhood, in the context of adolescence.

Adolescence in the *quince* is framed as a privileged time of life, as the apex of beauty, and the time to find a partner. The meaning of the celebration, almost universally for youth, and also consistently for adults, is to celebrate achieving adolescence. Youth are hesitant to say that they are becoming women, and more likely to describe the passage to fifteen years as a celebration for having made it to fifteen, as just a great party in which they are the star, and as a recognition of their status as adolescents. As one *quinceañera* put it, "it's when you, when supposedly before fifteen you're a girl and so when you turn fifteen you're an adolescent." And as another said, "it is like starting to be less of a girl or a kid and more like you can be crazy and sort of, I mean, within reason of course..." A real-life transition for her would be more likely to occur at eighteen, she goes on to clarify. Others refer to the time as becoming a "*señorita*" or a "miss." One adolescent commented that while people believe it is a change from girl to woman, it is really a change from a girl to "a young person, a *señorita*." Parents also consistently identify the *quince* as marking the entrance to adolescence, rather than adulthood. As one parent said, "you aren't a girl anymore, you are an adolescent."

The celebration is also about enjoying adolescence. Time after time, interviewees stated "because you will never be fifteen again" as a reason they ultimately decided to celebrate their *quince* with a big party, despite the cost in time and money. The phrase has the ring of a marketing jingle, but it is relevant at the least because it is repeated so often. Not only is it a repetitive citation of fifteen as a great, one-of-a-lifetime experience, but it also reflects an orientation toward enjoying adolescence. When asked whether the ceremony and *fiesta* had a more religious or social meaning, one interviewee explained the sentiments of many: "Yeah, it is the tradition and everything, but for me that isn't so important. It's more to say that I am growing now, well, just the party. The Mass is to give thanks to God that He let me live more time, that is the significance that I see, give thanks to God and celebrate that I am fifteen." Another described it as celebrating her entrance into "a better stage of life." She went on to clarify, however, that you don't need a *fiesta* for that, so it is really just to have fun and party with friends.

The fun of adolescence is partly about being with friends, family, and being a star or a princess for a day. Celebrants generally reported that fun with their friends was one of the primary pleasures of having had a *quince*, or one of the primary reasons to have one. One interviewee decided to postpone her *quince* in hopes of having more friends with whom to celebrate it the following year, when she expected to be in High School. Junior High was a painful time for her, in terms of making good and supportive friendships, and she hoped high school would be better in that respect.

As for males' reasoning behind participation in the event, *chambelanes* most often cited a desire to be a good friend or supportive family member. For example, one repeat *chambelan* took his role very seriously as being a supportive friend and defending the *quinceañera* against negative attitudes and criticism from peers. Boys and girls alike take pleasure in performing for an audience, as well. As one interviewee commented, he enjoys performing the role of *chambelan* "because I don't see it as difficult, I like to dance, I like people to watch me dance, I don't know why, I like when people clap." Even one *quinceañera* who was hesitant to celebrate her *quince* because she feared the dancing part later regretted not having performed her surprise dance at the last hour. Deciding not to perform the surprise dance was her one regret, because she had enjoyed the other performances so much.

The stage of adolescence is identified as one of more liberties, changing bodies, and dating. The liberties include the ability to go out with friends unsupervised on a more frequent basis, to talk to boys, date, or even have a boyfriend, and to wear makeup and more provocative clothing and high heels. As one interviewee explained, "you have more rights to have friends, to have a boyfriend, to go out and hang out." These freedoms are no small matter in Guadalajara because of the religious and social conservativism that Jalisco is famous for.

Changing relationships with males are especially significant. One girl explained the meaning of the *quince* as based on the changing relationships with boys: "They say that 'that girl that we had is going through changes now', like even in school and everything, there are different ways of getting along with guy friends at school." Another interviewee, giggling in embarrassment, expressed being unsure of what the Mass is for, but guessed—based on the Masses she had attended—that it is a chance for the father to recognize them and "give them his point of view that they shouldn't sleep around, that they should choose their guy friends carefully and all that." The *quince* hence serves as a moment to counsel girls on heterosexual relationships.

Through beauty classes, salon visits, and preparations with family members and friends, young girls learn about makeup application and the extra things they can do to make themselves beautiful. Through dance classes, choreographies, and practices, *quinceañeras* and their friends learn how to dance with a partner, how to perform for an audience, and how to emphasize their gender through movement. Through motherly guidance, girls learn how to be a gracious hostess, how to network, and how to negotiate with their sponsors (see also Stewart 2004).

In effect, the *quince años* is an opportunity for a *quinceañera* to acquire and practice her social skills, including appropriate dress, beauty, and comportment that put a gendered adolescence on display. The production and display at the *quince años* then feeds into the *quinceañera* machine, where guests pick up recommendations, ideas about traditions to adopt, and notions about what they do not want to do, in order to make their own party unique.

The *quince años*, centered as it is on the girl star, could be construed as simply the teaching of feminine norms. This, however, would be wrong. First, there are plenty of opportunities for socialization of boys as well. It is a family event, and cousins and brothers and uncles and nephews play roles as *chambelanes*, drivers, set-up, ushers, and masters of ceremonies. This is a gendered division of reproductive labor that is nowhere more clear than among the *chambelanes*. The *chambelanes*, playing the role of Prince Charming, are inducted into the masculine side of heterosexual romance and sexual relationships just as *quinceañeras* are taught about the feminine side. Prince Charming learns how to dance, how to lead, how to treat his princess as a precious treasure. He learns how to defend her honor to her critical peers, and how to make her look good in front of an audience.

Even more important than the direct socialization of boys who participate in the *quince*, however, the celebration contributes to the construction of masculine identities through the construction of gender as a system of difference. Recalling that gender is a social construction of difference built around the dichotomy of masculinity and femininity, the *quince años* plays an important role in socializing appropriate masculinity through what it is not.

Thus, the *quince años* is responsible for constructing a *gendered* adolescence. The *fiesta* marks a celebrant's transition to being a young lady, a *señorita*. The graces that the *quinceañera* learns, practices, and puts on display at the *fiesta*, such as beautification, hostessing, dancing, and networking, are the talents that are socially valued for women. Interviewees, asked about the ideals for feminine behavior, stated them to be friendliness, the ability to converse easily, the ability to listen well, studiousness, cleverness, good speaking abilities, good manners, and good advice-giving. Dancing is also a highly valued social ability. These behaviors and comportments are on full display at the *quince*, as a *quinceañera* asks family and friends to become sponsors, arranges guest lists, makes invitations, makes her debut, greets guests, poses for photos, receives gifts, and dances with her invitees.

One male interviewee could imagine a boy celebrating a *quince años*-styled event, but only for a young boy who wanted to change his sex and be presented as a woman; then, it would make sense. An effeminate boy could become another sex, and therefore be presented to society as a young lady at a *quince* celebration. A masculine boy, on the other hand, would not have a *quince* celebration, because it is about becoming a woman. This young interviewee explained that he does not discriminate, since being born another sex could happen to anyone, it isn't their fault. This interviewee's non-foundational idea about sex and gender was the most thoroughly articulated, but the idea that only an effeminate boy would have a *quince años* came up repeatedly in interviews. Most commonly, boys and girls and their parents simply responded that boys do not celebrate their *quince años* or their transition to adolescence. Boys just don't do it; it is not for boys. When asked if there should be a recognition, public or not, of boys' maturation, most demurred, repeating that that stuff is for girls. Boys are more likely to point to eighteen as an important life turning point, because they achieve more legal rights and responsibilities or finish high school.

The Mass is also a gendered obligation, because "women have to give more thanks to God and to their parents. A man is very different." The Mass serves as a vehicle for a woman's obligation to be grateful to her parents and to God. The *quinceañera* gives thanks publicly and before God, and then renews her commitment to be religious and pure in a series of promises to the Father. She finishes the ceremony by offering a bouquet to the Virgin Mary, a further sign of her commitment to be obedient and virginal before God.

The production of gendered social norms is not accidental. In addition to religious leaders, mothers, grandmothers, sisters, cousins, and friends take an active interest in teaching their daughters how to be women. One older sister made it a point to use the *quince años* as a medium for teaching her sister about makeup and making herself beautiful, gifting her with a personal beauty, manners, and comportment class. A good number of mothers, conservative and liberal, report trying to teach their daughters about sex and/or the value of virginity, and use the *quince años* to try to instill a sense of worth in their daughters so that they don't just get involved with any boy, do not get pregnant, and do not get married too soon. The teaching interests are not uniform, but they are all teaching about how to be a good woman.

Finally, whereas some families emphasize the religious elements and others the party, there is one rite of passage that is a common denominator for all ceremonies: the makeover. Indeed, the makeover is now a near-universal experience for young women in Guadalajara, suggesting that it meets the criteria for a rite of passage: a universally practiced, socially obligatory ritual that marks the passage to adolescence. The makeover, for example in the hair salon, even parallels the religious rite of passage with three stages: separation and cleansing; a transformation performed at a threshold; and reincorporation into society. Understood as a rite of passage, the beauty transformation has become a path to a secular beauty religion, wherein becoming beautiful leads to a new stage in life, creates a better future, and becomes an obligatory daily ritual that very few people in Guadalajara will disrespect. The *quince* is merely one way that girls in Guadalajara formalize the modern rite of passage of the makeover. To be sure, the *quince* and the beautification process it entails is an intensified process of makeover and self-presentation, almost incomparable to other experiences of makeover. However, participants in this study who did not celebrate their own *quince* also reported in substantial detail other experiences of makeover: a beauty pageant preparation, a sister's help, a friend's mentoring. Boys also participate in the makeover experience in and outside of the *quince*, albeit with significant gendered differences.

CONVENTIONAL BEAUTIFICATION IN AND OUT OF THE *QUINCE AÑOS*

In order to understand the importance of beautification, youth were asked when and where it was important to look good, what looking good means, and how it is achieved. The universal importance of looking good and the personal and reproductive labor invested in it led me to the conclusion that beautification was nearing the status of universal rite of passage in Mexico, and that, as the song says, "looking good is never easy."

When asked the most important times to dress up and look nice, interviewees almost universally replied that it was for family events and/or *fiestas*, one of which is the *fiesta de quince años*. Being both a family event and a *fiesta*, it is doubly important for all attendees and participants to dress nicely for a *quince*. *Fiestas* are usually held for major life and family events, such as baptisms, first communions, *fiestas de quince años*, graduations, weddings, and anniversaries. Other birthdays also often warrant *fiestas* with a rented *salon*, musical group, or catering, but rarely on the scale of the other *fiestas*. *Fiestas* are family events, but interviewees often also mentioned weekly Sunday meals with family and other social visits with family as important times to dress up.

Otherwise, interviewees answered "all the time" or "every day" as the most important times to look good. When pressed, a few of these agreed that one gets more dressed up for a *fiesta*, but many held on to their belief that looking good is always very important. The key for these youth, then, is that looking good is based on being appropriately dressed and beautifully appointed, whatever the situation. As one interviewee explained it: "It depends a lot on the occasion. A get-together with friends: dress fashionably, nicely, well of course, fashionably, with fashionable accessories. A family get-together: something more reserved, something more classic, I don't know, a button-up shirt, dress pants. A party: ...we go pretty elegantly, just a little. And then in parties that are more elegant, the men wear tuxedos/dinner jackets (*smoking*)."[5]

In sum, the *fiesta de quince años* falls into the category of the most important moments of life, for the *quinceañera* as well as attendees, for looking good. The *quinceañera* is involved in a process, usually spanning some months, of beautification for her grand entrance. *Damas* and *chambelanes* spend less time planning their performance, but they also often spend months learning their dances, dieting, choosing a dress, highlighting their hair, practicing hairstyles, putting on false nails, and learning how to use cosmetics. Attendees also report that a *fiesta de quince años* is one of the few events that warrant their most thoughtful and beautiful presentation. *Quinceañera* beauty standards can therefore be seen as both an expression of general standards of beauty and beautification, but also as an exaggeration or intensification of beauty standards and practices. That is to say, the *fiesta de quince años* includes a very important production of beauty that both reflects and exaggerates society-wide standards.

Also importantly, the *fiesta de quince años* teaches young women the process of beautification, from nails to hair to cosmetics to comportment, at the age when they become eligible to use, or use substantially more, beauty products and beautification techniques. The *quinceañera* is therefore a prism through which to see the construction of gendered beauty in one of its most concerted moments, and at the time when beautification is taught and learned.

The following section describes feminine and masculine beautification processes, in everyday life and for special occasions like the *quince años*, and reflects on how these relate to global trends in popular youth culture. The text focuses on how youth see their practices in relation to global trends, and how their practices feed into global trends. By taking the perspective of youths' lives, this research reveals how the globalization of fashion is driven by adolescents in their quest for identification with and differentiation from each other, rather than an external imperialism that corrupts them. The text then turns to an analysis of privilege in beautification processes. Gender and race are important categories of analysis of the beautification process, and they expose how the politics of gender and race among youth are present. At the same time, an analysis of race in beautification processes and ideals among youth brings into doubt the idea of an omnipotent globalization that spreads Anglo-American beauty standards. To the contrary, the globalization of beauty ideas, practices, and products introduces more diversity of ideas, practices, and products, not less.

LOOKING GOOD

Looking good for youth in Guadalajara, in addition to balancing their desires to be normal and to be unique, has two distinct dimensions. On the one hand, when asked about their own beauty practices and standards, interviewees repeatedly referred to "fixing oneself up" or "*arreglandose*" as the true measure of looking good. As one interviewee explained, one does not have to be particularly beautiful (*bonita*), but being well fixed up (*bien arreglada*) looks good and makes you attractive (*guapa*). As another explained when asked why it was important for her to look good, "A person should always look fixed up in order to, I don't know. The more fixed up you are, I feel like, the more you have. More people will like you." Young men are equally concerned with looking good, especially on special occasions like family events. The basic dimensions of *arreglandose* for girls, in addition to dress, are, as one interviewee put it, "*como se maquillan, como caminan, como se peinan,*" or cosmetics, walk, and hairstyle. For boys, being fixed up includes being well-dressed and well-coiffed. Often, though unspoken, it also means having a "*cuerpo de futbolista*" or a soccer-player's body.

On the other hand, there are some general beauty ideals underlying many of the youths' particular ideals, belied by some of their practices, if not their words. These general ideals include a set of norms based on imagined standards of beauty like pale skin, long pale hair, blue or green eyes, chest-waist-hip measurements of 90cm-60cm-90cm, thinness for girls, and tallness and soccer-players' bodies for boys.

The following sections discuss the standards of beautification or *arreglandose* as well as the underlying beauty ideals for the *quince años* and how they fit into youths' general set of beauty standards in five categories: cosmetics, hairstyles, dress, comportment, and body shaping.

Cosmetics

For a *quinceañera*, cosmetics are important, and heavily applied. Most of my participants had their makeup applied professionally or semi-professionally for their *quince años*. *Quinceañeras* gave numerous reasons for using makeup artists. Some did it "just because," others in order to feel special and pampered, still others because a family member or friend offered to do it, and, finally, some because they did not know how to apply it themselves. The *quince* is often the first time a girl will wear makeup, so she often does not know how to use and apply it.

Typical makeup application for a *quinceañera* looks something like stage or fashion makeup in Mexico. Watching the news or a *telenovela*, one sees this type of makeup application on the female protagonists. For a *quinceañera*, it includes bright eye shadow colors that match the color of the *quinceañera's* dress, dark and thick eyeliner, extensive use of shadow-coloring on the eyelid, eyebrow shaping, eyebrow color definition, and false eyelashes and/or mascara, all to make the eye look bigger and more pronounced. A more professional makeup artist might use color shading on the face to make cheeks look more hollow, nose bridges more straight, chins thinner, foreheads less prominent, or to otherwise "fix" imperfections of the facial features. Any cosmetician will use liquid foundation to make the color of a *quinceañera's* skin more even, powder to set and mattify the foundation, and cheek blush to give a rosy color back to the face and to make the cheekbones more prominent. She—the cosmetician is almost universally a woman—will also use lip liner, lip color, and a lip gloss to give a lasting, rosy, shiny, and sparkly pout to the *quinceañera*.

Makeup in the *quince años* reflects the importance of makeup to youth, but also exaggerates it. Girls this age are just learning to wear makeup, and experimenting with whether and how much they want to use it. Many of the interviewees were allowed to wear makeup for the first time when they turned fifteen years old. With four interviewees, this new privilege was not seen as particularly enticing, and they continued to wear little or no makeup. Others experimented with different amounts of makeup. A number of others, however, took full advantage of their privilege, and wore foundation, powder, eyeliner, mascara, color-coordinated eye shadows, blush, and colored lip gloss. Makeup for fourteen-to-sixteen-year-olds is often prohibited at school. Some girls will put on makeup during their last class at school, for their walk out and for hanging out after school. Trading school uniforms for stylish clothes, girls will match their eye shadow to their blouse-and-jeans outfit. The three female interviewees who did not attend school wore makeup from morning to night. While the *quinceañeras* almost universally apply fingernail extensions with rhinestones and small, color-coordinated drawings for their big party, very few will wear false nails daily, and none wore false eyelashes or eyelash extensions daily. Male participants did not wear makeup, and its use is believed to be outside the norm for a masculine boy (see below).

Hairstyles

The norm for *quinceañera* hairstyles is fixed "up." A *chongo*, or updo, is almost mandatory, as I never witnessed a *quinceañera*, live or in video, wear her hair loose and down. These hairstyles are based on a number of processes. First, clean hair is processed with some hair products to make it smoother and either a blow dryer, hair curler, or hair straightener to make its shape more uniform. During or after this process, all or most of the hair is gathered toward the crown of the head, making a sort of modern beehive that makes the hair look like mounds of curls or mounds of straight but stylistically separated locks of hair sprouting out of the crown, falling forward over the top of the head, and falling down or streaming down the *quinceañera's* neck and back. The new hair shapes are held in place with bobby pins, hair clips, gel, and hair spray. A variation on this might include a fauxhawk, where the hair on the top of the head is distressed or "ratted" until puffy, some straight hairs are smoothed over the "rat's nest," hair on the sides of the head is smoothed back, and the girl is left with a hairdo that is raised on the top of her head and slick on the sides. A less radical variation, a rising trend in 2007, uses the same techniques as the fauxhawk except it adds volume to the top of the head in a round, head-shaped form instead of in a mohawk shape. From this mound of voluminous hair, locks appear to fall loosely in curls or in waves or straight. In reality, the hair is not loose even in the "loose" hairstyles because so many products are used to keep the hair in place. In addition to her updo, a *quinceañera* will wear a crown or a hairpiece of flowers and glittery accessories.

Amazingly, variations of these almost supernatural hairstyles are often seen in the street on schooldays and in the fashionable stores. Not all girls wear these styles, and not all wear them daily, but in the beauty industries, fashion shows, and among the fashionistas on the street, it is not uncommon to see a fauxhawk with straight hair falling down the back. What is most common is *some* form of hair modification, be it curly hair that is straightened, straight hair that is curled with a curling iron or molded with a blow dryer, or hair of any style that is drenched in gel to give it a "wet" look that stays in place. As one informant explained, "since I have straight hair, I curl it or make it wavy." The important thing with hair is to modify it to some degree from its natural state.

As with makeup, many *quinceañeras* are just beginning to experiment with hair styling and hair modifications. Highlights and hair dyes are prohibited in some schools. But some *quinceañeras* will get their hair highlighted for their party, or, as with one group of friends, a *quinceañera* will get highlights and then her friends, one by one, will try it out.

Boys' hairstyles are shorter, and are generally less styled. The standard for a boy is to have a short haircut and to wear his hair styled with gel and a comb. As one participant informed me: "I think gel is my most important fashion accessory, because that is what I use to style my hair." This type of styling often has a "wet" look, and is usually firmly put, so that no hair falls out of place and the locks are hard to the touch. Despite their simple styling procedure, boys' hairstyles can still be quite supernatural. This includes a fauxhawk made with short hairs and gel, highlights, short spiky 'dos, and lots of soccer-inspired styles. One interviewee who was also a semi-professional performer and dancer reported styling his curly, longish, hair with a straightening iron, and I also saw this used on all of the male participants at a coed adolescent beauty pageant. Still, in mainstream styles it is highly rarified that a boy will go beyond the use of gel and a comb for styling. I observed it among those boys who would be going on stage.[6]

Dress

Quinceañera dress, or The Dress, is one of the most important aspects of celebrating the *quince años*. For the *quinceañera*, the chance to dress up for a *quince* may be one of her main motivations in having the party...Not having the chance to dress up for one's own *quince* can also be a sore spot. When asked whether she regretted not having celebrated her *quince años*, one sixteen-year-old girl responded that she only regretted not having had the chance to dress up. Another interviewee first discounted her own *quince*, saying that she hadn't had one. Upon further questioning, however, it became clear that she had had a special party, one like no other year, carefully planned with her mother's help. She did not, at first, feel comfortable telling me it was her *quince* because she hadn't had the opportunity to dress up in a princess dress. Nevertheless, she did put on her nicest and most favored dress pants and blouse, color-combined accessories and cosmetics.

Even if a *quinceañera* doesn't personally feel the urge to dress up like a princess or a movie star, family and peer pressure to do so is powerful. In this sense, the *quince* is sometimes used as a chance to intervene on a young girl's sense of style. One interviewee was sent to beauty school, against her initial wishes, as part of her transformation. Another, highly resistant to allowing herself to be beautified by her mother, eventually negotiated and submitted to professional hairstyling as appeasement for the dramatic liberties she was taking with her *quince*—no princess dress, no waltz, and no *damas* or *chambelanes*. To be sure, there are plenty of ways to celebrate a *quince*, and plenty of ways to dress. One participant who celebrated with a club outing with girlfriends chose a special cocktail dress.

Still, the most popular of the *quinces*, the prototype so to speak, is based around a beautiful ball gown. Planning or remembering their *quince*, almost all interviewees start with their dress. Imagining, designing, shopping for, ordering, and fitting the dress is one of the most central aspects to the *fiesta de quince años*, and is often the starting point for planning the event, anywhere from one month to a year ahead of time.

The dress, as it is marketed in *quince* magazines, the Expo Quince, marketing materials, and on television, is basically a ball gown with a tight bodice and a very ample skirt. Still, the most important aspect of dress selection is making sure it is unique, and uniquely suited to the *quinceañera's* taste. This paradox first struck me in an early interview when, being shown a *quince* portrait of a *quinceañera* in her pastel green, strapless, corset bodice, full-skirted dress, the *quinceañera* herself proudly reported to me that she was really happy with her *quince años* because she had had an original dress that wasn't like all the others. Responding to my gaze, which possibly revealed my slight puzzlement, she explained that she had looked a long time for this dress because she wanted it to be different, and had not seen anyone else with a dress like it. "Still," she said, "to this day I haven't seen anyone with a dress like this." I left still puzzled as to why a dress that to me appeared to fit the prototype perfectly was so unique, but came to appreciate that all the *quinceañeras* had a similar understanding of their dress as uniquely theirs. Some appeared more distinct than others, most looked very similar to me, but all were seen by their wearer to be reflective of her personal taste, personality, and style.

One fourteen-year-old, with little idea about her future *quince*, had her dress design visualized, based on an image of a dress in a Japanese cartoon. Another dreamed about a black gown, even as she doubted that her mother would permit her to wear one. She wanted to wear black, or maybe red or wine if her mother would allow, because it would be unique. In the case of a fifteen-year-old who traveled from California to Guadalajara expressly to celebrate her *quince* and the Christmas holidays with extended family, The Dress was found through browsing in the popular downtown *quince* and bridal dress district, locating a designer in her price range that she liked, drawing what she wanted with the help of her designer, picking out a fabric color that would be unique and "close" to her preference for black, having her measurements taken, and waiting for the designer, who probably used a dressmaker, to fulfill her order. She debuted her co-creation—a dark brownish-red with even darker highlights, strapless, corset-bodice, cake-topper dress and matching shawl and headpiece—in less than a month.

In terms of dress, the most important rule is color matching. As one participant explained:

> When you are going to get dressed, the clothing has to be matching nicely. If you are going to wear pink clothing, it should all match, from the shoes to the accessories: pink. The makeup...yep, also. Since you are wearing pink, you should wear pink eye shadow. Everything should match, even the rubber bands in your hair should match what you are going to wear, they should be the same color pink.

One group of friends has a rule that they wear a maximum of three colors at a time. As my interviewee informed me:

> You can wear a maximum of three colors. If you are going to wear blue, it has to be a color blue that matches with something. It could be white or pink or if you are going to wear orange it has to match with some other color. It could be blue, orange, and white, or if you want to wear black, it can be all black or black combined with two other colors, but those three colors have to look good together.

Wearing more than three colors, she said, looks disorderly, unkempt, or gypsy-like. Girls tend to have "their" colors, with my interviewees reporting such colors as pink, lavender, red, pastel green, purple, and black.

Strict color combination and color limitation is especially true for the *fresa*, or strawberry girl. A *fresa* at school is likely to be considered the most popular with the boys, the best dressed, and the target of other girls' jealousy. The term *fresa* has come to mean many things, and can be insulting in some contexts, but is generally regarded as referring to well-dressed, well-regarded, privileged, snobbish adolescent girls. To be a *fresa*, a teenager has to be dressed in color-combined clothing, preferably by brand-name makers.

The *fresa* prototype is based on when the term referred to the privileged girls who "had everything." For example, a *fresa* has the money to color-coordinate all of her outfits so that her accessories, her shoes, and her makeup match a two- or three-color scheme every day. The *fresa* girl also not-so-subtly favors European beauty standards as well because the privileged classes have historically been descendants from the area's Spanish, French, and other European colonials. Today, the *fresa* prototype has filtered into popular society, and represents the most popular beauty standard for youth in Guadalajara.

As the term has filtered down from the truly privileged to be a social phenomenon among youth, they have developed new words to distinguish "true *fresas*," or truly privileged youth, from all of the other "*fresas*." During the time of my research, the word *pepón*, referring to a big, sparkly doll, came to be used to refer to the really rich, as opposed to their many imitators. The word was so new that my friends at the *licenciatura* (Bachelors) level in university had not heard it, and most of my personal beauty class was stumped when I told them it was a new word that I had learned. Still, it was used in several interviews with aplomb. In another case, a youth explained to me that she and her friends are *cerezas*, or cherries, because cherries are even more expensive than strawberries.

The opposite of *fresa* is *naco(a)*. *Naca(o)* is a derogatory term used to mean many things, but generally refers to poor people with little education in the manners and tastes of high society. *Nacos* are therefore understood to wear mismatched colors and patterns; loud and ostentatious colors, patterns, and accessories; and over-done hair and makeup. A comedic parody of *naca* adolescents on a popular television show has the *nacas* chewing gum loudly and wearing tight, bright, multipatterned, multicolored clothing with numerous glittery accessories and gelled-down hair. In different skits they are servants in a big house, unemployed, and street vendors, and they exhibit their ignorance of grammar and good manners at every chance.

Mismatching colors and prints are not just a question of economic and social class, as in being a *naca*. There is also an ethnic dimension to the ridicule of the lack of color coordination, with an unmistakable correlation between being *naca*, being poor, and having darker skin, since indigenous and black people historically have held the least paid and least skilled jobs. Still, a *naca* is not an indigenous person per se. So, the insult that someone is *naca* is a reference to social class more than race or ethnicity, but with clear racial and ethnic implications. What is more, the many indigenous groups in the area who dress in a manner that identifies them as ethnically indigenous also use bright, multiply colored ensembles. The preference for wildly contrasting colors and patterns is stunningly beautiful to this researcher but either seen as outside of local social norms or derided by youth. Furthermore, the great majority of interviewees did not include indigenous groups in their definitions of Mexicanness[7] or in their analyses of beauty. When pressed, a number of interviewees begged ignorance, others specified that indigenous people are not the same as Mexicans, and still others dismissed indigenous dress and beauty with words like *sucios* (dirty), *fodonga* (sloppy or uncared-for), *fachosa* (weirdly costumed or gypsy-like), and *feos* (ugly). Other prejudices against indigenous beauty can be seen in the bias against short stature, especially for men, the prejudices against dark skin, large facial features, a bent nose bridge, and natural hair.

As is the distaste for mismatching colors a disregard for or rejection of the various indigenous styles that use color contrast. Color coordination is the general standard for *arreglandose* in Guadalajara. Most subculture aficionados, including emo, punk, *metalero* and rock, choose color coordination. *Psychos*, a subculture of electronic music aficionados, define themselves partly as countercultural through their use of mismatched colors.

Color combination is nowhere more visually conspicuous than in a *fiesta de quince años*. Choosing her color may be one of the first things a *quinceañera* does, along with choosing her dress. In the *quince años*, the dress color not only matches the *quinceañera's* eye shadow, fingernail polish, hairpiece, earrings, necklace, bracelet, ring, shawl, purse, and shoes. It also matches in color and shade the bouquet(s), the cummerbunds, waistcoats, and neckties on the *chambelanes' tuxedos (smoking)*, flower arrangements, bows on dining chairs, centerpieces, streamers, party favors, and other types of decorations. Color combining, always important, is even more so at the *quince años*.

Men's dress in the *quince años* also reflects the imperative to color-combine. *Chambelanes'* rented tuxedos, the most common *chambelan* attire, vary according to period themes. *Smoking* rental shops offer ten to fifteen styles of suits. One might be fashioned around a mandarin collar with a frock-length coat, another based on a military-style coat with tails, double-breasted. Each style cites a period or a theme, which is chosen to match the theme of the party, the dance, or the *quinceañera's* dress. All *smokings* generally incorporate a touch of color to match the quinceañera's dress. As rentals, these suits are made with the simplest of tailoring, and just a hint of style.

At the Expo Quince, an expo that serves the more extravagant spenders as well as many browsers, vendors exhibit more elaborate *chambelan* attire worn by hired *chambelanes* who are semi-professional dancers. Some of these styles include formal British Palace Guard attire, Napoleonic military wear, or Disney Prince costumes. *Quince* magazines also illustrate these types of extravagant displays with Disney character, popular Hollywood character, or military costumes for *chambelanes*.

Comportment

Another exceedingly important part of beautification for a *fiesta de quince años* is learning to dance the waltz and surprise dances. Historically, the *quinceañera* celebrated her new social status as a young woman by dancing a waltz with her father or with her escort, or both. This tradition has evolved into one of the most important parts of the production and the most anxiety-producing: the waltz and the surprise dance(s). Dance choreography, lessons, and practice is often the most time-consuming and engaging aspect of the *quince años*. It is often anticipated with excitement, anxiety, or a mixture of both. One interviewee planned not to celebrate her *quince* with a party because she did not want to make a dance performance. Another recalled that her only regret was not having danced a surprise dance, out of fear. At the time, she had only managed the courage to dance the waltz, but looking back wished she had done both.

The choreographed waltzes that I witnessed or was told about were danced with between two and eight *chambelanes*, or male escorts. *Chambelanes* are frequently hired from dance schools or dance companies or *chambelan* agencies for the waltz, but they are also often brothers, cousins, nephews, and friends. The non-family member boys who get asked the most are the ones the girls have a crush on, the tall ones, and the ones who know how to dance. This means that certain boys get picked often. For example, two interviewees who are friends shared a leading man.

The waltz begins as a dance with the *quinceañera's* father, followed by a dance with her *chambelan-de-honor*. The dance with her father, sometimes foregone and sometimes expanded to include dances with uncles, grandparents, godparents, and sponsors of the event, is usually unchoreographed and danced in closed embrace.

The second waltz, with her *chambelan-de-honor*, is usually choreographed to include her court of *damas* and *chambelanes*. These waltzes are based on a very simple set of steps. The main movement is back and forth, like a step forward on one count, step backward on the second count, or a step sideways on one count, and step back on the second count. The dances are choreographed for simplicity and visual impact. There is very little partner dancing in embrace, and much more theatrical use of space. The courts will fill up the dance floor and, walking around to the slow beat, use simple turns and back-and-forth movements to emphasize the *quinceañera's* star quality. If a *quinceañera* dances with multiple *chambelanes* and no *damas*, she generally dances for a short bit with each boy, perhaps being invited to dance on one knee, having him turn her and promenade her to dance with her next partner. The *quinceañera* and her court will then dance a less complicated number called the *brindis*, or toast, in which the *chambelan-de-honor* hands the *quinceañera* a champagne glass and the court as a whole begins the party by leading the room in a ceremonial, non-verbal toast tuned to her dance music.

Following the formal waltz and toast, the *quinceañera* will disappear for a moment to change her outfit for the "surprise dance." The surprise dance is a dance of the *quinceañera's* choosing, danced alone or with either friends or *chambelanes* after the waltz. It is not really a surprise anymore, because although it is considered optional, it runs against the norm to not perform one. The surprise, if there is one, is what type of dance the *quinceañera* chooses as her second dance. The surprise dance is a contemporary feature of the *quinceañera* tradition, dating to the late 1990s or early 2000s. The youngest mother interviewee celebrated *quince años* in 1989, and had never seen or heard of the surprise dance during her youth. Its first published mention may be in a 2007 memoir/documentary of the *quince años* in the Latin American diaspora in the US (Alvarez 2007).

The surprise dance showcases the *quinceañera's* dancing skills and interests, usually based on either classes that she takes or a choreographed dance that she learned for the event. One interviewee showed her extensive Arabic-influenced dance training with a couple of solo numbers, and one accompanied by classmates. Another showed her skills in Tahitian and Hawaiian dances. Some learned partner dances and danced choreographed tango or salsa numbers. Several danced hip-hop, pop rock, or jazz dances, also choreographed by their regular teachers and accompanied by their classmates or teachers and other professionals.

Girls have much more extensive experience to draw on in preparing the surprise dances; boys are more timid when it comes to learning and dancing the varied rhythms. The choreographed waltz, based on a forward and a backward step and some simple turns and some walking, is significantly easier to learn than the other, more stylized and faster dances. Also, once one waltz is learned, it is even easier to do it again, and the traditional waltz is repeated at party after party, making it simpler for *chambelanes* to perform one or more waltzes. The other rhythms, by contrast, are personalized to the tastes, and oftentimes-extensive training, of the *quinceañera*, and so it is not as easy for her to find male accompaniment among her friends and family. Furthermore, the costumes for the surprise dance, perhaps in particular for Arabic, Hawaiian, and Tahitian dancing, are intimidating for young performers. As one interviewee replied when asked whether she danced her surprise Tahitian dance alone or with her *chambelanes*: "I did it myself. I don't think they would have wanted to put on the loincloth." Therefore, accompaniment in the surprise dance is usually from girlfriends, dance class peers, dance teachers, and hired, professional dancing, *chambelanes*.

When the *quinceañera* returns to the dance stage for her surprise dance, she is usually wearing one of two outfits. One outfit is a shorter and sexier version of her ball gown. It is common for her dressmaker to include a mini skirt under or separate from her ball skirt, so the *quinceañera* removes the full skirt and puts on a puffy short skirt that matches her corset. In this, she can dance many numbers, like salsa or rock. The other outfit is a costume based on the dance, for instance a clingy black or red dress for tango, a shiny, flouncy dress for salsa, jean miniskirts and midriff-baring shirts for rock and hip-hop, '50s style skirts for a retro rock-and-roll reproduction, chiffon skirts and brassieres for belly dancing, and grass skirts and a coconut shell brassiere top for Hawaiian dancing.

Diets, Exercise, and Body Shape

A final area of beautification for the *quince años* has to do with body shape. Boys did not report any type of body modifications in preparation for *quince* celebrations. *Quinceañeras* and young girls, on the other hand, often discussed body ideals and how to achieve them. The most important body-shaping exercise for the *quinceañera* is the use of the corset. The corset, in combination with a puffy skirt, forces a girl's midriff into a curve and creates or accentuates an hourglass shape. As one interviewee recounted, even a chubby girl can feel beautiful in a corset. This birthday girl was very happy with her photos and her presentation on the day of her *quince años* because of the thin waist that her dress gave her, but also expressed to me that she could "hardly breathe" and it was difficult for her to move. This was not the norm among interviewees, but all of them did achieve a fairy-tale waist and hourglass figure with their dresses.

A couple of girls expressed their preference for an A-line or sheath skirt, although they did not connect their preference for a more form-fitting dress with their size or shape. One thought an A-line would be more elegant and less ostentatious, and another thought it would be more elegant and sexy. I would venture, however, that these girls would have chosen a slimmer profile partly because they were thin. This is because beauty ideals for these adolescents, more than anything, emphasize both thinness and hourglass proportions. This is true not just in the *quince* celebration but also in everyday life. Consistently, the conspicuously serious moments in interviews with adolescent girls came when we talked about weight and wanting to be thinner. As one interviewee reported as she choked up with anger, "your skin can be purple, but you have to be thin." Therefore, a girl who is already thin has the luxury of wearing a sheath gown or a smooth A-line and still showing off her thin, hourglass proportions. Another girl, however, will jump at the chance to be cinched into a corset and a full ball gown skirt.

Besides corsets, many interviewees, of all sizes, reported using diet and exercise to get their bodies in beautiful shape before their *quince*. Echoing the sentiments of a number of interviewees, one answered that "lose some kilos, that is the only thing I would change." Nevertheless, while a small number put themselves on diets to lose weight, most reported trying to eat a "balanced diet" all the time. Much more common than dieting, however, was the use of exercise to improve body shape and slim down. This included both general workouts such as Pilates, stationary-bicycle riding, kickboxing, and running to lose weight and/or stay slim, as well as body-part-specific exercises, such as leg lifts to "lift the butt" and abdominal exercises to slim the waist.

Despite some special preparations for *fiestas de quince años*, the preference for the slim, hourglass figure is not exclusive to the *quince*. Indeed, preoccupation with weight and shape is common even among the youth who do not or who have already celebrated their *quince*. One young interviewee repeatedly expressed distaste for prototypical beauty norms, the traditional *quince años*, and the social pressure on her to be thin and made up. It was this interviewee, in fact, that most made me question the generalizations surfacing from this research. Still, when discussing her sister's perfection in all things, calling her a superwoman, she qualified it by pointing out that the only thing her sister lacked was a body "like that."

This is not to say that interviewees were lying to me or that their informal conversations were more real, more honest, or revealed their true feelings. What is informative about the discussions about weight and body shape is that they were almost always very contradictory, both within interviews and between interviews and hanging out. Almost all interviewees stated that their own standards for beauty are based on personality and qualities of "internal beauty." Otherwise, they stated an oft-heard phrase that "no woman is ugly." Interviewees, particularly girls, repeatedly denied that they judge women by a set of beauty ideals. On the other hand, however, these interviewees were quick to explain how other people—by most estimations, everyone else but they themselves—judge women's beauty. Thus, there is a strong disinclination to judge women, especially other women, on their physical characteristics. At the same time, there was plenty of recognition that women are indeed criticized for their physical attributes according to society-wide standards. There was even the occasional slippage when a girl denied holding ideals of beauty for others but spent considerable time exercising to lose weight before her *quince*, or when she rejected society's' standards in an interview but expressed them informally.

For one participant who wanted to be either a plastic surgeon or a fashion designer for fuller-figured women, this contradiction was especially strong. Her desire to be a fashion designer was motivated by wanting to help women look and feel beautiful despite social pressures to be thinner.

Her desire to be a plastic surgeon was also motivated by the desire to raise women's self-esteem. But she saw being a fashion designer as thumbing her nose at social pressures, and plastic surgery as succumbing to them. She was not sure what she wanted to do. The contradictions that these participants expressed and exhibited led me to see a general, underlying contradiction between wanting to escape, even deny, social pressures to be thin, and the real pressure that they feel and may even perpetuate. This phenomenon of both rejecting and succumbing to society's pressures suggests a number of things.

First, the contradictions illustrate that girls are informed about adults' concerns for their health and well-being, especially around weight. "Balanced diet" has become somewhat of a code for "diet" these days as fad diet foods announce that they are "part of a balanced diet" and girls deny any weight loss measures "except for a balanced diet." A few girls anticipated my questions by denying any sort of eating disorders before I asked about them, even though it was not my intention to ask. Essentially, girls know that they and their body image are of central concern to researchers and adults, and they were reticent to share them, or more than willing to refute medical and feminist discourses about them. They know what a healthy body image is, and they repeatedly demonstrated that. Second, these contradictions suggest that, in addition to knowing what a healthy body image is, some of them still struggle with attaining it.

YOUTH NORMALIZATION VERSUS PARTICULARIZATION AND GLOBALIZATION

The standards and practices for "looking good" in Guadalajara in the early twenty-first century, as described above, are not static in time, nor universal among youth. Indeed, how current styles contrast with previous standards and practices is one way to view changing gender norms and practices. The contests among youth over what looks good provide some of the richest information about why and how standards and norms of gendered beauty change. The above description is, therefore, a description of a cultural reference point, a mainstream beauty culture that is widely described and accepted as socially dominant during this period in Guadalajara. The study of the process of beautification and the *quince* are not the study of particular styles so much as the process of style-making, its historical context and meaning. The process of how that mainstream beauty culture has come to be, how it changes, and its ties to the globalization of beauty products, images, and ideas, is more important to understanding the politics of the global economy of beauty.

Standards of beauty and beautification are not universal in *fiestas de quince años* because of tensions over standards and practices of beauty and because beautification plays two important identity-defining roles. The first tension is between tradition and individual taste. On the one hand, the *fiesta* is a traditional affair, with standards of presentation that are widely assumed as prototypical, especially by celebrants' parents. Additionally, the *fiesta* is a social event that calls upon celebrants, participants, and attendees to dress appropriately in order to maximize their social identification. On the other hand, the *fiesta* is organized around celebrating the adolescence and increasing agency of a fifteen-year-old. The fifteen-year-olds have substantially different ideas from their parents about what is beautiful and appropriate. They also have some degrees of difference in taste among one another, differences that lead some to not practice the *quince* or to alter it significantly. Furthermore, youth universally voice their desires to be unique and original, often expressing their individuality through their style of dress. As a result, there is plenty of disagreement and negotiation over originality versus custom in the process of achieving beauty for this traditional, social event.

A generational conflict comes up because there is tension between conservative tastes of tradition and the parents' and sponsors' purse strings, and the *quinceañera's* desire to personalize and make original her *quince años*. This tension between youth and adult standards of presentation is illustrated in the generational changes in dress design and beautification standards in the *quince años*. For instance, parents' generations, from the 1960s to the 1980s, all wore less form-fitting dresses with sleeves and higher collars. Few wore makeup, and if they did it was a little bit of blusher and/or lipstick. Their daughters, however, are accustomed to strapless corset bodices as the norm. Many mothers expressed discomfort with or surrender to the strapless gown, and at least insist on a shoulder wrap for the church service. But a *quinceañera* wants to personalize her dress. She may want to personalize by adding sleeves, but on the other hand she may want to make the ball gown skirt slimmer, the collar lower, and the color a dark red or black. This becomes a generational conflict over youth fashion and convention that is negotiated and worked out over time between the *quinceañera* and her parents and sponsors. The result is something of compromise, one in which the "tradition" is balanced with the tastes of a *quinceañera*.

One historical example comes from Texas, where, when the obligation to wear a head covering in the Catholic Church was lifted in 1970, girls in Texas reinterpreted their obligation by wearing a headpiece instead, in the form of flowers, ribbons, or other adornment (Cantú 1999). A crown, flower, or flower-and-ribbons headpiece continues to be the norm in Guadalajara. Thus, small transformations in the norms for feminine appropriateness and religious obligation can be seen through the changes in *quince* beautification practices over time.

The generational tension is also illustrated by attendees' dress. Interviewees universally responded that a *fiesta de quince años* is an important event, one at which personal presentation is especially key. Indeed, *fiestas* are the major social events for adolescent youth. This means that attendees will wear their newest, most fashionable clothing for the *fiesta*. And yet, adult interviewees consistently complain that their children's friends wear inappropriate attire, including denim blue jeans, low-cut blouses, and "even tennis shoes." It is, in fact, quite true that a *quinceañera's* friends will go decked out in their best blue jeans. To be sure, degrees of formality vary, usually depending on how close the attendee is to the celebrant, and whether an attendee's family is also in attendance. But the result is that parties are often full of adolescent attendees that dress fashionably according to their taste and social groups. By parents' standards, these fashions are considered too casual, sloppy, and not fixed-up. With their dress slacks or jeans, girls might wear a provocative top and boys a Polo-style or button-up short sleeve shirt. Depending on their style, girls or boys might wear name-brand sneakers or cowboy-style boots or high heels. And so, although all parties feel it is important to be well fixed-up for a *fiesta*, there are significant generational differences in what that means.

The tension over particularization versus normalization of beauty and style is not only generational; it is also a tension between being unique and social identification. The prototypical presentation of the *quinceañera* in 2006 and 2007 includes a pastel gown with a full, long skirt and a strapless corset bodice. It also includes mainstream hair and makeup design. Being fixed up appropriately for an event and seeking social acceptance by looking good are extremely important to youth in their search for social identification (see below). The *quinceañeras*, however, also yearn to express their originality and to make their special day "theirs."

The desire for originality was expressed in reference to beautification in the *fiestas de quince años* and in everyday life. Despite what is described here as a global beauty economy on the ground in Guadalajara, youth participants self-reported their participation in beautification regimes as a practice in originality and uniqueness. Some participants allow that others may be conformist to a popular ideal, but all expressed themselves as having a unique, personalized perspective on their likes and dislikes, potentially negating any claims that there are prototypes of beauty, standards of beautification, and that there are notable gendered and racialized trends within these. Asked whether her views on beauty applied to other people, one young woman stated, "'No', that's the way I am...I see myself as a person who exercises to keep in shape." A self-identified *fresa*, when asked whether she was a fan of RBD—one of the most popular music groups of the time—responded with a forceful negative and proclaimed "One has to be original...one has to be original, and they are way over." This young woman had been a big fan of the group; at another time, she had revealed to me that she had copied their lead singer Dulce María's red hair in the past. She had quickly moved on in her search for uniqueness. Like this interviewee, many young women strive toward originality through dyeing their hair different colors. They express both their unique individuality and their association with a style and youth culture, depending on the color of hair dye and the youth cultural styles of the moment. The universal desire to be and be seen as original and unique is palpable with these adolescents. Beauty and fashion are an important part of how youth identify themselves as unique.

The former Dulce María fan also illustrates another of the ways that youth experiment and display their uniqueness: through changing tastes rapidly. Dulce María and her red hair were still a popular trend at the time of this interview in 2006, but this participant had already moved on to find something more original. In 2007, this teen had again changed her style so dramatically she was no longer a *fresa*. Another participant went from being a disaffected, video-game-playing, dropout populist to a brand-name-only, club-going, devout Catholic in the short time I knew him. The rapid pace at which teens adopt and drop tastes would make any researcher dizzy. After an initial frustration with trying to pin down some of "their" styles, I came to understand that the search for new styles that could balance their need for social identification *and* differentiation was a bigger part of youths' styles than any particular trend.

The impulse to be unique and on the cutting edge, liking what is new and not what is out or old, is a strong feature of youth culture in Guadalajara, and it lends insight into the impetus behind the spread of global trends. As expressed by the young woman who rejected one popular rock band because they were "over," adolescents in Guadalajara are searching for the new and the unique. They are also very competitive with each other for originality, as exemplified by the young women who search ceaselessly until they find a dress for their *fiesta de quince años* that is unique from all of the ones they have seen before, and watch their peers afterwards to make sure that their own uniqueness holds up over time. This rush to originality inspires many youth to look to mass media and marketing for ideas. Quince magazines, the Expo Quinceañera, and fashion and celebrity magazines become important in the process of informing a youth's search for her unique style. She might even actively seek out a style that is unique from what is considered "Mexican." For example, one young woman has chosen her *fiesta* dress design from a drawing of a Japanese cartoon character that "isn't available here in Mexico." A boy liked to find images of and imitate the styles of pop stars from England, like Robbie Williams.

It is through this process of social identification and differentiation, both between generations and peer groups, that fashion is created. Here, Aubrey Cannon's conceptualization of fashion as a social process (1998) is useful. According to this conceptualization, fashion is a social process of group identification and differentiation rather than a specific mode of dress associated with the West (Cannon 1998). For example, the fashion process includes national identification and differentiation. Fashion is central to nationalist identity formation, as has been particularly shown through the now-global system of beauty pageants (Cohen et al. 1996; Banet-Weiser 1999; Leeds-Craig 2002), as well as ethnic and national dress (Rugh 1986; Root 2005). Likewise, the fashion process indicates belonging to social constructs such as modernity or tradition. (Basyouny 1998; Ossman 2002; Lukose 2005).

While the process of social identification and differentiation through fashion is facilitated by the fashion industry that emerged out of the Industrial Revolution, the use of fashion is not exclusive to industrial capitalism. Rather, it is a social process through which, in small groups, fashion functions as a signifier of belonging. In larger groups, it functions as a signifier of differentiation. This process of identification and differentiation is universal, although it manifests in different types of fashions in different contexts.

The framework of fashion as a social process is apt because it captures the dynamic of social belonging that is so important, particularly for youth. In addition, conceptualizing fashion as a social process of identification and differentiation breaks out of the staid model of fashion as solely a marker of social class. Early theorists of fashion saw it as a marker of social class through conspicuous consumption (Veblen 1945 [1899]) or a system of communicating class status (Barthes 1983). Fashion may mark social class, but it also marks many more areas of social status and belonging (Cannon 1998). This is easily illustrated, for instance, by the numerous accounts of fashions that identify and construct ethnic, language, and national group membership. The dynamic of social belonging through fashion is especially important because it brings into relief a central issue brought up by globalization in the beauty industries: how the expanding global sphere of material, social, and cultural exchange affects group identification and differentiation through fashion. This ongoing process of fashion identification and differentiation is therefore due to its centrality to changes in fashion and to youth's desires to connect with global fashions, the link between youth and the global beauty industry. Youth beautification creates both fashion and its globalization.

GENDERED AND RACIALIZED ADOLESCENT BEAUTIFICATION IN GUADALAJARA

Despite the central role that youth play in the construction of their own beauty norms and practices, the beautification practices and beauty ideals expressed in the *quince años* and by adolescents who participate in them are not egalitarian. Patterns of privilege and politics emerge in the process of beautification itself. For one, the use of beautification practices and beauty ideals is gendered in a way that emphasizes women's role as fashion consumers, as physically weaker, as being in need of improvement, and as sexually provocative. In addition, beauty ideals and beautification practices reveal racial hierarchies that favor Anglo-American bodies. These racialized ideals affect boys as well as girls in Guadalajara. The following discusses the gendered and racialized aspects of beautification and beauty ideals, in the quince and in everyday practices.

The adoption of beauty trends and practices is gendered first because the degree of involvement and time committed to beautification is more visible among girls than boys. As the star of the show, the *quinceañera* understandably puts much more time and effort into *quince* preparations. Still, the beautification techniques used by the *chambelanes*, who are playing the role of a typical fantasy man or Prince Charming, appear to be, by comparison, prescribed and even hidden. There is little room for creativity and investment in personal style or beauty for males. Interviewees who had performed as *chambelanes* explained their beautification process as nothing especially profound or involving. Boys' beautification processes are still present, but their prescribed and invisible nature make the gendering of boys' style based on their embodiment of a default, uninvested, natural look.

The suit uniform takes the personal investment and the outward signs of investment out of the *chambelan* dressing process, simplifying his beautification process with a social prescription. This does not mean that the decision to wear a suit is not laden with importance. A *chambelan's* first concern was often the price of buying or renting a suit. This led more than one potential *chambelan* to decline a request to perform, because he could not afford a suit. If he agrees to perform, his suit styling will be chosen to match the *quinceañera's* dress and tastes, again circumscribing his investment in the beautification process.

When asked what they had done to look good for their performances, boys almost universally indicated ignorance or indifference. Sometimes, with prodding, some reported shaving their facial hair and styling their hair with gel and a comb. A couple experimented with plucking some eyebrow hair, and one with straightening his hair. I never learned of a young man curling his hair. But the majority of boys found their fixing up as almost entirely unremarkable and "normal." They presented themselves as uninvested and uninterested in the topic of fashion. This also made it difficult to recruit male participants, since, as they told me, they were just not interested or felt they had nothing to offer on the topic.

Boys' curious silence about beautification should not be mistaken as a lack of investment in fixing themselves up. Boys fall into one of two positions on beautification: those who will share about their interest and experimentation with beautification techniques, and those who will not. Boys' interest in looking good was a cause for parents' concern and for friends and family to question their masculinity and their sexual orientation. Two of the three study participants who spoke freely about their interest in fashion also had their sexuality and masculinity questioned by a parent or friend, to me. At first I took this as merely an uncomfortable moment, since I never intended to discuss teenage sexuality with the teens or their parents or friends. Soon, however, it became apparent that this is a risk that boys run. If they are too interested in or too open about their interest in fashion and looking good, they are likely to have their masculinity and their sexual orientation questioned.

The most notable investment boys made in their *quince* preparations is in dance practices. A court often meets once or twice a week for one to three months, and every day for a week or two before the event to learn and practice their choreographies. This was another one of the major concerns for boys when they were asked to perform as a *chambelan*, due to the time commitment and the fear of dancing. Dance practice is clearly a fun time to socialize with peers, but it is also no small task in terms of time commitment and courage to learn and perform dances for an audience of between one hundred and three hundred people.[8] In addition, the leader's role in partner dancing requires a lot of practice, memorization, and focus to perform. In social dancing, learning and dancing as the leader is more time-consuming and difficult than learning and dancing in the feminine "follow" role.

The lopsided visibility of investment in beauty and beautification is equally if not more true in everyday life. A number of boys and only one girl reported that their appearance did not matter much to them or that they spent little time "fixing themselves up." As one young man put it, he only tries to look good when he does something special, like going to visit family. In his everyday life, it does not make sense to him to fix himself up, because he goes out clean and comes home dirty from playing soccer or riding his bicycle or other outdoor activities. Most of the young men do care a considerable amount about their personal appearance, often saying that it is important to look good every day and that it is important to wear brand-name clothing, but even so they spend less time directly fixing themselves up, and employ fewer visible techniques.

Additionally, appearance-making is gendered in the techniques and styles employed by youth. Many of the masculine techniques of appearance-making emphasize masculine power: piercings and athletic clothes and accessories are the commonly employed techniques of beautification used by boys in my study.

Both young men and women have piercings, a visible sign of subcultural group belonging and often defiance of authority, but there are some notable gendered differences. Eyebrow piercings are very popular among the young men of this age group, and seem to project, in contrast to the delicate adornments of the girls', a rugged strength, in addition to defiance. One youth proudly rejected his piercing as a question of fashion, saying instead that he "just did it." He had literally just done it, having a friend of his pierce it for him once, removing it on parental orders, and doing it himself a second time. To this young man, the pain was inconsequential, it literally didn't hurt, he said. On the other hand, young women talking about piercings often mention the pain as a factor to consider.[9] Another difference in men's and women's piercings is often size, with men using a larger barbell or a spikier spike and women often choosing a smaller barbell or ring.

Finally, athletic clothing and accessories, like baseball caps and bracelets that proclaim soccer team loyalties, are so ubiquitous as to almost appear universal among the young men of Guadalajara. Major sports brands like Nike and Puma are highly regarded, and athletic-branded and -inspired clothing and shoes are commonly used by fashionable young men at young people's special events, like parties and going to the movies. In 2005, plastic bracelets popularized by Lance Armstrong's Livestrong bracelet was the trend among young men. In 2006 and 2007, I saw more young men with cloth bracelets with soccer team colors and names woven into their fabric.

Young women's beautification employs much less in terms of athletic-inspired style and their techniques focus to a greater degree on skin, hair, makeup, tight clothing, and color combination. Skin care products are not exclusively used by young women, but it is far more common for women to use more than a skin lotion and more than one product, as well as to be conscientious about their products' brands.

Makeup among interviewees appears to be exclusively the domain of the women, although one mother expressed concern to me that her son was so preoccupied with looks these days and new fashions that he was even talking about using makeup. Another mother feared that her son's use of black clothing was leading him to be a depressive person, and that he might take up the use of black eyeliner. This was expressed as a disturbing idea to these mothers, and a sign of loss of order and tradition. Makeup among young men is used by the most fringe subculture, the Goths, a subculture that makes parents nervous, or by transgender youth, another subculture that makes parents nervous. Makeup among young men in Guadalajara is a highly rebellious, counter-culture undertaking; the norm is for women to wear makeup and for men not to.

It is rare to see a young man without a hairstyle that involves at least hair gel, but usually they make use of little else. Daily, and for special occasions, a young man will comb his hair into a shape using hair gel while his hair is wet from a shower, and let it dry. Young women's hair is treated as a labor-intensive project, requiring many implements and products, time, and creativity to create new hairstyles on a regular basis. Daily, straight-haired and curly-haired women straighten or curl their hair with hair irons and hair dryers and use clips and braids and rubber bands to put their hair in different shapes. For special occasions, a young woman will spend even more time and energy producing a unique hairstyle, have a friend or family member style it, or even go to a salon to have their hair professionally styled. For example, preparing for a special event, I spent forty-five minutes curling my straight hair with hot rollers, mousse, and hair spray, to arrive at a participants' house about forty-five minutes late but to great enthusiasm for my hairstyle. After we swept and mopped and did the dishes, the participant straightened her sister's wavy hair with a hair iron and smoothing cream, after which I began to straighten the participants' wavy hair. We were about an hour-and-a-half late, due to a combination of hairstyle production and household chores.

In women's dress as in other areas of beautification, gendered influences are also evident. The norm for young women is to wear very tight, form-fitting clothes that make them look thinner and/or closer to the 90-60-90 (cm) ideal feminine curvature.[10] Young women's color coordination is much more exaggerated than boys', because they match colors on shoes, socks, pants, blouses, jackets, and jewelry, always using some color combination of these items to convey that they are well-dressed.

Beautification practices are further gendered by the sources of media and marketing to young people. Young women use more sources of information and more often to gather inspiration for their "looks." They collect and share magazines, enter online chats on beauty, share information with their friends, all at a higher rate than the young men. Of media sources, men cited two magazines and the Internet as sources within which they might find beauty information. Women cited the Internet; numerous clothing, shoe and makeup catalogs; numerous television stations and specific shows; and eleven magazines. In addition, ostensibly gender-neutral media targets women as consumers of beauty information much more commonly than men. For instance, *Por Ti*, a youth pop culture magazine for young men and women, offers articles on pop stars and pop culture, and sections on beauty and fashion that are directed to the women.

In summary, beauty production and consumption is highly gendered among the youth of Guadalajara, meaning that young men's production and consumption of beauty produces a markedly masculine body, while young women's production and consumption of beauty produces a body that is recognizably feminine. The masculine body is notably stronger, more athletic, un-produced appearing, and less directly visible, while the feminine body is more directly visible through tight clothing, as well as visibly altered and produced through techniques of hair, skin, and makeup.

BEAUTY CONSUMPTION AND PRODUCTION IS RACIALIZED

One of the most interesting and challenging results from this research concerns youths' perspectives on race and beauty. Few youth explicitly expressed a preference for racialized beauty, although a majority defined prototypical beauty ideals *among their peers* in terms of "fine features," light eyes, light hair, thinness, hourglass curves for women, and broad shoulders and slim hips for men. Very few considered beauty to be a question of skin color, although to those for whom it was an issue, lighter skin was the preference. As with beauty in general, youth were disinclined to make judgmental comments about their peers and themselves based on racialized assumptions.

Among those few who did discuss racialized ideals for beauty, three were young men who evidenced as much or more concern with racialized ideals of beauty as the one young woman who expressed her desire for lighter skin. To the extent that these mainstream, *fresa*, boys, freely discussed their concern for looking good, their concerns revolved around looking wealthy and looking whiter, bigger, stronger, and more fine-featured. This suggests that the articulation of gendered body politics in Guadalajara is different from that in the US or Western Europe due to race and the place of Guadalajara in global flows of products, practices, and ideas. Whereas in feminist studies of disciplinary beautification in the United States scholars focus on how beautification both reflects and reinscribes gendered power relations, and intersects with race to differentiate women of color's experiences from those of white women, looking at ideals of beauty in a non-Western context highlights how gendered and racialized ideals affect men profoundly.

As a caveat, it is important to note that Anglo-American or Western ideals of beauty are not totalizing in Guadalajara. In preparing to investigate the politics of beautification among Mexican youth, even preparing to enter the field without prejudgments, I had much overestimated the degree to which Anglo-American norms would hold sway over ideas and ideals of beauty. In actuality, youth had a wide range of reactions to global flows of beauty products, practices, and ideas. One young man rejected buying imported fashion, a high-value commodity, out of patriotism. One young woman sought out advice on how to fix herself up through Internet chat rooms from young women in South America and other parts of Mexico. A young man and a young woman who do not know each other both use the Internet to learn about other countries' styles. The young man likes to adopt styles that are British; the young woman just likes to look. The main activities on Metroflog, a popular youth networking website (before the social networking website Facebook took over the market in 2008) are to put on display pictures of *oneself* for viewing and evaluating, and to view pictures of friends and write comments and leave a virtual signature on the photos viewed. Youth identified with different subcultures orient their fashion identification with global subcultures whose creative centers are in Scandinavia, London, Germany, Israel, India (Goa), and Japan (see chapter six).

Still, the three young men who spoke freely about their interest and investment in style also spoke freely about their concern with racial or ethnic identifiers, and erasing them. For themselves, the young men seek ways to remove signs of ethnicity to achieve their ideal look. These young men reported trying to stay out of the sun to keep their skin from darkening, using exercises to try to make them taller, and using a nasal prosthetic to make a nose with a down-turned bridge appear to be upturned. One boy assured me that his friend would not be able to accompany him to a fashionable nightclub because the friend was too dark skinned. He considered the idea that his friend might be able to dress like a very wealthy person in order to gain access, but was not convinced this would work. Most older men interviewees did not report these types of preoccupations, although one did recount how he had wished he were a tall blond, broad-shouldered, and thin-waisted man when he was a teen; he thought it would have been easier to get girls if he looked like a movie star.

Of young women participants, only one reported concern for the color of her skin, and used a skin-lightening cream and sunscreen combination to make her skin lighter. Still, another young woman expressed dismay at her pallor, saying she sometimes tries to tan. Some young women did, however, poke fun at young indigenous women, or women with "Oaxacan faces" as being particularly out of fashion. One mother laughed at the efforts of indigenous girls downtown who try to dress in a modern way—"you know, the ones who sell potato chips downtown and they try to change their clothes to fit in?"— saying that they could change their clothes but they still looked the same. A version of this conversation and set of comments recurred several times in varied contexts.

The diminishing or erasing of ethnic identifiers through bodily modification brings to mind the body politics as described by conventional feminist theories: it is the modification of difference, in this case defined as ethnicity, toward a normalizing ideal (Chapkis 1986; Bartky 1990; Bordo 1993) that privileges masculinity, but a very narrow vision of masculinity defined by whiteness, strength, and control over the natural world and women. In this way, skin lightening, heightening exercises, nose realignment, and even dress modifications can be read as acts of conforming to regulatory ideals of race and gender. To be attractive, these young men feel strongly that they should be tall, broad-shouldered, and with upturned noses and fair skin. Indeed, these young men take up the task of their racialized bodies in order to produce their ideal of masculinity, much in the way young women take up their bodies as tasks to produce themselves as recognizably feminine.

This evidence suggests that young Mexican men experience the racialized aspects of globalizing beauty ideals as powerfully as, or more than, young women. It raises the question of whether, in a non-Western context, and in the context of globalization, body politics are as much or more about race than they are about gender. These body politics are right at the intersection of race and gender; it appears to be through racial transformation that some young Mexican men seek to achieve a more powerful masculinity. Still, I hesitate to state unequivocally that young men's beauty is more racialized than young women's, since, as with body shape, girls are highly attuned to researchers' and adults' concern for their healthy body image.

They demonstrated knowledge of "healthy body image correct" answers more frequently than young men, and they may just have easily learned to have a "healthy" answer about race as they do about weight.

CONCLUSION

The *quince* is a tradition that constructs and puts on display a culturally conventional prototype of gendered, beautiful, adolescence. In Guadalajara, the growing list of symbolic rituals, exchanges, and theater that form part of the *quince años* and the months-long process of preparation demonstrate shifts in religious, gender, social, and familial relations in urban Mexico. Adolescence itself has emerged as a privileged category within the *quince*, replacing womanhood as the aspiration of the *quinceañeras* and manhood for the *chambelanes*. Through the lens of the *quince* and the process of beautification within it, the importance of the makeover to the construction of gendered adolescence is brought into relief. The makeover is now a central part of the formation of gendered adolescence, not least within the *quince*. Gender has always been a central part of the *quince* pageantry, but its enactment is shifting toward a made-up, actively constructed, overtly sexual, and publicly displayed set of characteristics.

The rising importance of the beauty makeover and dancing relative to church and familial rituals suggests that there are shifts in the substance of gendered adolescence in Guadalajara. The beautification process plays an important role in these changes, and contributes to the shifting meanings of gendered adolescence. This makes the global economy of beauty and its ties to the local processes of beautification, for example within the *quince*, that much more important. Categories of privilege and power are also important, both to the increasingly important process of beautification in the construction of gendered adolescence, but also to the global political economy of beauty. Categories of privilege and power are embedded in and reproduced by beautification, and are therefore embedded and reproduced in the globalization of beautification.

In addition to illustrating the rapidly shifting fashions and beauty styles, beauty standards and practices at any one moment illustrate that the keys to the process of beautification, invention of new trends, and dispersion of fashions are adolescent social identification and differentiation. The degree of importance and participation of youth in these processes illustrate that youth are the key to beauty globalization. More important than any single beauty standard or practice, the process of beautification and fashion trend setting, as seen through youth practices, indicates that youth are responsible more than any other group for beauty and fashion globalization.

Youth's incomparable role in beauty globalization is important because it upsets assumptions and assertions that beauty globalization is an external, unstoppable force. Youth are not passive recipients of marketing and media, consumption and ideas. Rather, their desires for uniqueness and belonging lead to them seeking and driving beauty globalization. In addition, youth even demonstrate an awareness of adults' worry about adolescents being corrupted by unhealthy external images, and exhibit savvy techniques of denying those assumptions. As opposed to being recipients of beauty globalization, youth act as idea entrepreneurs, and their practices drive the circulation of ideas, images, and products in the global economy of beauty.

Even given the agency that adolescents exercise in beauty globalization, it is not an egalitarian enterprise. Children learn racialized and gendered ideas about beauty from their parents, and deploy them in their search for fitting in and standing out among their peers. The availability of images, ideas, and products also shape the choices and contexts within which adolescents pursue their beauty entrepreneurialism. Given the presence and importance of familial guidance and conformation to older generations, as well as the pull to conform to social standards, youth innovation is seriously circumscribed by convention. In the case of beauty in Mexico, these conventions continue to include a history of strong gender dichotomies and racial hierarchy based on indigenousness and class. In sum, the globalization of beautification processes is driven by youth's desires, but shaped by both convention and their reach for innovation.

CHAPTER 3

Princess Dresses, Sexy Dances, and Eye Shadow: The Construction of a Global Political Economy of Beauty Through a Makeover

The importance of the process of beautification to the construction of gendered adolescence in Guadalajara means that the global political economy of beauty is that much more present and important to the *quince* and other forums for beautification*. In addition, one can observe many interesting things about the global political economy of beauty through the lens of the *quince años*. The global political economy of beauty is not "out there" in a fictional global space, but intimately connected to the production, consumption, and imagination of beauty in the *quince años*. The formal market in productive goods is important, but equally or more important are the semi-formal direct-selling markets, the informal markets in products and services, and reproductive labor by the *quinceañeras* and their families and friends. The production of the *quince años* also sheds light on the gendered processes of globalization. Globalization in the beauty industry is successful in large part due to gendered production, reproduction, and consumption in the beauty industries, demonstrating that the feminine gendering of the body itself is an engine of globalization. Linking the gendered body to gendered globalization illustrates the salience of linking

* "Beauty and the Quinceañera: Reproductive, Productive and Virtual Dimensions of the Global Political Economy of Beauty," by Angela McCracken. In Feminism and International Relations: Conversations about the Past, Present, and Future, edited by Laura Sjoberg and J. Ann Tickner, 194–211 (London: Routledge, 2011).

the reproductive, productive, and virtual economies (Peterson 2003) to understand the politics of globalization. It also highlights the importance of (gendered) bodies within globalization, and the important role of beautification in globalization illustrates how interdependent the reproductive, productive, and virtual economies are in the global economy.

Likewise, through the lens of the global economy of beauty we can see many interesting things about the *quince*. Through engagement with the global political economy, the *quince* of the twenty-first century includes symbols, rituals, and processes of preparation and, especially, beautification that were previously unseen in Guadalajara. Becoming a Mexican woman is no longer the same process it was in 1950. The result for the *quince* tradition and Mexican gender construction is, through ties to the global economy, a tradition and gender construction that is substantially more commercial, produced, and full of symbols than the *quince* and Mexican beauty of fifty years earlier.

THE REPRODUCTIVE, PRODUCTIVE, AND VIRTUAL ECONOMIES AND THE *QUINCEAÑERA*

In the *quince*, the productive economy of beauty is defined by market exchange in beauty products and services. The reproductive economy of the *quince* is defined by socialization in beauty practices, consumption, and information. The virtual economy of beauty is defined by the commodification and exchange of *quince* "traditions" and beauty ideals through media, marketing, and advertising.

The productive economy of the *quince* is immense. Those preparing for the *quince* purchase many products and services: catalogs and magazines; church services; party venues; lighting; dresses; makeovers; dance choreography and accompaniment; accessories; shoes; video and photography; music; invitations; decorations; transportation; food, drink, and cake; the "last doll"; jewelry; attire for the *chambelanes;* and a growing list of "extras" marketed to make a celebration unique. There are zones in the downtown business district dedicated to dress vendors; fabric shops; stationery printing; accessories; dolls; and party decorations especially for *quinceañeras* or *quinceañeras* and *novias* (brides; see figure 3.1). Beauticians, dance teachers and choreographers, videographers, photographers, suit rentals, party venues, and caterers are geographically dispersed throughout the city.

The role of the reproductive economy in the *quince* is also considerable. The church service reinforces the religious institution and hierarchy, even asking the participant to reaffirm her faith and commitment to the church. The reproduction of social networks is also important, as friends, extended

Figure 3.1: A *quinceañera* or a bride used in a flower shop advertisement

family, and family members' friends are customarily invited as a method of reinforcing social bonds and social status. The use of *padrinos* or sponsors for the party also establishes and reinforces social networks. Spending time with family and friends was most cited as the key aspect of the ritual for *quinceañeras*, *chambelanes*, and other participants. The preparation and execution of the event is organized by daughter and mother, and teaches skills such as networking, budgeting, priority-setting, and negotiation (Stewart 2004; Davalos 1996). Finally, family order is reinforced and reconstituted as celebrants and their parents negotiate freedoms and responsibilities of adolescence.

The virtual economy is also deeply tied to the *quince* through the images and ideas presented to celebrants in television, print media, street-level marketing, and through social networks. Television talk shows frequently incorporate *quince*-related content, such as beauty or essay contests to win a free *quince*. An MTV show has replicated the success of *My Super Sweet Sixteen*, which displays extravagant sixteen-year birthday celebrations of the children of celebrities and the super wealthy in the United States, with *Quiero Mis Quince*, which shadows celebrants in preparations and executions of their "dream" *quince*. Print media include weekly social column announcements, media directed at *quince* preparation, and popular magazines that young people use to obtain information about beauty and fashion. Federal, state, and local governments organize benefit *quinces* for poor or disenfranchised youth and create media campaigns around their own initiatives and the *quinceañeras*. The largest of these are sponsored by multiple cosmetics and hair product firms, as well as prestigious salons and cosmeticians, who donate products and services in exchange for publicity. In the nation's capital, the largest benefit *quince* is celebrated at the national performing arts center with a red carpet, simulcast on an outdoor screen, and televised. The local industry contributes substantial street-level marketing. And there are party seasons when a youth and her/his family will be invited to one or more *quinceañeras* per weekend for several months and experience the *quince* as a medium for beauty messaging replete with photography, red carpets, videography, and theater.

In three snapshots below, this text highlight the aspects of *quince* preparation that are most tied to the feminine gendering of the body: the dress, the makeover, and dance, and I apply a feminist global political economy lens to them. At the same time, I am applying a *quince* lens to the global political economy. I argue that the dress, the makeover, and the dance are shaped by and shape the global political economy through the intertwining reproductive, productive, and virtual economies.

The Dress

The dress industry is the most obvious aspect of the *quince* productive economy to a casual observer, as offerings are made in almost every business district, and there are well-known dress districts in the city center that attract customers from all parts of the city and from surrounding rural towns. While not all of the sixteen interviewees who had already procured their dress purchased it in the city center, all but three went to the downtown *quinceañera/novia* district to try on dresses. Two of the celebrants who did not travel downtown to look at dresses defined their *quince* celebrations as nontraditional partly because they did not buy the typical princess dress. However, one did head downtown and to the malls to look at evening gowns, eventually choosing a cocktail dress from a popular chain store. The other wore some of her favorite clothes. The third *quinceañera* who did not source her dress from the downtown shopping district borrowed a dress from a friend at the last minute.

Among those fourteen celebrants who viewed their *quince* as a more traditional endeavor, eleven bought their dresses downtown, and three chose a style at a store or out of a magazine and then selected a seamstress to reproduce their desired style at a lower cost. The story of how one dress was found illustrates several of the most important elements to finding a dress: the downtown dress district, budget, uniqueness, copying, and reliance on female social networks. After much searching downtown and elsewhere, this young participant found a dress in a shop in Tonolá, one of the municipalities on the eastern side of the Guadalajara metropolitan zone. The dress was unlike any other she had seen, but it was too expensive for her budget. She asked her mother's friend, a seamstress, to visit the store with her, and from memory the seamstress reproduced the chosen dress. Dress shopping downtown is the near universal starting point for a *quince* dress. At the heart of the city center and butted up against the largest shopping market in the city, young people in Guadalajara grow up seeing the dresses in windows and sidewalks. Dress copying is so common that dress shop managers will not allow photographs of their product and will not allow known seamstresses into their shops. Dress copying is done commercially by the vendors themselves, but even more frequently by home workshop seamstresses who are part of a *quinceañera's* social networks. For example, another celebrant's aunt sewed her dress, and they went downtown to one of the big fabric stores to pick out the fabric and design. She chose her dress design based on a composite of an evening dress she had worn before as a model and a corset ("which is the kind of thing used for the *quince*"), and, per her aunt's insistence, made it more modest for going to church.

The downtown district for *quince* dresses is divided roughly into two types of dress vendors: resellers of mass-production dresses and independent designers. The independent designers, more likely to be located in the upscale Chapultepec zone, offer personally designed dresses in the 5,000+ peso ($500+) category. These high-end stores also sell name-brand designer dresses imported from the US, Europe, or Mexico City. The girl and her designer, and usually her mother, will design the dress to satisfy the youth's desire for a unique look that expresses her personal style. Asked whether she had seen changes in the industry in the last ten years, a personal designer responded (from my field notes):

> (Emphatically)Yes, yes, many changes. The girls have become very daring and they no longer want a pastel gown with a large puffy skirt, they want black, red, they want it short, they want it daring and baring lots of skin, they like lots of dark colors and lots of contrast, red and black, white and fuchsia, fuchsia

and blue, things like that. They no longer come in and mom says, my daughter, put this on, wear this. Now, they come in and the daughter says: "No, I don't like it. I want it like this and like this" and they have ideas from the centers of fashion, Hollywood, many Hollywood stars, New York, Europe. They find pictures in magazines, on the Internet, and they say: I want this. She mentioned Penelope Cruz, Salma Hayek, Avril Lavigne, and the Cure as influences she has seen among her clients.

This designer explained to me that she will sit down with a client and her family with photos from international fashion magazines such as *Hola* (Spain) or *quince* magazines from Mexico City or Guadalajara, or a picture of a dress worn by a celebrity and published in magazines or on the Internet, and balance those desires with budgets and parents' requisites regarding fashion. From my field notes:

> She often negotiates with her client, as do the parents, to find something that the parents find acceptable and that she as a designer sees as fit for the figure and coloring of her client. She tells a story of a client who wanted an Avril Lavigne outfit, with a red skirt, white corset, and a small black jacket. The black was no good because the client had very dark skin, the parents didn't like the outfit anyway, so they put tulle under the skirt to make it more puffy and traditional, used fabric with black and white windowpane (*cuadrada*) and another white with black polka dots for the top, and dropped the black jacket.

The dress may be made by the designer, but the designer-made dresses are often actually subcontracted to seamstresses who sew for much less than the designer, or are even subcontracted to the very same factories that mass-produce the copies (see below).

The other main source for dresses is the dress shops that carry facsimiles of designer dresses. While their merchandise is jealously guarded from independent seamstresses who make copies in home workshops, these shops sell mass-produced dresses that replicate designer styles in *quince* magazines and at the Expo Quinceañera. These copy dresses typically sell at between 2,000 and 4,000 Mexican pesos, and are sold in dozens of shops at the heart of downtown. Shops don't sell the exact same dresses, but they are supplied by two main manufacturers outside of the metropolitan zone. These two manufacturers produce simplified copies of dresses that are featured in designer advertisements or magazines, and they sell models to the downtown vendors. Through vendors, *quinceañeras* can special-order models with variations and in different colors, making the dresses more customized. For example, a dress can be chosen with Top A, B, or C, with top X, Y, or Z, and in colors 1, 2, or 3. The number of options and combinations is virtually infinite. These dresses exhibit the same color trends that the designers use, although with less dramatic effects—for example, a single strong color. Although *quinceañeras* frequently expressed their desire for black and red dresses, among tens of shops visited several times and hundreds of dressed browsed, I only saw one almost-black dress hanging up on a dressing rack, and never saw one on display on a mannequin. I did see some red dresses for sale, although not in the main displays on mannequins and in windows. I myself never saw red or black dresses actually being worn, although a friend did see a red *quinceañera* dress on a celebrant taking pictures in the park. Mothers tend to disapprove of red and black dresses, and the negotiation over the dress color, shape, and degree of sexiness is a focal point in the negotiations over *quince* tradition and innovation.

The production of the *quinceañera* dress operates in close connection with the global reproductive, productive, and virtual economies. They are produced as part of the informal, flexible, or factory-based, and always-feminized dressmaking industry, or by female relatives. Their design is closely tied to the global virtual economy of signs through media and advertising.

The designer and the copy dresses are produced through a feminized and globalized chain of production that includes the virtual economy of signs. Such signs include fashion magazines, Japanese cartoons, the Internet, Hollywood celebrities, and international music stars. The abundant offerings within this market are the result of the shift in the Mexican economy since the 1960s toward specialization in certain industries, one of which is garment manufacture (Fernandez-Kelly 1983). Part of the success of the shift toward garment manufacture, and the reason for the industry's feminization, has to do with the low value given to women's reproductive labor in clothes-making (Mies 1986; Enloe 2004).

The production of the dresses cannot, however, be separated from the market that they serve: a demanding, informed base of youth. The desire for uniqueness is universal among interviewees and is reflected in advertising and sales pitches made by dress designers. Exclusivity of design is the thrust of designers' sales pitches. It is what their clients are looking for. Clients also bring with them images, literal and imaginary, of what they want, based on information they gather through media and marketing in magazines, television, and the Expo. The result is that now, as youth's access to information directs their search for unique expressions of their identities, the global virtual economy of signs informs their dress production.

Makeovers

Beauty salon services employed by *quinceañeras* typically include a hairstyle and a makeup session, acrylic fingernail fashions, and, often, hair coloring or highlights. Only the two *quinceañeras* who identified themselves as having a "nontraditional" party did not have their hair and makeup done by a professional. The other fourteen *quinceañeras* who had completed their *fiesta* received the professional services of a female relative or friend of the family, a beautician in their neighborhood, or in the case of one, a beautician near her mother's place of work. Every neighborhood in the city, save a few very exclusive well-to-do neighborhoods, has a handful of beauty service providers within a short walking distance, operating out of homes, garages, small salons, or malls.

As women enter into the labor market, they enter it based on gendered cultural expectations as well as gendered demands on their time. These factors make working in beauty services an attractive option because it uses skills that they have developed through learning about becoming a beautiful woman in their personal lives, gives them added cultural cachet as an expert in beautification—a highly prized quality in Guadalajara, and offers flexible work options that allow them to fulfill family obligations. Indeed, the most common type of beauty salon in Guadalajara is run out of a beautician's home. The beauty industry that serves the *quinceañera* makeover is also part of, shaped by, and shapes the global economy of beauty. The considerable employment of women in the beauty industry is part of the global trend toward flexibilization and feminization of labor markets, a product of the inextricable productive and reproductive economies.

Additionally, the majority of interviewees purchase at least some of their beauty products from friends and relatives selling as network distributors for companies including Avon, Jafra, Fuller, and Mary Kay. Direct sales through network marketing is being intensified, and successfully, in the Mexican market for health and beauty products. This increase in network-based direct sales is a further flexibilization of the health and beauty industries, based on a gendered type of flexible labor employment through which international companies engage women's supposedly "free time" at home to sell and distribute products outside of a traditional retail model, for commission instead of wages and benefits.

The growth in the beauty services industry is also closely related to the growth in the information and images circulating evermore rapidly and profusely as part of the growth and speed in the virtual economy. The financial sector motivates and shapes the growth of markets in emerging nations and among youth or emerging consumers, as they are important targets for growth in profits. The ideas about femininity that make beauty services or network–based direct sales a good, even a "natural," option for women influence why and how women are recruited into beauty services, sales, and distribution. For example, the overwhelming majority of images used in cosmetics advertising feature women. The proliferation of images, services, and products for beautification enable people, particularly women and youth, to learn about and participate in the beauty industry in ever more myriad ways. In addition, the exponential growth in beautification techniques encourages women to seek more products, and so they require spending money to buy them or the discounts that come with being a "distributor." In sum, the beauty services and products industries are shaping both the global political economy of beauty and the production of the gendered body, particularly for women and adolescents. The result is rapid expanding and populating of the beauty industry with women and young workers, and the multiplying of services and products within the industry.

Dance

Historically, the *quinceañera* celebrated her new social status as a young woman by dancing a waltz with her father or with her escort, or both. This tradition has evolved into one of the most important parts of the production and the most anxiety-producing: the waltz, toast, and the surprise dance. Ten of the fourteen girls who had already celebrated their *quince* used dance instructors to help them choreograph a waltz, and seven of these also choreographed one or more "surprise dance(es)." The choreographed waltz in all participants' cases was danced between the *quinceañera* and between four to eight *chambelanes*. As mentioned previously, *quinceañeras* frequently hire *chambelanes* from dance schools or dance companies for the waltz. A surprise dance is a dance of the girl's choosing that follows the waltz, and she often performs it with friends or *chambelanes*. In *fiestas* that I witnessed live, in video, or in photographs, *quinceañeras* danced tango, Hawaiian, Tahitian, Arabic, salsa, hip-hop, reggaeton, jazz, or even numbers from the movie *Grease* for their "surprise" dance. In photos and exhibits at the Expo Quince, many more themes emerged, frequently inspired by Hollywood movies.

The performance reinforces familial hierarchy as the *quinceañera* dances her final dance as a girl with her father. Her father then inducts her into womanhood by placing her in high heels and into the arms of her *chambelan-de-honor*. The dance also plays a symbolic role in her induction into heterosexual coupling as she dances with her *chambelanes* (Cantú 1999). The waltz is an important part of the reproductive sphere as it performs and reproduces ideals of familial, gender, and sexual relations.

The productive economy of dance is in some ways localized because teens generally prepare and learn choreographies for their *quince* at local dance academies. Many young girls are enrolled in courses well in advance of their fifteenth birthday, and most hire their dance academy teacher to choreograph the performances and teach their court of *damas* and *chamebelanes* in private lessons. The rest of the *quinceañeras* ask friends and family for recommendations for dance schools or choreographers that specialize in *quince* choreographies.

Dance teachers and choreographers are most often the brokers for professional *chambelanes*, recommending them from their networks of former students and friends. Alternatively, professional *chambelan* agencies recruit young men from dance schools, and advertise their service at the Expo Quince and through word-of-mouth. Professional *chambelan* troupes provide the whole package, from choreography, dancers, and costumes, to make the *quinceañera* shine. Or, celebrants may purchase special clothing or costumes that fit the theme and style of the surprise dances. As mentioned earlier, many *quinceañeras* will change to a shorter version of their ball gowns, paired with the same corsets, for their surprise dance. Other costumes might include rock-themed denim skirts and tank tops or belly dance, tango, salsa, Hawaiian, and hip-hop-themed details.

Despite the local nature of the dance economy, the political economy of dance is global, through its links to the reproductive and, especially, virtual economies. One surprisingly global aspect to the dances is demonstrated by their varied styles and execution. The traditional waltz tends to be more conservative, reiterating themes of colonial Spain and English and French aristocracy. It is danced in an upright, formal embrace where bodies only touch at the hands. Still, despite the tradition and conservatism inherent in the waltz, the urge to express originality is leading to a diversification of waltz styles. Some of the standards for *quince* waltzes are *Sobre las Olas* (Juventino Rosas 1884), *De Niña a Mujer* (Julio Iglesias 1981), and *Tiempo de Vals* (Chayanne 1990). *Sobre las Olas* is an instrumental waltz, and a traditional first dance for newly married couples at weddings. *De Niña a Mujer* is a classic ballad, the lyrics of which acknowledge, despite a father's resistance and lament, a daughter's growth from girl to woman. *Tiempo de Vals*, or "waltz time," is a song about waltzing being an occasion for going back in time, first loves, romance, and passion. These are the three classic waltz songs for a *quince*, and they are still frequently used, despite the trend toward modernization and more explicit focus on popular culture and sexuality. Notice, for example, the shift in themes between the songs originally popular in the 1950s (instrumental classical waltz), 1980s (a father's lament for losing his little girl to womanhood), and the 1990s (an ode to romance and passion). This illustrates a trajectory from buttoned-up and chaste romance to overt sexuality within the *quince*. Chayanne's classic is still heard probably every weekend at a *fiesta* in Guadalajara, but more and more youth are choosing unconventional music from popular culture to choreograph their waltzes. I saw or heard about Disney, pirate, and Arabian nights themes, with dances performed to film scores or Whitney Houston or Paris Hilton songs. These songs follow the trend toward more explicit romance and heterosexuality. Despite the changing music score, the waltz dance itself continues to play out a prince and princess theme and reinforce classical ideas about gender roles: a beautiful dance partner with a corseted waist taking dainty, controlled steps.

As mentioned earlier, the inclusion of "surprise dance(s)" in the *quince* choreography is a relatively new phenomenon, dating to the first decade of the twenty-first century. Despite their newness, the surprise dances are by far more common than not, and are now the more important part of the celebration, especially for *quinceañeras*. One mother complained that during the year her daughter and her daughter's friends turned fifteen, she was compelled to stop attending the *fiestas* because she would get so bored with seeing one surprise dance follow another, with the guests' dancing sometimes not starting until after midnight. Surprise dances are identified as special and exciting because they reflect the unique desires of *quinceañeras* and are used to show off their personal style and skills. While the youths' claims to originality are questionable, the surprise dances are important to them as sources of personal expression. It is in these dances that one can see the global virtual economy of signs best. Here, *quinceañeras* imitate popstars like Shakira and Beyonce and groups like Vaselina, and they achieve a striking similarity to the pop culture music video form: pop music, short skirts, short shirts, tight clothing, shiny shoes, and fashion that is generally designed to highlight waists, chests, hips and buttocks, and legs. Other surprise dances use the Latin American dance forms of tango and salsa, also danced wearing fashions that show off the body and in ways that emphasize sexuality. Finally, surprise dances often pick up on the Arabian, Hawaiian, and Tahitian dance forms popularized by Shakira and taught in dance academies across the city. Again, Arabian, Hawaiian, and Tahitian dances feature body-centric clothing and dance styles. The surprise dances are usually performed by a *quinceañera* alone or with a group of girlfriends; sometimes the dance will incorporate a *chambelan* or a few *chambelanes*, particularly in the partner-based salsa and tango dances, where a professional or semi-professional dancer will be hired to lead.

The surprise dances universally present a picture of the *quinceañera* that is in high contrast to the waltzes. First, she sheds the floor-length ball gown for something more revealing on the bottom, or makes a costume change that creates a new character, distinct from the dancing princess holding court. In these dances, she plays the solo star performing a dance on a stage. Or she plays the lead dancer in a hip-hop dance troupe or a group of booty-shaking divas. She plays the female lead in a romance choreography where two dance partners fight over her. She plays the reluctant lover in a tango. In these types of dances, she frequently dances solo as a celebrity, or as a lead dancer, or as the object of desire, and usually in a highly sexualized manner.

In sum, the local dance classes, teachers, choreographers, dancers, and costumes are produced or practiced locally, but are intertwined with the global economy of beauty, largely through the virtual economy of signs. The adolescent interpretation of the Viennese waltz, the global pop music score, and the music video have had a profound influence on the celebration of the *quince* tradition. In combination with the increasing use of photography and videography for the *quince*, the waltzes and surprise dances have added to the sense that a *quinceañera*, rather than making a dedication to her church or a debut on the marriage market, is more of a celebrity for a day, replete with makeover, costumes, red carpet entrance, paparazzi, an audience, and a pop performance. The waltzes and surprise dances can be viewed and criticized on video-sharing websites. Viewers can then copy or improve upon the dances. In this sense the dances enter into and contribute to the global economy of signs that influences young people's interpretation of this tradition.

As should be evident from these three aspects of *quince* preparation—dress, dance, and the makeover—how young women dress, modify, improve, and move their bodies is tied to the global economy of fashion and beauty products, images, and ideas. Not necessarily every aspect of the beautification of the *quinceañera* is global, but through the linking of the reproductive, productive, and virtual economies we see that the beautification process is indeed very closely linked to global exchanges. The dress shop downtown and the dance academy are local, but the Hollywood imagery and the European monarchies that inspire its style are part of the global virtual economy of signs. Likewise, the global gendered division of labor; the restructuring of state policies; the reorientation of national economic strategies toward dress manufacturing; and the brand piracy industry link the production of the dress to transformations in reproductive labor. The makeover might be conducted by a sister, cousin, or aunt, or in a local beauty salon, but the products, images and ideas are global.

The significance of the relationship between globalization and the bodily modifications and comportment of young girls in Guadalajara is twofold. First, it is important because it illustrates a diversification of expressions of gender in Guadalajara at the same time that traditional unequal gender relations are reinforced. The relationship of globalization to the gendering of the feminine body is complicated because it is at least partly *through* the gendering of the feminine body that globalization operates and reproduces existing inequalities. This can be seen through the operation of the reproductive, productive, and virtual economies in the *quince años*. Through gendered bodies, the productive economy relies on and supplies the reproductive economy and meets gendered consumer demands. This very process cannot help but reproduce those gendered divisions. For example, we see the increasing popularity of the *quinceañera*, which gives form to strict gendered ideas about women's relationship to the church, the family, their bodies, and sexuality. At the same time, however, the tradition is quickly evolving to incorporate new ways of "being new" for the girls. In their dances, this includes exaggerated sexuality, autonomy, and personal freedom. In their dresses, it means bright colors and black or red as increasingly common symbols of youthful femininity as opposed to white and pastels. In terms of beautification, their mothers' and fathers' ideals of a "natural feminine beauty" have given way to increasingly produced, unnatural, even alien-esque styles and the extensive consumption of beauty products. In short, while reproducing strict archaic gender norms, globalization is also undermining them, making them less natural, and creating more diversity among the young women of Guadalajara.

Secondly, it illustrates how the feminine gendering of the body can be seen as an engine of globalization. As postcolonial and postmodern feminists have noted, totalizing accounts of globalization as corporate capitalism writ large, including feminist ones, underestimate the power and participation of non-hegemonic forces in globalization (Gibson-Graham 1996; Chang and Ling 2000; Freeman 2001; Bergeron 2001). By the same token, the "ground-up" view must not be mistaken for a celebration of the local, difference, and women as the embodiment of agency (Freeman 2001; Bergeron 2001; Weldon 2006). By focusing on the way gendering of the body generates globalization, this text shows that globalization cannot be conceived as a totalizing or all-encompassing power. To the contrary, globalization must be understood as deeply intimate, indeed feeding into and being generated by all of our bodies and bodily modifications. Following Enloe's paraphrase of a feminist adage, the personal is political, the personal is economic, and the personal is international (Enloe 1989). In addition, in this case at least, it appears to be producing some diversity, albeit within a conformist gender imperative.

Figure 3.2: An alien-esque hairstyle advertisement at a home-based salon.

CONCLUSION

This chapter argues that the production of the gendered body, as seen through the *quince años* in Guadalajara, is shaped by and shapes globalization and that this process can be seen through reproductive, productive, and virtual economies. The links between the production of feminine beauty and the global political economy can be seen through the entire process of *quince* beautification, from dress and accessory selection to dance classes, makeup application to hair-styling, photography, and videography. Through ideals and practices of beautification, the production of gendered beauty in the *quince* is intimately shaped by the increasingly global exchange of products, ideas, and images.

A second argument is that the global political economy of beauty should be conceptualized using the RPV framing of the global economy. The RPV framing of the global economy as "intertwining and inextricable" reproductive (care), productive (market), and virtual (symbolic) exchange is useful to understanding how local beauty practices are simultaneously embedded in global markets, social reproduction, and exchange of symbolic information. The RPV framing is also useful in bridging the insights of feminist political economy and feminist cultural critique that inform scholarship on beautification. By combining the reproductive, productive, and virtual lenses on the global economy, we have a clearer picture of how globalization and the process of beautification in the *quince* are linked, and we also have a better idea of the politics of those links.

The close relationship between the construction of gendered adolescence and the global economy of beauty further builds on the argument, begun in chapter one, that the globalization of beauty is not a monolithic process. Whereas chapter two posited that youth's desires for social belonging and uniqueness drive beauty globalization, this chapter adds that the globalization happens through the bodily practices of dress, comportment, and makeovers, especially by girls. These very intimate acts of beautification are playing a role in constructing the global economy, and vice versa. Again, as discussed in chapter two, the result is the emergence of new expressions and substance of gendered adolescence in Guadalajara. There is more diversity in those expressions, as well as persistent conventions of privilege based on gender, race, and class.

CHAPTER 4

Beauty and the *Quince*: A Reproductive Economy View

Hostess Table Etiquette

1. Act sweetly, delicately, we are the hostesses.
2. Know how to chew delicately, without talking with a full mouth.
3. Know how to use the flatware, how to sit, how to use napkins.
4. Know how to converse.

Above are the major areas of social etiquette expertise, as taught to me at a beauty and personal development class at one of the most popular beauty schools in Guadalajara. To follow all of the rules and advice on how to be a good hostess in our daily lives would be outlandish in Guadalajara (I never saw a base plate in use), but the spirit of the advice is important: being a good host is a highly valued social skill, as are table manners and good conversation. Much of the advice from this class taught me new tools for accessing good social manners: letting my dinner partner walk to the restaurant table ahead of me gives him time to pull out my chair for me; telling my guests the hour that the meal will be served puts them at ease. But most of the advice is based on social etiquette that is primarily learned through the reproductive economy: families teach table manners, how to be a host, who pulls out the chair, and how to converse in a ladylike fashion. This class on social etiquette therefore brings into relief two things. First, feminine social etiquette, or norms of appropriate behavior, is not natural, but taught, learned, and practiced by reproductive labor. Second, the class illustrates a trend toward commercializing historically unpaid reproductive labor. For example, classes on beauty, manners, and comportment are now widely available in Guadalajara, as are classes on cosmetics, hair styling, and fashion. These two things, the teaching of femininity and the trend toward commercialization of that labor, are key elements to how the reproductive economy aids in the global circulation of beauty products.

This chapter extends out from the *quince* into the reproductive economy, which is responsible for the greatest part of the *quinceañera's* process of beautification. The reproductive economy includes biological reproduction, social and cultural reproduction through the education and rearing of young people, care work for the young, sick, and elderly, and production of unpaid goods and services for home consumption (Bakker and Gill 2003; Barker 2005; Hoskyns and Rai 2007). The overwhelming proportion of work and responsibility in the reproductive economy falls on women. Although the contribution to wealth made by unpaid reproductive work is overlooked by conventional political economy, reproductive labor is an essential activity without which the productive economy would not function as it currently does.

The reproductive economy in the global political economy of beauty is essential to understanding the depth of the economics and politics of beauty in women's personal lives. The reproductive economy perspective on the beauty industry is also important because it reveals how important unpaid work, women's work, and youths' work are to the global beauty industry. This approach foregrounds women's agency in building and driving the beauty economy through social reproduction. The beauty economy is not defined by women's passivity and consumption. Women are not victims of the global beauty industry, but rather its primary agents.

Reproductive work shapes the use of beauty products, the consumption of beauty information, and the formation of ideas about what is beautiful in the *quince*. The characteristics of the reproductive economy in the beautification of the *quinceañera* and the production of the *quince años* illustrate the centrality of the reproductive economy to the global political economy of beauty. Through its links to the global productive economy and the global virtual economy, the reproduction of gendered norms of beauty in the *quince años* is increasingly tied to globalization. The intersection of globalization with the reproduction of beauty in the *quince* has meant that reproductive labor is increasingly called upon, both as free labor when demands for beautification, beauty products, and beauty services rise, and as an industry to be commercialized. The intensification of demands on reproductive labor, the increasing commercialization of reproductive labor, and the role of the *quince* in the construction of social norms, means that the reproductive economy of beauty in the *quince* plays an important part in reproducing social hierarchies.

Structures of hierarchy in the global reproductive economy of beauty privilege narrowly defined masculinities and momentarily achievable ideals of femininity, the institutions of gender difference, marriage, family and church, and the ideologies of patriarchy, racism, capital commercialization, and individual consumption. Disagreement and negotiation between parents and adolescents over beauty and other ideals adds a twist to the reproduction of social norms, and shows one avenue through which change in the privileged institutions, ideologies, and identities of the *quince* may be occurring: generational rebellion.

REPRODUCING BEAUTY, REPRODUCING GENDER IN THE QUINCE AÑOS

The *quince* is produced through intense reproductive labor, and itself plays a significant role in the reproductive economy through communicating and teaching social norms. The *quince* is therefore both a product of and an input into the reproductive economy. The importance of reproductive labor in the production of the *quince años* is nowhere more clear than in the process of creating the beautiful *quinceañera*. Family and friends teach *quinceañeras* about beauty production and consumption. Ideas about what is beautiful, what products to use, and how to get beautiful are also passed through family and friends, through word of mouth, and via people in the newly commercialized reproductive industries—beauty services and personal product distribution (see chapter four). As *quinces* become more labor intensive and reproductive labor increasingly commercialized, the demand on reproductive labor, both unpaid and commercial, has increased dramatically.

The reproductive economy is important to the *quince* because orchestrating a Mass and a party is a lot of work and money. In fact, the amount of work and money they require can be prohibitive for most potential celebrants. When a family cannot afford the expense but still wants to practice the *quince* tradition, they might call on social networks and extended family to contribute their labor, gifts in kind, and money. One saw it as worth the effort because

> I would see my friends before their *quince*, I helped them get ready and everything, and I saw that they had to go rehearse with their *chambelanes*, that they had to go to find the dress, then the cake, then the invitees, then the dinner,

then something else, ugh, they were left with no, they didn't have time to do anything. But in the end I saw them and I saw that they were happy.

Just taking care of the basic elements of a party takes a lot of time for the *quinceañera* and those who help her.

Another *quinceañera* decided that a *quince* would not be worth the effort because she always saw people talking behind a *quinceañera's* back about something gone wrong after all her work.

> The *fiestas* are a lot of trouble because you have to be rehearsing a waltz, a surprise dance, take care of the dress, shoes, you fix up everything and it never comes out anything like you want or what you expect, and you can't please all the guests, there is always someone who leaves talking bad, or I don't know, that is what I have always seen.

The *quince años* takes a lot of money and reproductive labor, and the contentment of a *quinceañera* and her family is closely tied to the successful completion of the reproductive work and the accompanying social approval.

Extended families and friends, especially female, contribute a large part of the labor to make a *quince* possible. One of the major conduits for contributions is through the solicitation and participation of *padrinos*, or godparents/sponsors. A girl's baptismal godparents, or *padrinos de bautizo*, will often participate with a monetary contribution, and *padrinos* will hold a position of honor at the party and be announced by an emcee. The *padrino* (godfather), or a special *padrino* who sponsors the larger part of the *fiesta*, will often perform a special dance with the *quinceañera* after she dances with her father.

Depending on a girl's economic resources and her social resourcefulness, she may have many more *padrinos* for her *quince años*. One of the major developments in the practice of the *quince años* is the emergence of the use of *padrino* sponsors to make the party accessible to aspiring middle class families. As one father recounted regarding the differences between *quinceañeras* in his time, in the mid-1960s, and those of his children, "Yes, they are different, I think, because of the simple fact that before a *quinceañera* just stood up with her godparents and her parents at the church to give thanks and now, now I see that there are even 'cake' godparents, 'dress' godparents, godparents for everything." One girl protested to me that she did not want to celebrate the relatively new tradition of giving the celebrant her "last doll," saying that "are a lot of *madrinas*[1], for example for the cushion, for the drinks, for the ring, for everything. I would like to have one for the cushion, for the drinks, for the bible, for the album,... for the cake server and the knife, but not the doll, that doesn't agree with me so much." Many people contribute without being *padrinos* or *madrinas*, as well. A party might be held in the home of a friend of the family, or the party salon owned by a parent's work colleague, for example, to cut down on costs. All of these godparents and sponsors contribute a portion of the expense and labor to create a party full of details and an increasing number of traditions.

The cooperative nature of paying for a *quince* makes the overall cost difficult to estimate. One *quinceañera* borrowed a dress, and another used clothing she already had. It is more difficult to assess the cost of the less expensive celebrations because there are more sponsors and more gifts in kind, such as beauty makeover services, borrowed transportation, potluck, and borrowed event locations. A meal and party at home for a girl and her friends may cost as little as 500 pesos. With the help of an older brother of one *quinceañera*, I estimated one simple and low-cost *quince* to have cost about 8,000 pesos (800 USD) among the various contributors. On the higher end, a *quinceañera* bought a designer dress, hired professional *chambelanes*, rented a limousine, hired a musical variety show, a disc jockey, and a mariachi band, and rented one of the more expensive dance halls and church halls, for a party that I estimate cost over 130,000 pesos (13,000 USD), in addition to the cost numerous family members paid to fly from the United States. These costs are not, and are not expected to be, recuperated in gifts to the *quinceañera*.

Quince preparation involves a lot of cooperative effort, but when it comes to the beautification, it is female family members and friends who are responsible, from ideas to applications. Personal relationships, word of mouth, and close proximity are the keys to who ends up dressing and "fixing up" the *quinceañera*. A dress might be made by the friend of a mother, a sister's friend might do the *quinceañera's* makeup and nails, and perhaps a mother will find a salon recommended by a friend at work. A *quinceañera's* sisters might help her design her dress, or one of them might pay for it. One *quinceañera's* cousin donated skills that she was learning in beauty school, and another's cousin hired her own cosmetician. The cosmetician brought a hairdresser that she works with. Another *quinceañera* went to the makeup artist, nail artist, and hair stylist that her sister recommended, a place by their house. Yet another had her makeover done by an older sister, a professional cosmetician. One *quinceañera* borrowed green jewelry to match her green dress from a cousin who had also worn green, although of a different shade. Friends and family members gift and loan jewelry, makeup applications, hair styling, dress design, dress manufacture, shoes, flowers, dance classes, and all of the other elements of a party. In the cases where a cosmetician is contracted, it is without fail through a personal recommendation or through a beautician's salon in the neighborhood. All of the service labor involved in teaching beautification and comportment is essential to the production of the beautiful *quinceañera*, who is inexperienced in such things.

Mothers are, almost without exception, the central influence on a *quinceañera's* preparation. The refrain "my mom told me" or "my mom said" is sprinkled through discussions of *quince* preparation, dress shopping, makeup, and hair. As one interviewee recounted, "at first I said 'no,' that I didn't want one, that I would prefer if they gave me money, but my mom said 'no,' that she wanted to give me a party." I came to find out that at least two *quinceañeras* celebrated only under intense pressure from their mothers, while many more experienced their mother's desire to celebrate as merely one among many motivations.

One of the areas over which mothers exercise substantial influence is the dress. Mothers are the primary shopping partners for dress shopping, as observable in the downtown *quince* shopping districts. The three girls who wanted black dresses did not get them or did not think they would get them because of their mothers' protest. One mother convinced her daughter to choose a pastel green dress over the girl's favorite color because the pastel green "made her shine." One "nontraditional" *quinceañera's* mother picked out her dress for her.

Chambelanes also contribute significantly to the reproductive economy of the *quince años*, playing the very important role of Prince Charming in the party, as well as that of supportive friend through the preparations and at the party. One *chambelan* who had made two debuts and was planning on a third, explained that he likes to perform this role because "it is a nice thing, you know...you make the *quinceañera* feel good, when she is having trouble doing a dance step, you support her and you tell her that she can learn the dance step...it is true, the majority can learn the step, why can't she? Taking it easier and practicing more you can do it. It feels nice to me." This *chambelane's* sentiments, while more fully articulated than some others', are not uncommon. The boys dedicate many afternoons to repetitive dance rehearsals, hours and hours of flirting, and making the *quinceañera* feel special. At rehearsal after rehearsal I witnessed considerate and patient *chambelanes* encouraging the *quinceañera*, trying to increase her confidence, and teaching choreographies to newly added members of the court or to ones falling behind.

Friends are also a significant source of information and help in the preparatory stages. One *quinceañera* reported her first motivation to have a party based on her friends' encouragement. Another went from a basic, simple party to a theme-driven, all-the-bells-and-whistles party after she went with friends to the Expo Quince and they prodded each other on. Most celebrants choose their choreographer from a dance school near their house, perhaps one where they already take classes. Others, however, find them through their friends who have hired choreographers or through parents, often talking at *quince años* parties. One celebrant hired her choreographer through word of mouth after attending a friend's *quince años* with her mother. In another case, a *chambelan* had contacts with choreographers from a previous *quince años*, and when his *quinceañera* and her court became disillusioned with their choreographer and dance instructor, he used his contacts to rehire someone from the dance company that had trained him at the earlier *quinceañera*.

This word-of-mouth and friends-and-family approach to the *quinceañera's* preparation and makeover hit home when, as my attendance at a beauty school became known, my services were sought to make up and style hair for an interviewee at her beauty contests. Then, at the big event, I quickly became a last-minute helper for other contestants who had not contracted professional services. Nervous and hesitant about my own skills, I was reassured by my young participant that she knew nothing about makeup and hair, so anything would be fine.

Cosmeticians, whether hired, family members, or even acquaintances, play an important role in choosing styles and teaching inexperienced girls about makeup, hair styling, and nail application. As one girl explained about her salon experience:

> Actually, I didn't do anything. In the salon, they plucked my eyebrows, they fixed me up in the salon, they did everything for me. They did my makeup, they did my hair, they plucked my eyebrows. I chose the hairstyle. The makeup too, but that was more her idea than mine. The hairstyle I did pick out, something out of the ordinary. There are always up-do's, I said no, I told her that I wanted something like that, but original and pretty, something that was like a little ponytail, a half-ponytail, but the other half of the hair down. I was walking and I saw the salon and I went in, I went in and I asked...I was looking for a good service, economical, and to see how the place was, because if it was like an ugly place, well, no.

As an assistant to the beauty pageant contestant, I even got to help the interviewee practice her modeling walk so that she looked more comfortable and confident in the high heels that her friend loaned her, two sizes too small. I shared with her what I learned in beauty class: hold shoulders back, but not too far back, steady, but not tense. Let arms drape down naturally, and then swing *just the forearm below the elbow*, each arm synchronized with the opposite leg. Look forward and maintain a gaze that shows you are not worried about your feet or worried about your arms or worried about falling. Place heels first, then toes. Walk with confidence and a steady gait, not too fast, and not too slow.

Ideas about what is beautiful, what products to use, and how to get beautiful are also deeply influenced by the reproductive economy, passed as they are through family and friends, by word of mouth, and by people in beauty services, dressmaking, and beauty product distribution. Through personal recommendations and services performed by sisters and mothers, word of mouth plays an important role in informing *quinceañeras* about practices and ideals of beauty. Sisters are especially important. As one fourteen-year-old put it, "Like, it is like... 'wow, look, how pretty that looks, I want to put on makeup, too'... so for, well, I don't know, my sister, sometimes she tells me 'oh, I am going to put this on you,' and she puts it on me. Or I say 'oh, look, let me make up my eyes'." Sisters are responsible for checking a *quinceañera's* clothes before she leaves the house, sharing fashion magazines, clothes, makeup, exercise DVDs, and most importantly, advice.

Quinceañeras also exchange a significant amount of information between themselves: "for example, my friends were the ones who got me to do it, they told me 'you know what, pluck your eyebrows, do your makeup like this, dress like this'.... yes, they taught me makeup and now I am all made up, to pluck my eyebrows, they taught me a lot of things, even how to hook up with boys." Another recounted how her cousin, also her best friend, told her to pluck her eyebrows and sat her down and did it for her, and taught her makeup and fashion. This young woman had not worn high heels, either, and her cousin showed her how. One *quinceañera* shared information among friends through another friend who sold clothes and shoes by catalog. The girls look at catalogs but they also buy out of friendship because "that is what [she] works in, that is why we buy," illustrating the importance of the social network to marketing and sales.

The influence of network–based direct sales marketing on spreading information and advice is not small. Out of twenty-eight girl interviewees, twelve of them—or an older family member—mentioned the use of network–based direct sales as a source of beauty and fashion products, from Herbalife to Avon to Fuller to Flexy shoes. Among twelve boy interviewees, only two connections to network marketing and sales were revealed to me, one by the mother of a boy whose sister sells makeup, and one by another boy whose sister sells

Avon. Although network-based marketing was not a specific line of questioning, it emerged as a consistent pattern in interviews and field notes without asking; had it been given more attention from the beginning, the pattern of sales and consumption would likely have been more pronounced (see chapter five). The overwhelming majority of participants' direct sellers were friends, family, and friends of family. Only one participant sold through direct sales herself, but many immediate family members did. In addition, only one interviewee mentioned purchasing her makeup from an Avon vendor who sold door-to-door. This girl is in a position of privilege among her peers, because Avon and Mary Kay brands are prestige brands among aspiring middle class youth.

The reproductive economy in beauty information is not exclusive to *quinceañeras*. Boys and girls find fashion by seeing what other youth are wearing, as expressed by one girl who commented, "I don't know, I see people here and there and I get ideas." Boys also borrow hairstyles from their friends and cousins and people in the street. As one said: "I hardly look at magazines, I see them maybe when my friends or my cousins have them." Another reported that he borrows ideas, "like the hairstyle that my cousins had. I say 'wow, that looks cool,' you know, and I try to do the hairstyle and if I like how it looks on me I keep using that hairstyle." Where boys differ is in the degree of services and products that they employ. All boys use hair gel, but beyond that, very few use more styling products, and they rarely get their hair done by a professional. The only instance in which male participants reported using beauty services beyond a haircut was when one was going to perform a dance show, and an experienced friend straightened his hair. I also witnessed professional stylists straightening and styling all boys' hair in the beauty contest that I helped with and another modeling show that I witnessed. Boys' sources of information, therefore, are less centered in the beauty services industry, and their efforts at beautification remain less visible.

In sum, the reproductive economy shapes the use of beauty products, the consumption of beauty information, and the formation of ideas about what is beautiful in *fiestas de quince años* and among *quinceañeras* and their contemporaries. Family members, friends, people on the street, and network marketers play a central role in the provision of advice, information, services, and products. The role of the reproductive economy in beauty production shows that beauty consumption, beauty ideals, and beauty production are not naturally occurring, but instead produced through teaching, advice, and practice in the reproductive economy.

THE CHANGING ROLE OF THE REPRODUCTIVE ECONOMY

The imperative to be beautiful puts a premium on reproductive labor necessary to produce the beautiful *quinceañera*. But it has not always been this way. The historical changes in the celebration of the *quince años* are illustrative of the major changes going on in the reproductive economy of beauty. As the extravagant *quince* has become popularized, there has been a concomitant commercialization of services and commodification of products to make the *quince* special and the *quinceañera* beautiful. Likewise, there has been increasing demand on reproductive labor to make up the difference between family economic resources and the demands of an extravagant *quince*.

There are three types of *fiestas de quince años* described by parents who reached fifteen between the early 1960s and the early 1980s: the social debut, the party in the streets, and the family and godparents going to Mass and sharing a meal at home. The practice of the social debut was reserved for those with significant economic resources. This "presentation to society" was practiced by the upper classes, included fourteen *damas* and fourteen *chambelanes*, and was highly esteemed though seldom seen. One parent from a relatively well-off family had attended such a debut in her youth, but otherwise interviewees saw these debuts only from a distance. They were known to occur, but their practice was not economically possible for one mother's family, the source of social envy for another mother, and was simply outside of the social circles of the rest.

As the big party has been popularized, the wealthier classes have practiced it less. Older adults often refer to the practice as having been one of the upper social classes, who now often eschew the practice as below them, preferring instead a vacation or a car. One mother, a high school teacher, captured the difference by recounting how her students in a well-off school ridicule the practice as vulgar or overly sentimental, while her students in another, public, school dream about their *quince años* with anticipation.

The party in the streets was practiced in villages and in some residential neighborhoods of the city. This second type of party is associated with rural tradition, and continues to be practiced on the outskirts of the city and in the villages that form a web around the metropolitan district. In this type of *quince*, a family closes off the street in front of their house and invites everyone in the neighborhood or the village to the party. Some families offered a meal, similar to the rural style wedding, of a typical food such as *birria* or *mole*, and everyone was invited to eat and then dance. If there wasn't money for a meal, family members pitched in for sodas or *aguas frescas* and the neighborhood danced. Music might be provided by a local mariachi band or by a stereo. In these parties, the dancing was less formal, although the *quinceañera* started the dancing by being invited by a local boy or by her father.

The final style of *quince* celebration, which was, according to one mother, much more common in the 1960s than any type of *quince* celebration now, is attendance at Mass and a family meal. In these cases, a *quinceañera* would give thanks to God and renew her faith in the presence of her parents and godparents. The family would then have a meal and maybe dancing at home, among family. Then, as now, dancing is a major measure of success of a party in Guadalajara. As one *quinceañera* put it, "It would be really cool if everyone would dance...if everyone sitting down, instead of being, like, 'oh look at that,' would say...'I want to dance, too,'" thereby signifying that the party was fun.

The major change in celebrating the *quince* over the last fifty years has been the popularization of the big, extravagant *quince*. Among youth interviewees, the big debut-style *quince años* is seen as the "traditional" *quince años*, the prototype against which their *quince* dreams and desires are measured. As discussed above, the presentation to society is understood to be an antiquated meaning, although it is fun to imitate. The big party is, more accurately, a big party, a lot of fun, a moment, and a chance to be a princess or celebrity for a day.

The differences between parents' *quince* practices and those of their children illustrate how the role of the reproductive economy in the globalization of beauty products and practices is changing. First, there is a premium on all of the reproductive labor required to pull off the popularized big celebration. Second, the premium on reproductive labor has led to two trends: there is an increase in unpaid reproductive work dedicated to celebrating the extravagant *quince*, and reproductive labor is increasingly commercialized in the service of *quinceañera* production.

The first trend in the reproductive economy of beauty is the increase in reproductive labor, illustrated by an increase in unpaid reproductive work dedicated to making *quinceañeras* beautiful. The amount of reproductive labor dedicated to making the *quinceañera* beautiful generally increases in inverse proportionality to the celebrant's family economic resources. The increased investment of unpaid reproductive labor in beautification makes the celebration possible, or possible on a grander scale, despite limited economic resources. "They couldn't give me the waltz, the dress, the Mass, I tried to understand it because it was my dream. My siblings talked to me, they told me 'look, there isn't any way right now to do the fiesta, how would you like it if you invite a friend, and we make a meal?' And we did make a meal, we danced the waltz, my brothers and I, my mom. But it was really nice that day I remember...they made a sacrifice to make me feel special, so yeah, sometimes it doesn't matter if you get a *fiesta* in a rental hall, but what matters really is the love." As an opportunity to participate in an expensive endeavor, a lot of families and extended networks make up for the lack of financial resources by donating reproductive labor. This makes reproductive work the bridge between feeling poor and feeling able to celebrate the *quince*. So, for some poorer families, the added reproductive work is not only a source of income, but also a mechanism to close a resources gap and display upward mobility.

The second trend is toward increasing commercialization of reproductive labor. This is when reproductive labor is turned into a form of income production, often in the informal or semi-formal markets. Examples of the trend toward reproductive labor turning into commercial informal labor are housework (Mies 1986; Prugl 1999), domestic labor for hire (Pettman 1996; Chin 1998), international sex services (Pettman 1996; Agathangelou 2004), and international marriage markets. The commercialization of reproductive labor is part of a broader trend of informalization in the global economy. Informalization includes the search by corporations for cheaper labor through flexible work arrangements like homework or piecework. It also includes the trend toward commercializing previously unpaid reproductive labor, like sex and house cleaning. In the global political economy of beauty, we can see increasing commercialization of reproductive labor can be observed in dressmaking, makeup application, hair styling, and dance.

In the global economy of beauty there is widespread commercialization, including commodification of previously uncommodified articles and the commercialization of formerly unpaid reproductive labor, as well as informalization of product distribution by large corporations. The "commodification of everything" (Wallerstein 1995) in the beauty market includes creams that replace homemade food- and plant-based skin treatments, cosmetics that replace charcoal and berries, and a huge arsenal of recently invented necessities such as hair, nail, and eyelash extensions. The trend toward income generation through beautification services constitutes commercialization of beauty based on service labor that was previously not performed or performed in the private, unpaid economy. For example, three mothers who were interviewed learned to be seamstresses as young women. One mother learned as a young girl in the 1960s and worked as a seamstress and housemaid for rich relatives in exchange for room and board in the city, until she met her husband. She made her daughters' dresses for special events until her youngest daughter, a participant in this research, turned fifteen, and the family sent the dress to be made by a professional seamstress. Another learned in the 1970s because her husband's family would not allow her to continue studying toward a medical degree in the university. Her husband's family allowed her to study sewing and cosmetology, which she did in order to keep her mind occupied and to feel useful. She did not sew her daughter's dress, although a second daughter who also studied cosmetology did donate her cosmetician's services. A third mother learned her seamstress skills in the 1980s, to earn money on the side in order to help her family. She also hired a seamstress to sew her daughter's dress. What these stories illustrate is the historical transition from sewing and wearing homemade dresses to the commercial use of sewing skills to earn income, formally or informally, and the purchase of commercially manufactured dresses. Not one of my interviewees had a homemade dress, although their mothers had worn homemade dresses daily.

Beauty services likewise illustrate this movement from homemade treatments and makeup and long, undone hair, to the application of all kinds of extensions, corrector creams, foundation, at least three colors of eye shadow, face shading powders, eyeliners, mascaras, blushes, lip liners, lipsticks and lip glosses, hair sprays, hair gels, hair creams, flat irons, curling irons, and all manners of lifting and shaping hair. The explosion in beautification practices entails both the commodification of previously non-commodified products and the commercialization of services, such as beauty classes, makeup application, hair styling, nail application, and nail decoration.

Dancing is also now both commodified and commercialized, as young people take classes from professional dancers instead of learning from their mothers and fathers, hire professional dance accompaniment, and buy special outfits to make their dance stand out. The type of labor that has historically been performed in the reproductive economy is increasingly commodified and commercialized as people, mostly women, develop their labor as entrepreneurs.

In sum, the reproductive economy plays a central role in the economy of beauty. Reproductive labor teaches beautification practices, which products to buy and use, and ideas about what is beautiful. Reproductive labor is increasingly called upon to make up the difference between family economic resources and youths' middle class social demands. Finally, reproductive labor in beautification is also increasingly a source of income generation through its commercialization and growing demand for beauty services.

STRUCTURES OF PRIVILEGE IN THE REPRODUCTIVE ECONOMY OF THE *QUINCE*

Both through its reliance on reproductive labor and through its role in constructing social norms, the reproductive economy of the *quince* also plays

Table 4.1 SUMMARY OF HIGHLY VALUED IDENTITIES, IDEOLOGIES, AND INSTITUTIONS IN THE REPRODUCTIVE ECONOMY OF BEAUTY IN THE *QUINCE*

Highly Valued...	Reproductive
Identities	Breadwinner, metrosexual masculinities, fashionable consumer, *quinceañera*/fashionista, beautiful
Ideologies	Patriarchy, individual consumption, capitalist commercialization, racism, nationalism
Institutions	Family, gender difference, church, heterosexual dating and marriage, social networks

an important role in reproducing axes of social hierarchy. As summarized in Table 4.1, the reproductive economy privileges some identities, institutions, and ideologies over others. Structures of privilege in the reproductive economy of beauty privilege masculinities and momentarily, if at all, achievable ideals of femininity. The reproductive economy also privileges the institutions of gender difference, heterosexual marriage, family, and church, and the ideologies of patriarchy, racism, capital commercialization, and individual consumption. The age of adolescence can be seen to hold a certain amount of privilege that, intersecting with structures of hierarchy, lead to contestation and change of some norms, although the status of youth is temporary.

Privileged Identities

The RPV framework builds on feminist scholarship that argues that the privileged identities in the global reproductive economy are those of masculine breadwinner and the Northern consumer. The masculine breadwinner, usually a man, is valued for his work and his time through higher monetary rewards, jobs of higher prestige, and authority in the household. The less privileged vis-à-vis the breadwinner is the housewife whose work is not recognized, monetarily or otherwise, as critical to the global political economy. Northern consumers are privileged through their purchasing power, to which developing countries must appeal to earn foreign exchange. The appeal to the Northern consumer often puts women in the position of selling their domestic, sexual, or service labor in order to make ends meet, while consumers enjoy the privilege of being courted and gaining the fruits of low-paid reproductive labor.

The privileged identities in the *quince* reflect somewhat these generalizations of the RPV framework, while also offering some more specificity by focusing on the global beauty economy. The breadwinner masculinity is privileged in the *quince años*, inasmuch as fathers and the patriarchal family (see below) are privileged. Interestingly, another type of masculinity, the fashionable, cosmopolitan, metrosexual, is also present as a model of privileged masculinity through the modern *chambelan*. The most valued femininities are based on beauty, youth, fashion, and social grace.

At first glance, the reproductive economy of beauty appears to privilege some women, some of the time. Women are the beauty experts, holding positions of influence through their knowledge about beauty products and practices, and the sharing of informed opinions. Women are most often the teachers of *quinceañeras*, both within the family and through professional beauty services. They are also most often the entrepreneurs in commercializing reproductive labor. By employing the skills they learn in the reproductive economy, they become income earners and help their families.

Women also express a sense of well-being and empowerment achieved through beautification. When asked why they fix themselves up, the most common response was to explain that it feels good and that it makes them feel good about themselves. Whether they saw getting fixed up as a question of personal satisfaction, social necessity, or both, was often unclear or contradictory in the interviews. But in the end, all of the respondents saw getting fixed up as a way to make themselves feel better. Some took it further than just feeling better, as one identified it with increasing her self-esteem, and one identified it as a mask that she uses to protect herself from criticisms by her peers. Looking good, in effect, presents an opportunity for women and girls to improve their social status.

There is evidence that beauty is helpful in finding employment, and this seems to be true in Guadalajara, as well. A few of my interviewees took great pride in their looks and their ability to get fixed up because it allowed them to participate in the large industry of models and *edecanes* (product demonstration models). Models and *edecanes* work at Expos or other commercial events as product promoters, made up with the exaggerated stage cosmetics of a *quinceañera* or a *telenovela* actress and wearing a sexually provocative uniform with the product logo. They are usually in their late teens or early twenties, and their thin hourglass figures, smooth skin, youthful faces, fancy hairstyles, and skillful application of makeup put them at the pinnacle of conventional beauty in Guadalajara.

Apart from this small group, however, working interviewees did not invest much in fixing themselves up for their jobs because they worked in family businesses or in the home. Yet as they grow into the labor market, they will find that employment announcements often list "good presentation" as a work requirement, along with age range and background requirements. The requirement for good personal presentation is especially high in the female-dominated employment sectors of fashion retail sales and beauty services.

In sum, the reproductive economy of beauty in the *quince* and among *quinceañeras* privileges the women and girls who have knowledge of beauty products and applications, women and girls who are good at fixing themselves up, and women and girls who are considered beautiful: the fashionistas. In the *quince* celebration, the beautiful *quinceañera* plays the star part, that of fashionista, inhabiting this role through contracting beauty services, having a dress made for her, and becoming the star of the show as her beauty and grace take center stage. As she embodies the ideals of beautiful and graceful feminine adolescence, she represents the ideal of Mexican womanhood.

Beyond the immediate reproductive economy of beauty in the *quince*, however, there are larger structures of hierarchy that make beautiful girls and beauty experts' apparent privilege and empowerment in the beauty industry less certain. To be sure, signs of gendered inequalities are noticeable even in the interviews. One *quinceañera* had gone to a male stylist who was supposed to be good because, "you know, they say, like, the gays are supposed to be good." As a friend who was opening a beauty salon explained to me, and a high-paid male stylist corroborated, men are supposed to have naturally gifted hands in any task, including when it comes to making women beautiful. The high-paid stylist complained to me that male beauticians are considered to be not only better than their female counterparts, but also gay, putting them in a hierarchy above women but below more traditionally masculine men.

Looking at the industry from a wider perspective, these signs of privileged status, seemingly paradoxical, show their roots. Men in beauty services, while few by comparison, feature prominently in the industry. Men are considered to be the best hair stylists. The most prestigious hair salon and hair styling academy in the city, *Patrice*, is populated by a dramatically higher proportion of male hair stylists than the more typical neighborhood salons. Likewise, the modeling and beauty school that a participant and a friend called the most prestigious in the city, *Clase y Estilo* (Class and Style), is run by Aurelio Lozano, a locally renowned makeup artist who also has a newspaper column, radio show, and television show. Despite their virtual absence in neighborhood salons, male aestheticians are frequently interviewed as stylists and makeup artists in the pages of national and international beauty magazines.

These positions of prestige and expertise, disproportionately occupied by men, also carry greater economic reward. Alejandro L'Occoco, a successful hair stylist, has parlayed his success with celebrities and in national and international competitions into the city's other name-brand salon, a successful beauty academy, salon franchise, and name-brand products. To illustrate the difference in cost and prestige, a haircut with a hair stylist at Patrice costs 450 pesos, a haircut at a L'Occoco salon 300, a haircut at a *fresa* salon of some prestige 250, and a haircut in my downtown neighborhood 100 pesos. In the aspiring middle class suburbs of town, 100 pesos is a lot to pay for a haircut. This is not to say that the male stylists at Patrice are only being paid for their gender, but rather that the industry suffers from vertical segregation, where men and women self-select and are channeled into differently valued positions, and that men's and women's work is valued differently.

There is also an element to national hierarchy evident in the beauty services industries, where Europe—particularly France—and the US are privileged sources of expertise and talent. Patrice Mulard, founder of the Patrice salons and academy, is French by birth and was educated in France. Aurelio Lozano, the renowned makeup artist, was educated by "European teachers" (Lozano 2008). International training, competitions, and exhibitions are constantly cited as sources of prestige and legitimacy in promotional materials and print media. Among the beauty academies peppered throughout the city, titles that include references to Europe, France, and Madrid are popular (see figure 4.1). The global foci of the fashion industry remain centered in Western Europe and New York, and Spain retains a special status as the source of Mexico's colonial aristocracy.

In sum, the local, middle class, reproductive economy of the beauty industries privileges some women's beauty and beautification, but in global perspective they remain at the bottom of a long chain of vertical segregation. The higher the degree of prestige and economic return associated with beauty services, the higher likelihood that a man is performing them, or that they are associated with Europe and the US.

The age of adolescence, however, is a final category of identity that could be construed as holding a certain amount of privilege in the *quince* economy. Adolescence is, after all, one of the primary points of celebration, and the *quinceañera's* desires are central to the event. As discussed in chapters two and three, youths' desires can differ dramatically from those of their parents. Tensions between parents' and youths' desires can be seen through, for example, the traditional waltz and the surprise dance as well as the dress and the surprise dance outfit. Differences of opinion over dresses, colors, and sexiness, among other things, result in challenges to conservative gender norms of circumspection, modesty, and piousness.

Figure 4.1: The *Instituto Internacional de Belleza y Moda Paris* is an example of European or United States references common in the beauty industry.

The special status attributed to adolescence and youths' desires in the *quince* results in some space opening for a slow transition to *which* identities, institutions, and ideologies are privileged during the event. The hip-hop surprise dances draw a great deal on Black American and Caribbean culture, and the popularity of Beyonce, Tyra Banks, Shakira, and Latina Hollywood celebrities has made an historically racist and white-dominated media landscape more diverse. The center of attention is shifting away from the Mass toward the ever-more-complicated, choreographed, and dramatic dances. Necklines are dropping, corsets are popping, and short skirts are coming out from under the ball gowns. The net effect is that, in comparison to *quince* celebrations of forty years ago, metrosexual masculinities are more visible vis-à-vis breadwinner masculinities, fashionistas are replacing princess debutantes as the teen dream, consumption and commercialization have subsumed once-hidden reproductive labor, the Church is losing prestige, and the family is struggling to maintain control over teenage sexuality and individualism.

The apparent privilege of adolescence, however, is dampened by the accompanying investment that the celebration makes in the institution of the hierarchical family and other traditional, or conservative, institutions, identities, and ideologies. Notably, gender difference as an institution, while showing some cracks, remains resistant to change even among the minds of counter-hegemonic youth (see chapter six). In fact, the *quince* celebration, inasmuch as it favors "tradition," reinforces gender differences and esteems conservative social institutions, including marriage, family, and the church. To the extent that the celebration and its traditions are contested and changed by youth, the *quince* is an instrument that upsets and undermines social institutions and their norms.

The privilege of adolescent beauty is further dampened because the *quinceañera's* beauty and special status is necessarily temporally limited.[2] The *quinceañera's* special status as princess lasts one day. Her beauty is the result of intense investment in that one day, and her youth, which will last for some time but is also limited.

Privileged Ideologies

The RPV framework identifies patriarchy, racism, and capitalism as the privileged ideologies in the reproductive economy. For example, patriarchy as an ideology protects the patriarchal family, heterosexual marriage, and gender difference as social institutions in the reproductive sphere. It also protects the privilege of masculine identities. In the case of beauty production in the *quince años*, the ideologies of patriarchy, capitalism, and racism are manifest in small ways.

Patriarchy, or the ideology of masculine power and privilege, is manifest symbolically and materially. Symbolically, there is the weight given to the patriarch(s) throughout the event. For example, there is the ritual wedding-like presentation of the girl by her father to her *chambelan-de-honor*. Materially, family reliance on women's unpaid reproductive labor to cover the labor and expense of the *fiesta* reproduces a gendered division of labor that relies greatly on women's unpaid work, which is not honored with the same prestige as the patriarch's and godfather's financial contribution. Through its dependence on the reproductive economy of beauty and its pageantry, the *quince* acts out, reinforces, and naturalizes the gendered division of labor.

Racism and nationalism also manifest as ideologies shaping the *quince*, primarily through the reproduction of a gendered beauty norm based on monarchic beauty ideals: the Venetian Waltz, the Buckingham Palace guards, the dainty-waisted Tudor princess. These Old European princesses, knights, soldiers, and Disney and Hollywood fairytales evidence a long-standing tradition, dating to colonial times, of racial preference for and privilege given to European aristocracy, Europeans, and European-descendent Mexicans.

Privileged Institutions

The privileged institution in the global reproductive economy is the family. The family is the institution to which service and sacrifice in the reproductive economy is made; the institution that reinforces the separation between productive, breadwinner work, and reproductive, housewife work; and the first institution that socializes children into structures of hierarchy such as patriarchy and racism. In the reproductive economy of the *quince años*, the institution of family is clearly favored, as are two institutions that play a traditional role in the family: gender difference and heterosexual marriage. Finally, the Church also occupies a place of honor in the *quince* tradition, although its influence is fading.

The institutional privilege of the family in the reproductive economy of the *quince* is most clear, as it is in the name of family that the *quince* is carried out. Girls' obligation to their parents and parents' obligation to their girls are the most frequent and compelling reasons given for such a significant outlay and expense. The family reproductive economy is largely responsible for the investment of money and labor in the *quince*. Bringing family together socially is also one of the primary reasons for celebrating the *quince*. Family networks are strengthened through sponsorship and involvement in the *quince*, and family members' ideas and desires for the *quinceañera* are important. The result is that the family as an institution is reinforced.

In addition to the family, the reproductive economy of beauty in the *quince* also privileges the institutions of gender difference and heterosexual marriage. Each of these institutions is foundational to any conception of a *quince* celebration. Gender difference, as discussed above, is one of the ideas framing who celebrates a *quince*, and how. Therefore, the girl celebrant, the princess dress, the Prince Charming dance partners, the hostessing, and the gendered division of responsibilities and symbolic rituals all establish a serious investment, both in preparation and in execution, in teaching and practicing gender difference based on a conception of princesses and princes. Gender difference becomes naturalized and assumed, much as the tradition of the *quince años* is assumed, to have lasted forever.

The institution of heterosexual marriage is also privileged in the reproductive economy of the *quince*. The assumption that the *quince* is a debut of a girl of dating age is now antiquated. Still, the assumption remains that a *quinceañera* who celebrates a ball-style *quince* is to begin dating. She dances a symbolic last dance with her father, who, as mentioned above, often ceremoniously gives her a pair of high heels before she begins to dance with her *chambelan-de-honor*. *De Niña a Mujer*, a popular song played at a *quince años*, sometimes during the father-daughter dance, recounts a father's sadness because he is going to lose his daughter as she becomes a woman, presumably as she replaces him with a male partner.

The Church is also a privileged institution in the *quince*, although it is losing its place as the most central institution. It is virtually unheard of to celebrate a big debut-style *quince* without having the Mass first. But, the one-time tradition of celebrating a *quince* just by attending a Mass with parents and godparents is also virtually unheard of today. The party, meal, and dancing are the more public and socially important part of the *quince*. Despite the lip service and fanfare invested in the Mass, more and more guests skip the Mass and attend only the party. In the United States, this shift has led to Church leaders refusing to perform *quinceañera* services or requiring *quinceañeras* to attend religious classes in order to qualify to receive religious services. I did not hear of this trend in Mexico until the aunt of a *quinceañera* complained to me about the mettlesome priests in the United States who insist on religious classes in exchange for *quinceañera* Masses. In her opinion, it was a reason to celebrate her niece's *quince* in Guadalajara rather than California. Napolitano (1999) also reported that parishes in Guadalajara may refuse to perform *quince* services because it does not meet religious standards.

In sum, the *quince años* celebration illustrates how the reproductive economy in action reinforces itself by reinforcing the institution of family, but also through the naturalized institutions of gender difference and heterosexual marriage that underwrite the institution of religious matrimony.

IS THE REPRODUCTIVE ECONOMY OF BEAUTY GLOBAL?

The question still arises as to how the reproductive economy plays a role in the *global* economy of beauty. At first glance, the reproductive economy of beauty in the *quince años* appears to be highly local. The family, the parish, and social networks are the key reproductive actors and stakeholders in the *quince*. Few study participants involved transnational families in their *quince* preparations. The transformations in the reproductive economy of beauty over the last fifty years, however, indicate that the reproductive economy of beauty is also global. The reproductive economy is responsible for teaching *quinceañeras* about beauty ideals, practices, and consumption. And beauty ideals, practices, and consumption have transformed dramatically due to globalization in the last fifty years.

The links among the reproductive, productive, and virtual political economies are what tie and illustrate the essential role that the reproductive economy plays in the global economy of beauty. First, reproductive labor teaches about beauty ideas, practices, and products, shaping consumption of products, services, and information in the global productive and virtual economies. Further, the reproductive economy is increasingly tied to the productive economy through the trend toward commercialization of reproductive labor, the trend toward commodification of formerly homemade goods, and the efforts by families to use reproductive labor to make up the gap between economic resources and social desires. The commercialization of reproductive labor and goods has been driven by transformations in the global productive economy—demands on women to earn income, growth in the informal economy, and the flexibilization of the beauty industry (see chapter five). As a result, the reproductive economy has become a source of entrepreneurialism, leading to the commodification of homemade goods and wide-scale commercialization of historically unpaid reproductive labor: teaching social manners, beautification, hair styling, and cosmetics application, for example.

In addition, the increase in demand on reproductive labor in the beauty economy is shaped and driven by the global information economy and youths' desires to compete and connect with other youth globally through their beauty and fashion statements. The reproductive economy becomes a medium for the global virtual economy, through which information is gathered and passed on. Thus, through the reproductive economy's ties to global transformations and virtual economies, it is itself global even as it remains local.

CONCLUSION

By extending out from the *quinceeañera's* beautification and into the reproductive economy, we can see that reproductive labor is not only important to the process of beautification, but is central to the global economy of beauty. The reproductive economy shapes the norms of beauty and comportment in the *quince*, and it is the context for youths' resistance and innovation. It is also an economy of increasing commercialization. The intensification of reproductive labor in the *quince* and beautification in general has led to increased demands on reproductive labor, and multiple opportunities for the commercialization of reproductive labor. Within the commercializing and globalizing reproductive economy, social privileges and hierarchies are reproduced, but also undergo pressure from change, particularly from youth.

Since the reproductive economy of beauty is central to beautification regimes, transformations in the reproductive economy of beauty are necessarily indicative of transformations in norms of feminine beauty and beautification. The ever more commercial and produced process of beautification is therefore consequential to beauty and gender norms. The commercialization and intensification of beauty labor makes beautification both more important in terms of time, money, and investment, and more important in terms of its centrality to the construction of gender.

Just as beautification is more central to gender construction, both beauty and gender construction are more closely tied to the global economy of beauty. The interdependence between beautification and globalization means that both beauty and its globalization are significant to the reproduction of structures of hierarchy along lines of identity, institutions, and ideologies. Existing hierarchies privilege narrowly defined masculinities and momentarily achievable ideals of femininity, the institutions of gender difference, marriage, family, and church, and the ideologies of patriarchy, racism, capitalist commercialization, and individual consumption. The importance of the reproductive context, particularly competition between parents and adolescents over beauty and other norms, creates space for slow transformations in beauty norms and practices. The trends in this transformation are toward more artificial, and more varied, beauty ideas, products, and practices.

CHAPTER 5

Beauty Has a Price: The Global Productive Economy of Beauty

Beauty has a price . . .
—Jimmy James, *Fashionista*, 2006

The productive economy of beauty encompasses the production and exchange of services and merchandise such as cosmetics, hair products, and clothing, for a price. The productive economy of *quinceañera* beautification includes almost every aspect of the beauty economy imaginable, from fingernail sparkles to eyelash extensions, from diet aids to perfumes. As illustrated through beautification in the *quince*, there has been an explosion in the beauty products and services offered in the beauty marketplace.

Extending out from *quinceañera* beautification into the global productive economy of beauty, this chapter looks at just a slice of the beauty economy: cosmetics. Cosmetics are arguably the most important part of a *quinceañera* makeover. They serve as a proxy for the beauty economy because, due to their importance, they easily garner the most accessible, well-documented, and comparable data within the global beauty economy. As seen through the lens of the global productive economy of cosmetics, this chapter addresses two questions that are central to this book: How do beauty products circulate between the global economy and *quinceañeras* in Guadalajara, Mexico? Does the beauty industry in Guadalajara privilege groups by race, class, gender, and nation?

The most common medium for cosmetics circulation is a close female. The cosmetics makeover is conducted in a beautification class by a cosmetician, or by a female family member or friend who will teach a *quinceañera* about the products and their use. Most *quinceañeras*, after their transformation, amass considerable stores of cosmetics, acquired through or shared with friends and female family members, and will themselves go on to share their expertise and products. Personal services, sometimes paid and sometimes donated, are the most important method of learning about products and their use. Several multinational companies dominate the market for cosmetics, but direct sales of cosmetics through social networks is the single most important method of product distribution.

This chapter makes two analytical observations about the productive economy of beauty. First, there is a blurring of lines between the public market in goods and services and the private exchange of products and favors for *quinceañera* beautification. When looking at how cosmetics are bought, sold, and used on the ground, personal services play an overwhelmingly important role in shaping the productive economy of beauty. The personal services that shape the use and exchange of products are sometimes private, sometimes public, or often in-between. The most striking example is the rapidly expanding direct-selling industry for cosmetics, through which makeup and diet aids are sold by women to their friends and family, out of their homes or place of work, or otherwise through social occasions. This undefined boundary between public and private exchange illustrates how the politics of the global economy of beauty cannot be understood through the public economy alone. Much to the contrary, the beauty industry is successful because it intertwines productive, reproductive, and virtual economies.

The second observation on the productive economy of beauty is that it does provide opportunities to some women. The beauty industries are clearly not trivial in economic terms. But cosmetics sales and personal beauty services are neither the clear economic opportunities for women that proponents claim them to be, nor the exploitative abuse of women's insecurities that detractors claim. The beautifying industries provide some women with opportunities to empower themselves, albeit through channels that funnel their efforts into a hierarchical structure that benefits some women at the expense of others.

Based on these two observations, I conclude that the global political economy of cosmetics illustrates how intimately interdependent, and how gendered the global reproductive, productive, and virtual economies are. Employment patterns in the productive economy are profoundly shaped by dynamics in the reproductive economy: the gendered division of labor, assumptions about caring labor, and assumptions about women's time. Success in the productive economy of cosmetics is dependent on the exchange of virtual signs through marketing and media, as well as the successful performance of privileged identities such as "fashionista," or the knowledgeable fashion consumer. From paid work to semi-informal direct sales, to the home, the market, and the body, hierarchical femininities and masculinities are being produced in the cosmetics industry.

GLOBALIZING PRODUCTIVE ECONOMY OF COSMETICS

As discussed in chapter three, the cosmetic makeover is now a universal rite of passage, but never more so than for a *quinceañera,* for whom cosmetics become an explicit sign of feminine maturity. The months-long makeover has become the most time-intensive and important element of the *quince,* but it is also a universal practice for young women regardless of whether or not they practice the *quince.*

The cosmetics makeover usually begins with a professional or semi-professional cosmetics application, in which a young woman learns about the products and how to use them. She will learn about and use products such as cover-up, powder, blush, lipstick, eyeliner, eye shadow, and several other cosmetics for the face, hands, and hair. The productive economy of beauty on the ground, therefore, includes products, their sales, and service employment in cosmetics and cosmetics application.

Eye shadows play a very prominent role in the cosmetics trade, although tens of product categories are used in the makeover. In beauty class, for example, participants were shown a professional application of makeup that included sixteen shades of eye shadow. This, however, was an advanced application, and as beginners we were taught makeup applications that typically included only between four and six shades of eye shadow per application. For different color schemes, however, we would need approximately a half dozen other shades, and thus were encouraged to buy dozens of eye shadows during several weeks of class. We also bought and used skin-colored cream foundation and skin-colored or transparent powder as a base for the makeup application, several shades of cheek colors or "blushes," black or brown eyeliner pencils, mascara, lip liner pencils, lip colors, lip glosses, and utensils for application. The utensils for application included sponges and brushes for applying creams and powders, tweezers for removing hair, and, in one surreal moment, a ruler with an adjustable marker so that we could measure the widths of our nose bridges, our eyes, and the distance between our pupils and our nose bridge, in order to determine the symmetry of our eye shape and whether we had wide-set or narrow-set eyes before employing corrective makeup techniques.

Quinceañeras who have undergone this level of induction into cosmetics typically own between thirty and fifty products, usually shared between family members. Less trained users typically own between ten and twenty products, again, shared with family members.

For a *quince,* girls will use more products than almost any other time. Extras such as false eyelashes or eyelash extensions are common, as are additional sparkly powders and paints on and around the eyes. Cheek coloring with blush is usually augmented with contour shadowing underneath cheeks, which makes cheekbones stand out more. The total effect is close to the television makeup of a *telenovela* star. In daily use, *quinceañeras* who attend school usually employ fewer products, usually after school or on weekends. Outside of school, or for those not attending, about one third of this study's participants used an equally heavy makeup application, and the rest, save a couple, used less makeup on a regular basis.

How do so many cosmetics end up on young women's shelves? In addition to taking lessons from professionals in beauty classes or in beauty salons, *quinceañeras* learn about cosmetics from older sisters and cousins, mothers, friends, and friends of their mothers. Most products are acquired through these connections. Many products are acquired as gifts from female relatives and friends, and others are purchased from lesson-providers, in *tianguis* (open-air weekly street market), or through family and friends who sell products from direct sales companies like Avon, Jafra, and Fuller.

Direct sales through networks calls upon individual contract-based employees and their social networks to build retail distribution and sales networks of consumer goods. Companies use slightly different models for recruitment and compensation of direct sales representatives, but they all generally pay a commission to the sales representative for product sales, and a commission to her for recruiting sellers. Recruits are members of a seller's "downline." In exchange for recruiting and training, a portion of downline sales commissions go to the seller(s) responsible for their recruitment, their "upline." This method of distribution not only outsources sales and distribution, but also recruitment and training of new distributors.

The importance of direct sales to beauty product circulation was an unexpected but important finding from field research. Prior to observations in Guadalajara, I had no idea that direct sales would be important to the provision and procurement of beauty products and services. Even in the middle of research, the importance of direct sales was lost on me for some time, as I tried to avoid unwanted sales pitches from friends and neighbors. Eventually the omnipresence of direct sales in cosmetics and other beauty aids was unavoidable. Direct sales consumer goods thread through daily life through bus-stop marketing, television advertising, neighbors' product recommendations, friend and family pitches, recruitment meetings, and personal consumption. A few impressive success stories, like the billionaire Omnilife (diet product) founder Jorge Vergara in Guadalajara and the multimillionaire Herbalife (diet product) distributors in Zacatecas, Enrique Varela and Graciela Mier de Varela, beckon to the poor with the awe-inspiring possibilities of being at the top of a multilevel direct sales marketing business. It was through this immersion that I learned that direct sales are an integral part of how products circulate in Mexico and of how people learn about product usage. They are, indeed, the single most important formal mechanism of beauty product distribution among the aspiring middle class in Guadalajara.

Extending out from the productive economy of cosmetics on the ground, one can begin to see even more clearly how important the personal instruction in and introduction to beauty products is to the productive economy of beauty. By applying a feminist political economy lens, these patterns begin to show more clearly how inextricable the productive economy is from the reproductive and virtual economies. One can also observe that the privileged institutions, identities, and ideologies of the beauty economy are shaped by gender.

The bulk of the cosmetics industry is concentrated in several large companies. The eight cosmetics and toiletries (C&T) companies with the largest market share in Mexico hold a combined 68.2 percent of the Mexican C&T market (see Figure 5.1). Four of these eight (Avon, Mary Kay, Vorwerck,

Top Company Shares C&T Mexico 2007

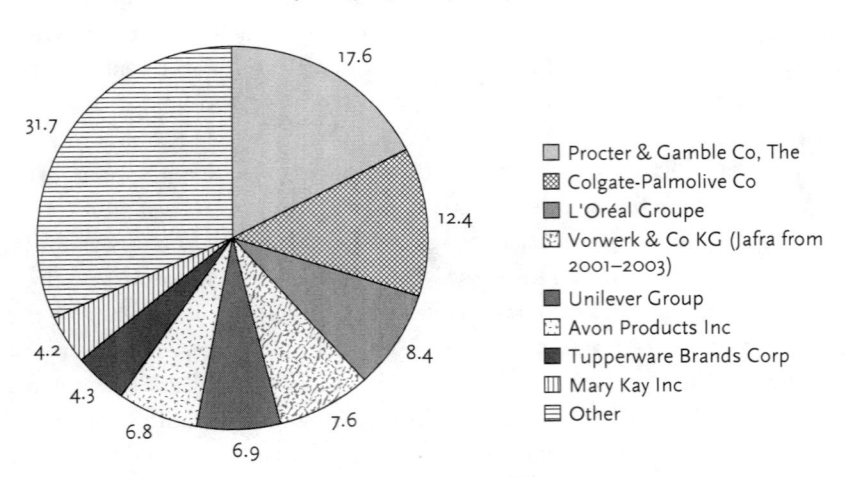

- 31.7
- 17.6
- 12.4
- 8.4
- 7.6
- 6.9
- 6.8
- 4.3
- 4.2

- Procter & Gamble Co, The
- Colgate-Palmolive Co
- L'Oréal Groupe
- Vorwerk & Co KG (Jafra from 2001–2003)
- Unilever Group
- Avon Products Inc
- Tupperware Brands Corp
- Mary Kay Inc
- Other

Figure 5.1: Top Company Shares, Cosmetics and Toiletries, Mexico 2007. Source: Global Market Information Database, Euromonitor International, 2008.

and Tupperware) distribute through direct sales networks (GMID 2008). Avon's Mexico manufacturing is used as a platform for the Latin American market. Vorwerck's manufacturing in Mexico serves as a platform for Latin American and North American markets. Of the top eight companies, all but Vorwerck's Jafra Cosmetics and Tupperware's House of Fuller cosmetics are considered within the trade press to use a global branding strategy (Kumar et al. 2006, GMID 2008). They all use a global supply chain to source, manufacture, and distribute cosmetics in Mexico and Latin America. These corporate strategies, as has been observed in other industries, increasingly rely on the services sector, such as market research, design, marketing, and distribution. Direct sales, in terms of both quantities of product movement and worker participation, is the single most important mechanism of beauty product distribution.

An added dimension in the beauty industry—the short product life cycle—makes innovation in marketing, design, and formulas an especially important part of the political economy of beauty products. The short product life cycle is highly manufactured by the fashion industry in order to keep sales high. Through magazine advertising, "editorials" in beauty magazines, in-store displays, and incessant new product launches, the cosmetics industry maintains a high demand for its "new" products, even if they are only marginally new (Gavenas 2002). This high demand for new innovation or new fashion leads to reliance on design, marketing, and collaboration with tastemakers such as news and beauty editors at magazines. In order to maintain sales momentum and growth, the industry relies on professional services in the fields of research, design, and marketing.

Due to corporate strategies in the beauty industry, primary producers and manufacturers are losing importance relative to professional services. Industry analysts argue that, due to corporate consolidation, primary material providers and independent manufacturers' bargaining power with the corporations "ranges from low to medium" (Kumar et al. 2006: 300). This move toward monopolization puts downward pressure on suppliers' terms, and puts more economic power in the hands of global corporate leaders. As consolidation continues through acquisitions and centralizing design and marketing strategies, independent producers' bargaining power will only decrease (Kumar et al. 2006).

As can be seen in observations of the cosmetics industry, economic activity in the productive economy of beauty is concentrated in the services sector. Due to global corporate strategies, research, design, and marketing add more value to the product than does manufacturing. Owing to the flexibilization of production, manufacturing does not have to be carried out in Mexico for products to be sold in Mexican markets, and Mexico is used as a manufacturing platform for other markets.[1] Manufacturing activity is dwarfed by distributive and personal services activity.

The increasing importance of services in relation to production is not only evident at the corporate level. A 2006 survey of businesses in the cosmetics and toiletries industry chamber of commerce reported a distribution of 51 percent industrial producers, 43 percent distributors, 17 percent *maquiladoras*, and 14 percent primary producers (CANIPEC 2006: 61).[2] The percentages add up to more than 100 percent because some companies engage in more than one activity; production and distribution is the most common double dedication (CANIPEC 2006: 62). The CANIPEC survey also attempts to account for the informal market, a serious concern to CANIPEC members (see below). Measured in sales, it accounted for 3.8 percent of the market in 2006 (CANIPEC 2006). The informal industry is overwhelmingly made up of retail distribution services in street markets (Pastor and Wise 1998).

CANIPEC data, however, does not take into account the two largest parts of the cosmetics and toiletries industry: direct sales and personal services. First, it does not consider the very large distribution machine that is the direct sales force. Direct sales are particularly popular for health and beauty products and diet aids. Approximately 1.9 million Mexicans were reported as "direct sellers," or network marketing salespeople. Complete employment data for the cosmetics and toiletries industry is not available, but the CANIPEC survey is illustrative of how important and yet overlooked direct sales are to the beauty industry. The thirty-four businesses surveyed by CANIPEC reported 20,843 workers, 17 percent of whom worked in administration; 18 percent subcontracted through employment agencies; 28 percent in production; and 31 percent in sales. Apart from these numbers, CANIPEC reports 722,728 independent representative employees, mostly in direct sales. Figure 5.2 graphs the relative employment patterns described by these data. The direct sales force clearly swamps every other category of worker, all categories combined and is even more important in urban areas like Guadalajara, since approximately 78 percent of direct sales representatives are in urban areas (AMVD 2008).

Personal services are a second area of high employment in the cosmetics and toiletries industry that is not represented in CANIPEC data. Because beautification needs to be learned, personal services and education in beauty play an important role in the industry. In Guadalajara, personal beauty services include many that have already been discussed, such as hair coloring, hair cutting, hair styling, false nail design and application, manicures, pedicures, and makeup application. Special services might include facial cleansing, false eyelash application, eyebrow shaping, or tattooing

Relative Employment in C&T Mexico 2006

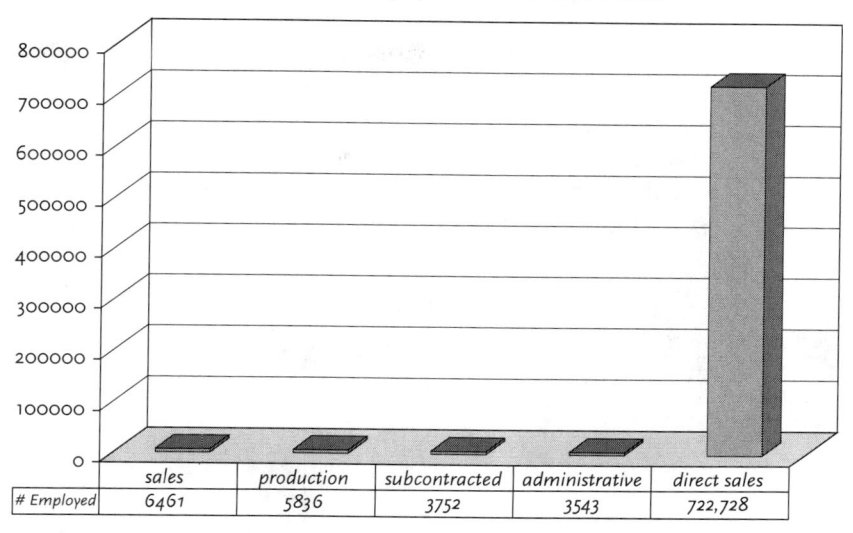

	sales	production	subcontracted	administrative	direct sales
# Employed	6461	5836	3752	3543	722,728

Figure 5.2: Relative employment patterns in Mexican cosmetics and toiletries industry, 2006. Source: CANIPEC 2006.

makeup. Spa services, a growing niche market for wealthier people, offer a variety of services from removal of unwanted body hair to skin exfoliation to reducing the appearance of cellulite. Personal services make up a large part of the industry and are carried out in beauty salons and spas. In interviews, all female participants had either patronized a neighborhood salon or employed the professional beauty services of a family member in the business.

The preponderance of beauty salons is evident in urban areas such as Guadalajara, where they are found at least every couple of blocks in every neighborhood of the city except for the two very wealthiest and some new private planned communities (see for example Figure 5.3). In addition, beauty services academies can be found in every city sector and number more than ten in the city center. Finally, direct sellers take on a combined role of distributor and personal service provider, as they use demonstration techniques in their quest to win clientele (Wilson 1999; Hennessy-Fiske 2008). Due to personal services and direct sales, therefore, by far the largest employment in the market is in distributive and personal services.

In sum, economic activity at the top rungs is increasingly research-, design-, and marketing-oriented. Furthermore, the employment pattern is overwhelmingly reflected by service employment that is on the lower end of the value scale in terms of pay, benefits, and security. Personal services,

Figure 5.3: A home-based beauty salon.

such as personal beauty service, are generally perceived as very low-skill and low-remuneration. This has meant that the increase in service-sector employment has had uneven development impacts. The service sectors that make up the bulk of the beauty industry, direct sales distribution and personal service, are typically the less valued service jobs or direct sales marketing jobs.

Structural Inequalities

These trends in the beauty industry, as in the global economy, tend to favor certain identities, ideologies, and institutions (see Tables 5.1 and 5.2). Structural inequalities of gender, race, ethnicity, class, and nation shape the dynamics of inequality in these sectors. This generally results in a privileging of masculinities, as well as some categories of national status, social status, economic resources, and race. A closer look at these service sectors reveals in more detail the global structural inequalities manifest in the beauty industry.

Table 5.1 HIGHLY VALUED IDENTITIES, IDEOLOGIES, AND INSTITUTIONS IN THE GLOBAL COSMETICS AND TOILETRIES INDUSTRY

Highly Valued...	Productive	Reproductive	Virtual
Identities	Global corporate professionals, upline	Sales entrepreneur, beauty expert, thrifty and savvy consumer	Fashionistas, celebrities
Ideologies	Profit, competition	Patriarchy, capitalist entrepreneurialism	Fashionable consumption
Institutions	Global companies	Family	Advertising firms, media

Table 5.2 LESS VALUED IDENTITIES, IDEOLOGIES, AND INSTITUTIONS IN THE GLOBAL COSMETICS AND TOILETRIES INDUSTRY

Less Valued...	Productive	Reproductive	Virtual
Identities	Producers, downline	Unsuccessful, financially insecure, unkempt, poor, narcissistic	Unfashionable, uninformed
Ideologies	Sharing, social distribution	Feminism	Subsistence consumption, no consumption
Institutions	Small companies	Caring work	Manufacturing industry, political institutions

Gender is the most central dimension of inequality; women are most likely to be employed in the least remunerative, most insecure jobs. Another axis of inequality is social class status, where poorer and less educated women occupy the lower rungs of the beauty industry. A third axis of inequality is national: the bottom of the employment chain is held by Mexican nationals, while the bulk of assets are earned by multinational companies.

A horizontal segregation by service sector, in which women tend to occupy jobs in sectors identified with "women's work," is a gendered pattern in most sectors of the productive economy. The beauty economy is no exception. Gender segregation is very noticeable in the service sector, between highly paid financial services providers and domestic personal service providers. In the service sectors of the beauty industry, we see even deeper patterns of inequality, particularly pronounced due to the dynamics of the direct selling business, but also in personal services.

Direct sales of beauty and fashion illustrate the importance of personal and distributive services, as well as its stark inequalities. Recall that in Figure 5.2, 722,728 direct sales representatives were reported as opposed to 20,843 regular company employees, with 3,752 of those subcontracted.[3] This ratio would be less impressive if one were to believe industry and popular arguments that direct selling is a hobby job, or merely supplemental, part-time income earned in women's free time. Direct sales income is jealously guarded by direct selling companies, long under attack for deceiving its sales force with unsubstantiated promises of easy wealth. There are no statistics on number of hours worked in direct sales, but there are indicators that it is still the major source of gross income and growth in the cosmetics and toiletries sector. Of C&T sales in Mexico in 2004 and in 2006, the largest market share, 33 percent of sales, was in direct sales (see Figure 5.4; CANIPEC 2006, 2008). In 2006, of the top eight C&T companies in Mexico, four of them are based on direct sales networks (Vorwerck & Co., Avon, Tupperware Brands, and Mary Kay), for a total of 22.9 percent of the market share. Clearly, direct sales are a substantial part of the beauty economy.

The reverse is also true, as the direct sales industry in Mexico is overwhelmingly constituted by the beauty industry (see Figure 5.5). Cosmetics

Distribution Channels - Mexico 2004

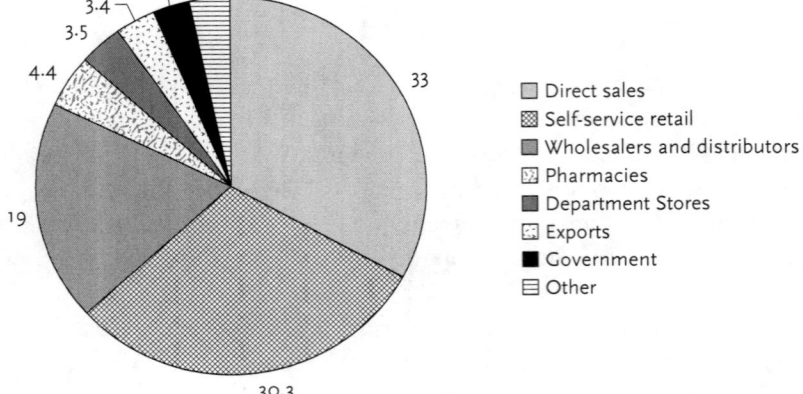

- Direct sales: 33
- Self-service retail: 30.3
- Wholesalers and distributors: 19
- Pharmacies: 4.4
- Department Stores: 3.5
- Exports: 3.4
- Government: 3.2
- Other: 3.2

Figure 5.4: Distribution Channels, Mexico 2004. Source: CANIPEC 2008.

Direct Sales Percentage by Product Category

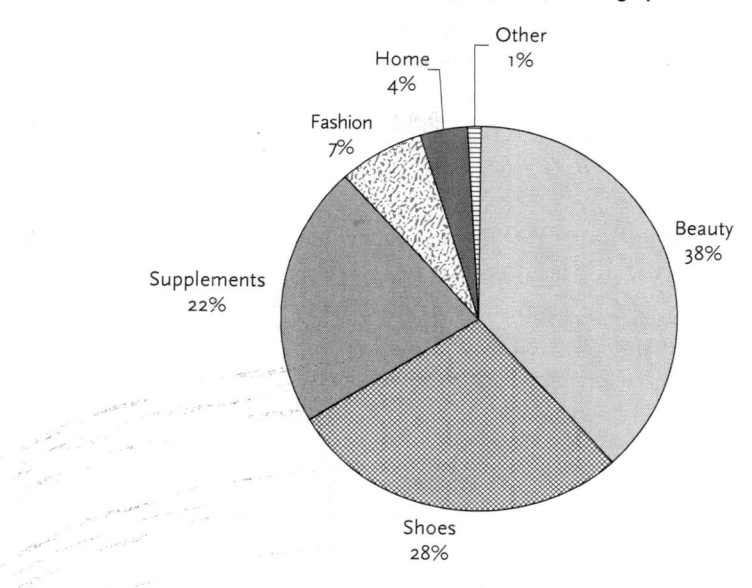

- Other 1%
- Home 4%
- Fashion 7%
- Supplements 22%
- Beauty 38%
- Shoes 28%

Figure 5.5: Direct Sales by Product Category. Source: AMVD 2008.

constitute 38 percent of sales, with shoes and fashion another 35 percent. Additionally, the 22 percent of sales in the supplements sector includes the largest single distributor, Herbalife, a weight-loss aid that reached $373.2 million in sales in Mexico in 2006 (Dickerson and Yi 2007). The Mexican Association of Direct Sales (AMVD) reports that total direct sales reached an estimated $44,581 million pesos (over 4 billion USD) in 2007 and that approximately 1.9 million Mexicans are "related in some way to the Direct Sales industry" (AMVD 2008).

Direct sales are not exclusively, but are overwhelmingly, made up of beauty industry sales. They are even more important in the sectors of the cosmetics and toiletries industry oriented toward beautification, as opposed to hygiene. A 2006 study by the cosmetics and toiletries chamber of commerce in Mexico (CANIPEC 2006) found that the perfumes & fragrances and makeup categories counted an estimated 77 percent and 72 percent of sales through direct sales channels. Oral hygiene, hair products, and hair color products, at 1 percent, 1 percent, and 15 percent had much lower percentages of direct sales. In sum, direct sales are of paramount importance to the beauty industry in Guadalajara, just as the beauty industry is central to the success of direct sales. Direct sales are also the major channel for the circulation of beauty products in Guadalajara as discussed in chapters three and four.

The direct sales industry is doing very well in Mexico as in other parts of the developing world, an easy extension of neoliberal globalization since the 1970s (Hilsenrath 1996; Wilson 1999, 2004; Fadzillah 2005). While markets in the US have been considered low-growth since the mid-1980s, company strategies have focused on expanding into new markets in middle-income countries and into the Spanish-speaking market in the United States. The $113 billion global network marketing industry (WFDSA 2009d) is relatively more important in developing than in advanced industrial economies (compare Figure 5.4 with Figure 5.6), because developing economies are considered the economic frontier by both global direct sales marketing businesses such as Avon, Amway, and Mary Kay, and proponents of market-based solutions to global poverty (Hammond and Prahalad 2004; Prahalad 2006). Network marketing in the developing world is also important materially, because sales in advanced industrialized economies have plateaued, relatively speaking, whereas sales in developing countries are growing significantly. For instance, while Avon's 2008 sales rose 3 percent in the United States, they rose 25 percent in Latin America.

The expansion of direct sales into emerging economies is both a strategy increasingly recommended in the business press and pursued by global corporations. According to the business press, while developed economies

Global Distribution Channels C&T 2006

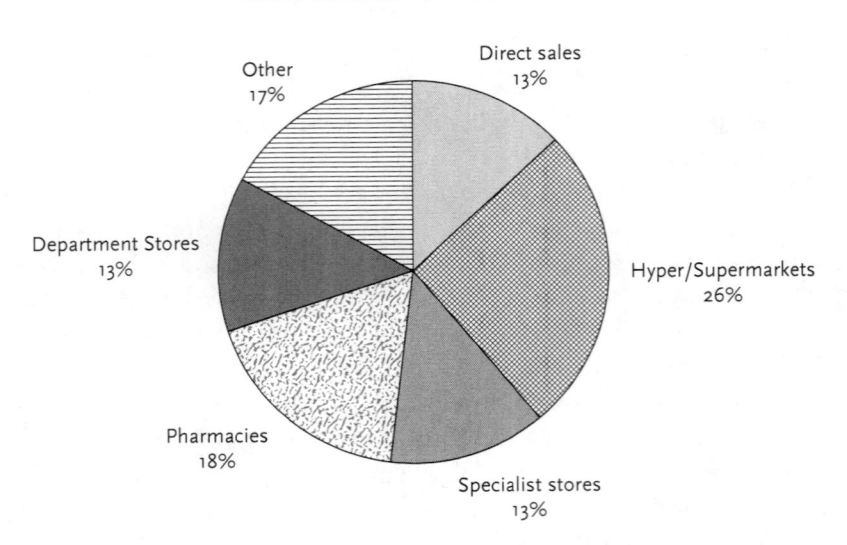

- Direct sales 13%
- Other 17%
- Department Stores 13%
- Hyper/Supermarkets 26%
- Pharmacies 18%
- Specialist stores 13%

Figure 5.6: Global Distribution Channels—Cosmetics and Toiletries 2006. Source: Global Market Information Database, Euromonitor International 2008.

are saturated with retail outlets and competition for a large consumer market, developing economies have large untapped markets, have fewer competitors, lack retail and distributive infrastructure, and have higher levels of unemployed people needing extra income—making developing countries well-suited to direct selling ventures (Wilkinson et al. 2007: 23-24). Hammond and Prahalad (2004) argue that direct sales are an opportunity to tap into the buying power among the global poor. Direct sales can tap this "fortune at the bottom of the pyramid" by overcoming obstacles such as regulatory tape or incompetence, lack of infrastructure, illiteracy to marketing, and "tribal, racial, and religious tensions, as well as rampant crime," that make business operations risky (32).

Direct sales are also a frontier for expanding capitalist entrepreneurialism. As proponents Hammond and Prahalad contend, direct sales are both profitable for businesses and charitable to the poor as they are "(e)nding the economic isolation of poor populations and bringing them within the formal global economy [to] ensure that they also have the opportunity to benefit from globalization" (37). The expansion of direct sales is, therefore, considered a win-win for global businesses and poor entrepreneurs wanting to become capitalists. Wilson's (1999) ethnographic and discourse analysis of the direct sales industry in Thailand describes the spirit of such neoliberal discourse as the "logic which has propelled the formation, growth and global expansion of the industry as a whole" (402). In this discourse, "the central figure of this logic, the direct sales distributor, embodies and enacts two central axioms of contemporary economic logic: entrepreneurship and decentralized distribution" (Wilson 1999: 402). The expansion of the direct sales empire, then, is part of neoliberal expansion that constructs the seller as a capitalist entrepreneur and the industry as a market-based development strategy.

The spread of network marketing to the developing world is closely tied to processes of globalization in the global economy. The intersection of aggressive global business strategies with revolutions in information and communication technologies, open economies, the movement of people, and individuals searching for income-producing activities, contributes to the widespread success of network marketing. Neoliberalism, deregulation, economic liberalization, privatization, lower trade barriers, increasing communication technology, and increasing travel infrastructure, all contribute to a direct-sales-friendly global environment. In this sense, the rise in network marketing and its growth in the developing world should be understood as part of several shifts in the global economy since the 1970s: a shift toward information-based production, flexibilization and feminization of production, and neoliberalism as the predominant economic ideology. The flexibilization of direct sales is in distributive, as opposed to productive, services.

It is important to note that network marketing and sales is not simply an expansion of global corporate power and capitalist logic to exploit women. It is also a strategy pursued by women in times of economic hardship, as in the case of Argentina after the monetary crash in 1999, when "unemployment climbed into double digits in 2001 and 2002, [and] direct selling grew as people sought other ways to make a living" (Ponder 2005, cited in Wilkinson et al. 2007: 23). This was also reportedly the case in the 2006–2009 recession, as unemployed and underemployed people turned to network marketing to cover decline or loss of income (Change 2009; FT 2008, 2009).

This widespread incorporation of women as entrepreneurs in the world of direct selling, however, is still highly unequal in its processes and outcomes. While the direct sales force accounts for about 97 percent of the workforce in the beauty industry, returns on that portion of the industry are at about 33 percent (CANIPEC, AMVD 2008). This means that, in terms of remuneration, direct selling is one of the least remunerative economic activities in the beauty industry, despite its prevalence as a form of economic exchange and importance to global sales. Still, one might point out that, according to company literature, direct sales are meant to be supplementary income, a source for extra cash flow that requires virtually no time commitment (e.g., Avon 2008, AMVD 2008). According to this logic, the lower levels of remuneration are justified. The products sell themselves; women do not have to labor to sell them. Data are not available to evaluate the ratio of time spent selling to income earned, but signs indicate that the claim that direct selling results in easy side money does not withstand scrutiny. Feminist perspectives on reproductive labor lend insight into why direct sales are not a wealth of easy money.

Direct selling is highly gendered. Until the 1920s, door-to-door peddling in the US, the precursor to the network marketing business strategy, was almost entirely carried out by men (Biggart 1989). Beginning in the late 1800s, women business entrepreneurs began to develop cosmetic products and direct sales methods that would eventually become the centerpieces of the network marketing industry. In 1886, the California Perfume Company, later Avon, under the direction of Mrs. P. F. E. Albee, began to recruit women to purchase and resell perfumes and cosmetics door-to-door in their neighborhoods. At the turn of the century, Annie Turnbo Malone developed and sold hair products for African American women through door-to-door sales, as well. Malone, along with Madame C. J. Walker, one of her former sales agents, innovated and developed the multilevel network sales method for door-to-door cosmetic sales, instituting incentives for sales agents to recruit and train new agents (Peiss 1998). Women-targeted products and women-oriented sales grew steadily, and after World War II, multilevel direct sellers began shifting to sales through "home parties," and the female seller, particularly the "housewife," became the typical target of recruitment and sales (Cahn 2006: 287)

Network marketing today largely consists of sales of cosmetic, diet, fashion, and household goods to women, the sales force is made up almost entirely of women and their social networks, and a high percentage of economically active women are typically involved in network sales. A 2004 survey of network sales representatives in Mexico estimated that 90 percent of approximately 1.9 million (about 1.7 million), representatives were women (AMVD 2008). In 2004, 37.5 percent of Mexican women, nearly 15 million, were "economically active" (INEGI 2004). Thus, not only are women the overwhelming majority of network marketers in Mexico, more than 10 percent of "economically active" women work in the industry.

The direct sales model, particularly within cosmetics, diet, and household goods, also uses femininity and masculinity to operate, and as a result has some gendered processes and outcomes (Wilson 1999, 2003; Fadzillah 2005). For example, youth direct sales marketers in rural Thailand are accessing an alternate ideal of femininity through their use and promotion of Amway and Avon cosmetics, a femininity that Fadzillah (2005) argues is based on modern Western beauty, familial independence, and urban cosmopolitanism. At the same time, network marketing is transforming youths' material circumstances as they become independent earners, recruit older family members as underlings in their network, and amass relative wealth. As a consequence, network marketing not only presents a way to access new ideologies of femininity, but also transforms material circumstances, gender norms, and family hierarchies. Direct sales marketing is therefore important to the expansion of markets as well as gendered capitalist subjectivities.

The employment of and marketing to women in direct sales and personal services in beauty and fashion can be seen as part of the global trend toward flexibilization and feminization of labor markets, as well as gendered consumption. Gendered network marketing involves a flexibilization of the health and beauty industries, outsourcing the costs of training, employment, and infrastructure to women. Through this type of outsourcing, international companies employ women's supposedly "free time" to sell products in a "volunteer, for-profit" model of sales (Bartlett 1997). Why is this model of unpaid labor particularly gendered? Beyond the obvious observation that an almost exclusively female workforce is asked to volunteer their time to make sales in exchange for the chance at some profit-sharing, there are several more ways in which this labor process is gendered.

First, gendered expectations about women's time being free, unoccupied, and nonproductive, operates both to motivate companies to seek women's free labor and women to accept it. As women enter into the labor market, they enter it based on gendered cultural expectations as well as gendered demands on their time. The same factors that make working in beauty services attractive make working in direct sales attractive: it uses skills that women have developed through learning about becoming beautiful in their personal lives, it gives them added cultural prestige as experts in beautification, and it proclaims flexible work options. These factors make working in network marketing attractive because it proclaims flexible work opportunities that allow women to fulfill their obligations to family—through reproductive labor—as well as the increasingly common second shift in the paid labor market.[4] Network sales of nutrition and diet aids rely on a woman's personal experience of consumption, weight loss, and/or health improvement as the major selling point (Cahn 2006). And finally and perhaps most importantly, network sales depend on the most valuable sales tool for word-of-mouth marketing and sales: women's social networks (Biggart 1989).

This gendered division of labor, however, can also be an obstacle to making easy money during free time. Some argue that women's entrance into the labor market leads to overall improvement in women's lives and empowerment (e.g., Gray et al. 2006). This is an argument of liberal feminist theory, which posits that women's equality can be achieved through legal and formal institutional equality (Tong 1998). Socialist, postcolonial, postmodern, and critical feminist scholars maintain, however, that deep social inequalities exclude the possibility of achieving gender equality through legal equality or equal labor market participation. These feminists contend that recruitment into the productive economy has been premised on gendered social expectations that funnel women into jobs with low pay, fewer benefits, and higher insecurity (Elson and Pearson 1981; Safa 1981; Nash and Fernández-Kelly 1983; Enloe 1995, 2004 [2000]). These scholars are therefore skeptical that women's increased formal employment will lead to a fundamental change in gender inequality.

In addition, feminists argue that entrance into the labor market leads to a double or even triple workday. After labor market entry, women work in the productive economy, but also remain largely responsible for caring labor and subsistence living. In addition, economic pressures add to the load of care and subsistence work, where the burden of structural adjustments is carried. Finally, many feminists reason that the stress of economic pressures puts stress on emotional relationships in households, leading to extra emotional work or even domestic violence (Hochschild 1997; Gonzalez de la Rocha 1994; Chant 1991). In short, women's widespread entrance into the labor market through network marketing is not a case of women achieving economic or social parity with men, or finding an easy way to make money in free time, but rather a restructuring of women's activities and obligations, often characterized by an increase in workload and a decrease in economic security.

One of the problems with informal employment is its lack of protections and benefits, and associated risks. In 1994, the *LA Times* reported record cosmetics sales of $465 million in Brazil, then Avon's largest non-US market. The greatest area of growth at the time was in the Amazon region, with $70 million, or 15 percent of national sales, a rate credited to the lack of previous commerce and the flexibility and opportunity of direct selling for women with little education and work experience. By local standards, the $250 to $700 estimated monthly earnings provided a sizeable income and an alternative to menial labor. On the other hand, the relatively high income did not come without business costs and risk. Three Avon representatives had been robbed and killed, and one had narrowly escaped death in an overturned boat. Malaria is also a constant threat (Harris 1994). What this dramatic story partially illustrates is that women and men assume risks, sometimes tremendous, to make their sales incomes. Were the lack of benefits, such as health insurance, as well as the costs of doing business in rural areas, calculated, the sales earnings would undoubtedly be much less.

The feminization of the direct sales industry illustrates women's complicated relationship with globalization; women are not universally winners or losers in the beauty sales economy. In the direct sales model, the empowerment of successful network marketers is vis-à-vis their less-successful social network, women in their "downline." For example, the teenagers in Thailand who become high earners in their family and subsequently disrupt family hierarchy do so by selling to and employing in their downline family and friends, necessarily closing off the opportunity to the people they employ in their downline. The big winners are only those who get in the business first. Depending on the corporation's pricing and incentives program, it is often actually more lucrative for a salesperson to dedicate herself to recruiting other sellers and skimming off a commission rather than selling merchandise. These multilevel direct sales techniques exploit women's social networks in order to sustain profit, and implicate their saleswomen in a complex web of exploitation among themselves. Thus, the assumption of women's empowerment through direct sales marketing neglects to interrogate the (more numerous) failures. While Hammond and Prahalad, on the one hand, exaggerate women's potential for empowerment through access to consumer goods, Fadzillah overstates the potential for women's empowerment through access to selling consumer goods when that empowerment is based on upstaging other network marketers. The direct sales downline is an example of how women are integral to the growth in the global economy, not simply as exploited workers or consumers, but also as complex intermediaries.

CONCLUSION: PRODUCTIVE, REPRODUCTIVE, AND VIRTUAL DYNAMICS

Considering the above analysis of the productive economy of the beauty industry, politics of the globalization of beauty products cannot be understood isolated from the reproductive and virtual economies. First, employment patterns are shaped by the gendered division of labor, assumptions about caring labor, and assumptions about women's time. Women are recruited into and seek out beauty and personal services as an extension of their personal lives and skills. The work of direct sales is premised on the assumption that the time women spend outside of paid employment is "free time" that can be put to more productive use. Direct sales and the larger part of salon services are conducted out of "private" spaces that blur the distinction between public and private work.

Second, women are the primary actors in economic exchange in the productive economy of beauty. The beauty industry is a case in which women are the chief beneficiaries of women's personal services, the primary consumers of beauty products, and the main distributors and retailers of beauty products and services. Whereas the gendered division of labor is marked by men being the usual beneficiaries of women's personal services (Peterson 2003: 55), using the beauty industry as a lens on the global economy makes clear that there are sectors of personal services and retail wherein women are the primary workers and the primary clientele. The sectors are almost entirely feminized, although there is still marked vertical segregation illustrated by the fact that men occupy the top positions both at the corporate level and in beauty salon services. This is a highly gendered division of labor and division of consumption that highlights that women occupy distinct and contradictory positions in the global economy.

Third, in the case of the beauty industry, the privileged identities are not only the capitalist entrepreneurs but also the informed fashionistas, the fashionable consumers.[5] The creation of these identities relies not only on access to products but also on beauty instruction, information and communication technologies, media sources, and advertising, as well as access to catalogs, retail outlets, and audiences. The exchange of signs between close individuals leads to the increased circulation of beauty products. The ideas about women that make beauty services or network marketing a good, even a "natural" option for women are implicated in the global exchange of signs. The exponential growth in beautification techniques and products is propelled by global strategy targeting women as network marketers, encouraging women to seek more and more products and expertise, and to become beauty entrepreneurs in order to become successful women. Likewise, it enables them to seek more products, and the spending money to buy them or the discount associated with being a direct sales distributor.[6]

In sum, through woman-central selling, woman-central advertising, and woman-central consumption, the beauty industry is a through-and-through example of how the reproductive, productive, and virtual economies are inextricably linked. The beauty industry is also extremely gendered, making it absolutely central to the reproduction of femininities. From paid work to semi-informal direct sales, to the home, the market, and the body, femininities are being reproduced. The beauty services and supply industry is directly linked to both globalization and the production of the gendered body, illustrating a mutually constitutive process whereby femininity and feminine roles in the global economy are co-constituted.

CHAPTER 6

Different Brands of Beauty: Subcultures and the Global Virtual Economy

It is about 11 am Saturday morning, and my excitement surges as I turn the street corner and see a young adolescent, dressed mostly in black, walking in front of me. A group of three teens heads in the same direction on the sidewalk on the other side of the street. I catch up to the group, now waiting to cross the street. One of them is carrying a backpack fashioned out of half a bucket. Among us all, there is enough black cloth to build our own dark room. We are headed to the *Tianguis Cultural*, the city's hub of youth subcultures. The *tianguis*, or street market, is a weekly outdoor event set up in a small plaza in downtown Guadalajara. Here, in what is really an oversized street median, mostly young people converge every Saturday to sell their wares, to browse, and just to meet up, hang out, and wait until the band starts at around three o'clock. I love coming here because I could not ask for a more appropriate site of immersion for my research. This market *is* youth, fashion, and culture in Guadalajara. Ironically, it is like nothing I see all week in the rest of the malls and plazas where youth gather, hang out, and shop for fashion. Even a few blocks away, the streets look "normal," but as I turn that street corner, I feel the excitement as, seemingly from nowhere, young people in outlandish outfits begin to emerge as if from thin air, multiply, converge, and liven up this otherwise dreary and dangerous plaza downtown.

The *Tianguis Cultural* in many respects is the epitome of the commodification of culture, argued by many to be a hallmark of postmodern globalization. But as a case study in cultural commodification, *el Cultural*, as it is referred to by regular visitors, and its subcultures illustrate that the global politics of cultural consumption is more complex than the marketization and depoliticization argued to be the effect of commodifying culture. To the contrary, the cultures of style among youth in Guadalajara shed light on an aspect of global politics that is often overlooked or undervalued: the globalization of diverse beauty ideals. Youth fashion subcultures exemplify a global political economy of beauty and fashion that not only commodifies and markets a thin, white, Anglo-American ideal, but also facilitates the broadcast of a diverse range of fashion and beauty ideals. This is not a broadcast from powers-that-be in the music and fashion industries, but rather the fruits of youths' own entrepreneurialism. The virtual economy of beauty is so open and so diverse that it enables the transformation of some social norms. The intersection of globalization with youths' open yet resistant attitudes toward social norms opens up space for transformative change with respect to gendered norms of appropriateness.

GLOBAL VIRTUAL ECONOMY

The global virtual economy encompasses three "modes," or areas of virtual exchange: finance, information, and cultural signs. This incorporates the exchange of symbols, including monetary, informational, and cultural, in the global economy. These types of symbols share in common their virtuality, which gives them shared characteristics; deterritorialized and dematerialized, the exchange of symbols is extremely rapid and extensive, but also uneven and in a context of unequal access.

This conceptualization of the virtual economy is based on critical and cultural studies that argue that how we value symbols, for example money, is not objective or politically neutral. Rather, the values that we place on signs are highly subjective, being shaped by cultural identities, institutions, and ideologies. The virtual economy, therefore, is critical to political economy as it shapes the use of money, investments, technology, communication, and consumption. Indeed, "globalization is most visible when we consider the transborder flow of information, symbols, and communication" (Peterson 2003: 113). This is no less true for the globalization of the beauty industry, where the information about, symbols of, and communication about beauty are woven throughout daily life.

Despite their visibility and its importance, global virtual exchanges are the least integrated into analyses of global political economy. Virtual exchange in finance has been the province of business and administration studies (c.f. Aitken 2007), contributing to the naturalization and depoliticization of international finance. The global exchange of signs, including that of beauty signs, has been the province of the humanities, particularly anthropology and literature studies.

The RPV categorization of these three types of global virtual exchange share their virtuality, the context of the information revolution that makes their exchange in real-time unprecedented, and similar patterns of power and prestige within their networks of exchange. The categories of financial exchange, and information and cultural symbol exchange, however, diverge significantly in their effects in the global economy of beauty. Financial markets are undoubtedly important to the management of the global beauty and fashion industry, shaping investment in firms and business and consumer credit. They therefore influence outcomes in the beauty and fashion industry, and are likewise affected by trends in consumption and production. Financial exchange, based in the use of currency exchange in real-time as an element of global capitalist profit-seeking, pushes for beauty product companies to enter new markets, including the global youth and emerging country markets. Financial rationale also makes the volunteer sales force of network marketing a sensible investment strategy. On the other hand, the exchange of information and cultural symbols is characteristically more popular, open to the participation of anyone in the global economy of beauty, and comprising the very substance of beauty globalization—exchange of images and ideas about what is beautiful.

This chapter focuses on just one category of the global virtual economy: the exchange of information about beauty and the exchange of signs—cultural symbols—about beauty. Information about beauty ideals is now rapidly exchanged and critiqued between youth through the virtual economy. Information exchange shapes beautification by opening access to new ideas about beauty. The exchange of signs encompasses the exchange of meaning and value that are infused into commodities when commodities are exchanged. The exchange of signs, being based on cultural meaning and aesthetics of consumer goods, therefore influences the social and identity-forming value of the fashion process. For example, when a *quinceañera* puts on a black dress for her surprise dance, she signifies her identification with a social group, and her difference from others. The politics of the virtual economy of signs lie in how value and meaning are assigned to cultural symbols or products, who sets the values, and who benefits.

The exchange of signs and information are the modes of the global virtual economy that are most central to the functioning of the virtual economy of beauty. The exchange of signs is also what is most central to the function of fashion as a social process of identification and differentiation; youth use their brand names, red hair bows, or black band t-shirts as ways of signifying belonging to their preferred social groups, and their rejection of their parents' norms. Through the information revolution, the signs of beauty ideas, images, and products have globalized, globalizing cultures of beautification as social markers. The information economy shapes new technologies for communication and marketing in particular, and provides the material for the trends toward increasingly differentiated, stylized, unnatural, and produced techniques of beautification.

Globalizing fashions are an excellent illustration of the global exchange of signs. It is through the increasing commodification of fashions, adornments, and cosmetics—signs of beauty—that the industry continues to grow. The commodification of beauty signs illustrates well how value becomes less about the product and more about its cultural meaning, as red hair signifies inclusion in a group and affection for a rock band. Or, to use Peterson's example, "it is not the durability of the jeans but the visibility of the designer brand-name that matters" (Peterson 2003: 141). In addition, it is through the cosmetics and fashion industries' excellence at producing desire for virtually identical but "new" products every season (Gavenas 2002) that it thrives, and does relatively well even in times of recession. The image of the product, the desire it conjures, and its cultural symbolism are as important as the product itself.

Peterson, along with many other scholars, uses fashion as an example of global virtual exchange (2003: 140-141), but does not explore the politics particular to beauty globalization. As discussed in the introduction to this book, the politics of beauty include group membership, intersectional personal identities, and the construction of gendered adolescence. If signs of group membership, personal identities, and gender are being deterritorialized and dematerialized and exchanged in the global economy, what type of effect does this have on those group memberships, identities, and genders?

This chapter extends out from the ideals espoused by youth in Guadalajara to the global virtual economy, focusing on sources of information and aesthetic inspiration that these youth cite as important to the formation of those ideas. These sources of information and ideas, although global, evidence some structural inequalities. Europe and the US are favored and valued sources of images, information, and ideas. Within the mainstream, *fresa*, culture, thin, white, and slight-featured beauty ideals dominate the virtual economy of beauty. Beauty advertising and images of beauty in media favor a thin, white, ideal. In effect, cultural signs in the virtual economy of beauty privilege an exclusive set of beauty standards that have been shaped by years of global and regional racial and national privilege. In addition, production of those images is disproportionately controlled by creative and professional classes in advanced Western industrial countries. These phenomena are no doubt mutually reinforcing, where privilege and access to media and marketing have contributed to the favoring of particular looks of beauty in the virtual economy, and vice versa.

While on the one hand globalization is spreading images of beauty, fashion, and femininity that are disproportionately influenced by Anglo-American norms of beauty, on the other hand it facilitates an increasing diversity of images and ideas. A limitation of scholarship on beauty and fashion globalization is its focus on "beauty pageant" or "fashion magazine" variety ideals. This focus on hegemonic beauty standards assumes an authentic, different, local context that is at risk of homogenization and erosion. At the same time, the focus on the globalization of conventional ideals conceals the otherwise diversifying effects of globalization in the global virtual economy of beauty and fashion. As illustrated in this text, locally situated youth are themselves powerful engines of fashion globalization and, as will be shown in this chapter, their fashions are more varied than ever.

In order to move away from this paradigm of homogenous global and authentic, different local, much of this chapter is dedicated to the beauty practices of youth outside of the mainstream. The subcultural focus provides a look at differences among groups, not just the most mainstream fashionistas, showing diversity and rapid change both at the global and local levels. Many youth are not adopting mainstream beauty standards, but their subcultures are equally if not more globalized. Subcultural globalization illustrates that beauty globalization is not exclusive to the mainstream, fashionable youth. In addition, resistance to hegemonic norms is not solely the terrain of transnational networks and organized groups, but is also part of everyday life, as simple as getting dressed up at night.

The case of the *Tianguis Cultural* illustrates that the commodification of culture does not necessarily depoliticize through promoting consumerism. Consumerism and the diversity in consumer markets achieved through extensive cultural commodification also help spread diversity. This diversity is not necessarily good, but in the beauty economy of Guadalajara, diversity does provide alternatives to conventional beauty standards, and therefore enables change in gender socialization. Still, even among subcultural groups, certain hegemonic ideas about feminine appearances persist. This chapter, by focusing on globalizations outside of the mainstream, illustrates some of the cracks in the idea of a hegemonic globalization, some of the probably limitless opportunities for resistance, and some of the social conventions most resistant to change.

VIRTUAL ECONOMY OF BEAUTY SIGNS

The trends in the global virtual exchange of signs has been in two movements: toward increasing commodification, or the fusion of culture and commodity through the increasing importance of cultural symbols in marketing commodities globally, and toward the production of increased consumer desire (Peterson 2003). In the beauty economy, the result is the increased use of images of femininity and masculinity to market goods, as well as the increased use of cultural branding to sell goods (Klein 2000; Holt 2004).

The fashion consumption economy is concentrated in urban and suburban zones like the Guadalajara Metropolitan Zone (ZMG), which includes eight physically continuous municipalities. Outside of the metropolitan zone, numerous towns and villages contribute to the metropolitan economy. The *Tianguis Cultural* is the center of the regional subcultural economy, being a source for artisans to sell their wares and for wholesalers who come to buy for resale in Guadalajara's main resale market, San Juan de Dios, and other mid-size cities such as Juarez, Durango, Queretaro, and Monterrey.

Increasing consumer demand drives the global consumer economy. This demand must be created, requiring heavy investment in marketing to foster desire. This helps explain why a private marketing research company like Euromonitor has better, more detailed statistics on consumption than the Mexican government. Companies like Euromonitor collect data from business associations, chambers of commerce, published research, the government, and independent research, and they compile them into systematic information on consumption patterns and behaviors to sell to marketers or companies that use consumption data to drive their investments and marketing.

The production of desire for consumption naturalizes the consumption economy, particularly through marketing campaigns and through television. The flood of admiration for the lives, consumption, and look of the rich in media and marketing naturalizes consumption for pleasure and status. Consumption becomes associated with wealth, even the source of wealth, despite the politics of unequal access to and benefits from the consumer economy (Peterson 2003). Thereby, the practice of the *quince* has become a hallmark of aspiring middle class consumers, even as it is less-and-less practiced and associated with the elite class of the mid-twentieth century.

But the politics of the global exchange of fashion symbols does not stop with the commodification of beauty and production of consumer desire. For one thing, mainstream beauty globalization is historically associated with the diffusion of ideals of whiteness, thinness, hourglass curves, and Anglo-American-associated features (Jones 2010). The promotion of white, especially Anglo-American, ideals of beauty in Mexico dates at least to post–World War II advertising by major international cosmetics companies, when "US cosmetics companies used endorsements by white American celebrities to sell products" (Jones 2008: 141; Jones 2010). Thin, white, and slight-featured beauty ideals continue to dominate the virtual economy of beauty in Mexico, even when the product's association with the United States or Europe is only by advertising association (Winders et al. 2005).

Without doing justice to the variety of media and marketing available and seen by youth in Guadalajara, there are a few indicators that this claim is true. Participants' female idols and symbols of beauty are largely international pop stars and movie stars from North and South America. Some key names include (in no particular order) Shakira; Fergie; Hannah Montana; Hilary Duff; Belinda; Belanova; RBD and its members Anahí, Dulce María, and Maite; Aracely Arámbula; Beyonce; Paris Hilton; Lindsay Lohan; Nicole Richie; Britney Spears; Janis Joplin; Lucero; and Jessica Simpson. Admirers of Janis Joplin and Lucero described themselves as "odd" for their admiration. What does appear unmistakable with this group of beauty and fashion idols is that generally, they share a thin, hourglass body, and pale skin, light hair, and light eyes by comparison with most of the population of Guadalajara. Male idols include Harry Potter; Ronaldo; Ronaldinho; Robbie Williams; Chayanne; Ricky Martin; Orlando Bloom; Brad Pitt; Tom Cruise; Ben Affleck; and Matt Damon. These idols share the soccer-player's body, slim features, and the admiration of many women. They also frequently grace the covers of the popular teen and fashion magazines, and several of them perform in Mexican *telenovelas*.

Curious about the supernatural hairstyles advertised on beauty salon signage, I took photos of the signs for a period of roughly three months, in every area of the Guadalajara Metropolitan Zone. This survey revealed a surprising pattern: There were virtually no definitively Mexican hairstyle models. None of the salons' signage appeared to represent a Mexican beauty, but rather an "ethnically unidentifiable" beauty (see Figure 6.1). Signs were most often produced by multinational companies like L'Oreal. One could say that the trend in beauty salon displays is to advertise "ethnically ambiguous"[1] hairstyles, but the term and concept is misleading. Ethnically ambiguous suggests correctly that the ethnicity of the model could potentially be Mexican, and that the true ethnicity of the model cannot be deduced. But the ethnic ambiguity does not cover the fact that the model will not be mistaken for Asian, African, or indigenous American. The

Figure 6.1: An "ethnically ambigious" advertisement in the Medrano district, the most popular fashion district among the aspiring middle class in Guadalajara.

ambiguity overwhelmingly favors the features, body, and hair seen among white Europeans and European-descendents. Most graphics featured models with blond, platinum-blond, or red hair.[2]

Europe and the United States are overwhelmingly the sources of *fresa* fashion inspiration. Occasionally, participants did cite Japanese cartoons and comics as fashion icons and one participant expressed a love for Arabic-inspired fashion because she has Arabic ancestry and takes Arabic dance classes. Otherwise, I had to go deep into the webs of subcultural fashion commodity knowledge in order to find sources of inspiration outside of Western Europe and the United States. US brands and Western European brands dominate the landscape. One good key to the popular brands is to see which ones are pirated and copied most: Coach (US), Versace (Italy), Chanel (France), Converse (US), Levi's (US), Diesel (Italy), Abercrombie & Fitch (US), Hollister (US), Ocean Pacific (US), bebe (US), Juicy Couture (US), and Baby Phat (US) were the popular name brands displayed during one jaunt through the *tianguis* of Santa Teresita, the most central *"fresa* fashion" *tianguis* in the ZMG. In effect, US and Western European commodities, brand commodities, and advertising dominate the mainstream virtual exchange of signs.

DIFFERENT BRANDS OF BEAUTY [143]

And yet, outside of the mainstream beauty and fashion industries, youth are spreading ideas about appearance, dress, and comportment that defy both the supposed depoliticization of commodification and the bias toward Anglo-American signs. Consider, for example, the trend of making homemade t-shirts with local artists' images to sell at the *Tianguis Cultural*. Several young women (between sixteen and eighteen years old) have commercialized their art and their sewing skills, creating several competing stalls of original designer clothing for 30–130 pesos (3–13 dollars), putting on fashion shows, and becoming image-makers locally. Their locally-produced fashions are exported by buyers to regional and international markets, and copied by more commercial enterprises. Their styles reference Japanese and American kitsch and punk culture, but their designs and styles are decidedly Guadalajaran, featuring local points of reference like local bus routes, Mexican currency, and local graffiti art. Youth use the information economy and their own marketing and media skills to diffuse alternate visions of beauty, fashion, and the values and belonging that they profess.

Some scholars see the globalization of the beauty industry as a homogenizing force or as an industry that contests or disrupts local, indigenous, and "authentic" cultural traditions. In a similar vein, Peterson characterizes the movement to a consumption-based market and increasingly commodified cultures as reinscription of structural hierarchies of access to and benefits from the global economy. If we conceptualize fashion as a social process of identification and differentiation, however, it becomes clear that beauty, rather than homogenizing, is always socially constructed based on social context, and also always indicates both inclusion and difference. Therefore, it is less useful to think of globalization of beauty as a homogenizing force and local context as contesting or local tradition being undermined. Instead, it is more helpful to conceptualize the global beauty economy as a set of parallel beautification globalizations competing for recognition and authenticity in local-global contexts. The key to globalization in this case, then, is that the global economy of beauty changes the context within which beauty fashions are articulated, the media available for the dissemination of beauty ideals, and the availability of alternative signs of beauty.

The transforming global context is important to the beauty economy because it makes inclusion and exclusion from social groups easier and more difficult, respectively. For example, *metaleros* (metalheads) now have to struggle to maintain their treasured sense of exclusivity because anyone can get their music from the Internet, rather than going through the laborious process of sending away for international mail order cassette recordings or earning the privilege of borrowing from a hard-won friend. Because of the media available for fashionistas, and the ease of access, the numbers and types of subcultures in Guadalajara are multiplying. The result is a proliferation of alternative beauty cultures.

El Cultural

The *Tianguis Cultural* illustrates how in some markets consumption and commodification are politicized. *El Cultural* was instituted as a market for artisans to earn fair prices for their work, circumventing resellers. It was created to commodify culture, and yet it has also established and maintained a political outlook on commodification. And, while consumption itself is naturalized, consumption at the *Cultural* is not unpoliticized. Through the diffusion of counter-cultural beauty/ fashion ideals, the subcultures of the *Cultural* politicize norms of appropriateness and commercial entrepreneurialism.

Consider the *metaleros*. Like other subcultures in the *Tianguis Cultural*, the *metaleros* profess a unique set of values, often expressed as moral and aesthetic superiority, as a way of life. *Metalero* is a general term for someone who is a dedicated fan of heavy metal music, but there are numerous distinctions among heavy metal lovers that make them *dark, goth, glam, death, vampiras, poser*, or any combination like *death-glam* or *glam-death-vampira*. I cannot make many of the distinctions myself, but with the help of a small group of *metaleros* I learned that there are insider signals that make a *poser*, someone who is trying unsuccessfully to fit in, stand out from people with more subculture credibility. And there are small signals that indicate one's musical and subcultural affinity. For instance, some *metaleros* wear white tennis shoes. Unbeknownst to outsiders, white tennis shoes are worn by a couple of bands, so their fans have adopted that style, making it a signal of knowledge about their favorite music and bands. Other fashion signals include corsets and the details that they convey, such as which vendors' stall in the *Tianguis Cultural* they are bought from and the style in which they are worn. For instance, a corset from one local designer carries a halter-top. Corsets from another local designer use more lace. Before spending time among the *metaleros*, they all looked very similar to me. However, it quickly became clear that there are many divisions among them over their types of music and the specifics of their style.

The biggest signal to subculture insiders is the band t-shirt. The band t-shirt announces a musical interest, and has grown into its own aesthetic. For *metaleros*, the band t-shirt is screen printed with elaborate, macabre aesthetics, on a black background. Men wear their t-shirts loose and long. Women wear their t-shirts tighter and with more design features, even tied up under a corset. The *metaleros* are just one example of how the fashion process is at work creating group identification and differentiation. Their symbols link affinities between people on the streets, in the *Tianguis Cultural*, and at concerts.

In speaking about their style, *metaleros* characterize it as a global, highly exclusive, way of life. They say it grew from bands in Scandinavia, but is now global, with many of their favorite bands being local, or from South America or the US. Their style is very dark, using a lot of black. The most common accent color is blood red. Prints on their clothes often utilize symbols of religion and death. They see their tastes as so specialized and so superior that membership in their circle of friends is very exclusive. They do not want to be associated with any *poser*, and often criticize other subcultural groups for their taste in music and their way of life. For example, *hippies*, *grunge*, and *rastafaris* are too dirty, too idealistic, and use drugs. *Metaleros*, by contrast, are clean, realistic, and drink a lot of alcohol but disassociate themselves from the use of street drugs. According to one, *metaleros* can be "any color" or from any country, but they have to share some of the core values discussed here.

The *metaleros* express these differences from mainstream society and other subcultures in part through their fashion and comportment. The more obscure a band, the more exclusive the beautification process. They laugh among themselves as *fashionistas* buy band t-shirts of bands they do not know just for the t-shirt design. One vendor in the *Tianguis Cultural*, after admitting that exclusivity can be bad for business, explains to me that he still prints a small set of limited edition band t-shirts in order to fulfill his desire to maintain exclusivity, even though it makes less financial sense for him as a vendor. The rest, he produces according to demand. This exclusivity is further maintained because *metaleros* do not like to share music. Perhaps as a throwback to the days when purchasing new music was difficult, international mail order unreliable, and local sources of music unsatisfactory, *metaleros* routinely express their distaste for sharing new music, even with friends. *Metaleros* actually lament the information revolution for making their music accessible to anyone, so any little kid can just download it and become a *poser*, liking the music and the fashions but not holding true to the social and philosophical values of a true *metalero*.

Other ways that *metaleros* symbolize their nonconformity are through tattoos, the heavy use of black, jewelry, hair dye, and makeup. Tattoos and body adornments often play tongue-in-cheek reference to religious symbols and death. The heavy use of black and secondary use of red in clothing and hair dye stands out in Guadalajara, where vivid colors or pastels, carefully combined in groupings of three colors or fewer, is the apex of fashion. *Metalero* makeup could be described as severe; it features pale tones of facial foundation and/or powder, and black eyeliner. Some of the *metalero* subcultures use black lipstick, others red, others none. The *metalero* aesthetic is part of the nonconformist values often espoused by *metaleros*. For *metaleros*, their subculture is not just a style, but also a "way of life." The bodily practices symbolize the belief that religion is a sham and a system of social control that keeps people from thinking independently. Society is too idealistic, so *metaleros* embrace death and pessimism. Their contrariness to social norms means that it is more difficult for them to find employment, and that they find romantic partners among similarly identified youth.

The *metaleros* are an example of the diverse subcultural trends in Guadalajara, although not each subculture espouses the same set of values, and they express themselves through fashion differently. For instance, the skateboarder or *skate* style in Guadalajara shares with the *metaleros* an affinity for black, tattoos, and religious skepticism, but are distinguishable for their athleticism, piercings, and more colorful use of screen-printing and accessories. "Old-school" and "new-school" skateboard riders are distinguishable by the style of their pants, the older style being looser.

As a market, the *Cultural* is the epitome of the commodification of culture, widely argued to be a hallmark of postmodernity (Harvey 1989) and contemporary globalization. Literally translatable to "cultural market," the *Cultural* is where cool is for sale, in the form of black vinyl corsets for *metaleros* and *darks*, deconstructed t-shirts for *punks* and *emos*, second-hand vintage imports for alternative music lovers, neon bead bracelets for *psychos*, tattoos and piercings for everyone, and the latest token of cool for the fashionable set and tourists. The most successful market stalls have drawn out their niche by offering exclusivity and authenticity of subcultural style to their clients. Clients are youth from all corners of Guadalajara, resellers in other parts of the country, and increasingly, tourists and students from abroad. The *Cultural* is the place that youth from all over the city will go to buy a piece of a subculture identification.

But the *Cultural* is also the major weekly social event, a characteristic of the commodification of the lifeworld. Even more than the popular malls, the weekly market is teeming with flirting, music-playing, eating, smoking, chatting, and watching young people. Many days, as the market winds down, a live band starts up, entertaining a mostly under-age group in the afternoon. This is, according to many authors, the definition of the commodified culture, where cultural artifacts are increasingly commercialized, and commercialization becomes the center of cultural activity (Peterson 2003). The *Cultural* is the equivalent to a commercial mall, but for subcultures. This commodification of culture is often read as the superficialization of culture for the benefit of corporate profit and at the expense of the marketization of everyday life. It is seen as part of a shift in public spaces being used to "further private consumption not public/civic interaction" (Peterson 144). But the *Cultural* and the subcultures that occupy it offer a chance to see globalization, even the commodification of culture, in a more optimistic light. As argued above, commodification of fashion and its globalization spread difference and social contestation. Difference and social contestation are not necessarily good, but they do present an opening, particularly with respect to challenging long-standing social inequalities and the naturalization of gendered differences. Furthermore, like the *quince* beauty industry, the *Cultural* provides an opportunity for youth entrepreneurs to spread their ideas and earn income.

Globalization is not undermining an authentic, traditional, morally superior set of local cultural ideals. First, culture is not a static formation, but rather a socially constructed web of meaning. This signifies that culture is always changing based on competing and cooperating identities, institutions, and ideologies. The process of social identification and differentiation within fashion is one example of how ideals of beauty and fashion is always socially constructed based on social context, and also always indicates difference. There are no authentic, traditional costumes that purely represent ethnicity (Borland 1996), nationality (Cohen et al. 1996), or sexual orientation (Higgins 1998). The process of using fashion to create social identification and differentiation is part of the process that creates authenticity as a social construct. Authenticity is not prior to the fashion process, but rather a result of it. Therefore, particularly in a post-colonial[3] context like Mexico, there is no set of authentic local ideals, but rather trends shaped by previous social context and innovation.

In support of this argument, consider historical gender and beauty ideals in Guadalajara. Conventional Mexican historical ideals of femininity are composites of various influences, deeply shaped by Mexico's indigenous and colonial roots, and its proximity to one of the major post–World War II global powers. Historical gender ideals in Mexico are not easily or simply described because they cannot be understood without an understanding and acknowledgment of diverse and competing identities and interests. Still, my argument that globalization is increasing the diversity of beauty and gender ideals warrants some summary historical notes.

First, gender ideals in Mexico, both contemporary and historical, have been influenced significantly by the colonial legacy. Authors have linked the two dominant archetypes of Mexican women, *la malinche* and *la virgen* to the colonial legacy that introduced European patriarchy as well as Christianity (Leal 1983; Arrizón 1999). *La Malinche* was the indigenous mistress of the Spanish conqueror Hernán Cortés, and her memory is invoked as a self-interested, traitorous, raped, unpure, woman (Paz 1950). The archetype of *La Virgen de Guadalupe*, on the other hand, is that of a maternal ideal, pure, virginal, "suffering, humble, and passive" (Leal 1983: 232). The revered ideal of the *Virgen de Guadalupe* helps explain the cultural ideals of femininity, such as motherhood and chastity, in Mexico.

In 1973, Evelyn Stevens articulated the Mexican ideal for womanhood as guided by *marianismo*, "the cult of feminine spiritual superiority, which teaches that women are semi-divine, morally superior to and spiritually stronger than men" (91) as the female counterpart to *machismo*, a cult of virility for men. *Marianismo* is based on reverence for the Virgin Mary (María). Stevens argued that *marianismo* is equally as prevalent as, although less well recognized and understood than, *machismo*. Indeed, *machismo* has become global shorthand for excessive patriarchalism in men (Gutmann 2007). *Marianismo* includes

> ...near universal agreement on what a "real woman" is like and how she should act. Among the characteristics of this ideal are semidivinity, moral superiority, and spiritual strength. The spiritual strength engenders abnegation, that is, an infinite capacity for humility and sacrifice. No self-denial is too great for the Latin American woman (Gutmann 2007: 94).

The cult of *marianismo* suggests that feminine virtue in Mexico is measured in self-denial, commitment to the family, and spirituality. Since Stevens' articulation of *marianismo* as the ideal of Mexican womanhood, much more research has been conducted on Mexican women's roles in society and households, showing that women do indeed perform feminine virtue through self-sacrifice and prioritizing their family's needs before their own; *marianismo* translates into women's assumption of responsibilities as reproductive workers, educators, and transmitters of culture (Bellón 1994; González de la Rocha 1996; Craske 1999).

Machismo, on the other hand, has long been considered the archetype or hegemonic ideal for Mexican manhood. According to Chant and Craske (2003),

> [T]he forging of asymmetrical sexualities in men and women starts early in Latin America. Long before puberty, girls in many parts of the region are controlled, kept within or close to the home in their play, encouraged to be demure

and deferential, and to build up a solid repertoire of domestic skills. Boys, on the other hand, are allowed greater spatial and social freedoms, and receive positive endorsement of aggressive and ostentatious behaviour..., that would meet with serious disapproval among their female counterparts (144).

Differential gender socialization is especially important for youth because these patterns are reinforced closer to puberty (Chant and Craske 2003).

Based on the differential treatment and socialization of boys and girls, the concept of the *macho* as the ideal of masculinity in Mexico has been popularized. Octavio Paz (1950) perhaps most famously argued that "the essential attribute of the *macho*[4] —power—almost always reveals itself as a capacity for wounding, humiliating, annihilating" (Paz 1950: 23). Subsequently, scholars have challenged the idea that the *macho* is so violent, and that it is the only or most important ideal of Mexican masculinity (Guttman 2007). Rubenstein (2002) argues that Mexicans also appreciate another ideal of masculinity, the counter-*macho*. According to Rubenstein, "El Santo," the iconographic wrestling actor from 1940s to the 1980s, "personifies a particular image of the good Mexican man: the virtuous man, in stereotype, as the opposite and twin of the stereotypical Mexican macho" (576). In contrast to the *macho*, the counter-*macho* is self-controlled, orderly, celibate or monogamous, nurturing, sober, and humble. His power comes more from "quiet command and self-discipline" (576) and he does not fall to the temptation of his many admirers. Both *macho* and counter-*macho* are patriotic, adored, and powerful.

Historical ideals of beauty in Mexico also reflect the influence of colonialism and religion. Cyntia Montero Recoder (2008) describes nineteenth-century ideals of feminine beauty as tied to expectation of marrying and becoming a mother. Women were considered beautiful when they embodied characteristics of youth, prudence, modesty, seduction, decency, moderation, truthfulness, sweetness, humility, grace, virtue, quietness, and pleasantness. Highly prized physical features included delicate and skillful hands, small feet, thin waist (Recoder 2008), pale skin, light eyes, light and wavy hair (Santamaria 1997; Carrillo 2002). Woman's beauty was also seen as closely tied to "nature" (Santamaria 1997). In postcolonial Mexico at least until the 1910 revolution, European fashions were markers of higher social status (Randall 2005). Since the 1960s, US influence in media and in the beauty and fashion industries has increased relative to European market share, although European names, celebrities, and sources of information remain highly valued in popular fashion and gossip magazines.

These historical constructions of femininity illustrate women's precious, but unequal, role in society. These ideals naturalize gender difference, constructing women as fragile, putting the burden of moral and religious correctness on women, and condemning women's sexuality, among other things. They also illustrate the multiple historical and social influences on gender constructions. So while Mexico's increasing globalization through trade, investment, flexible specialization, migration, and media production and consumption, has changed the social context for the construction of ideals of femininity, such change should not be seen as a corruption of previous social constructions, but rather a normal effect of changing social context.

Globalization has fostered growth of and diversity among subcultural groups that challenge historical and conventional doctrine about religion and gender. Through the design, production, distribution, marketing, and consumption of fashion, the global virtual economy makes important elements of subjectivity and group identification available for sale. What is novel, then, is that fashion commodification is so diverse and varied. Now, fashion signifies more than social class, nation, ethnicity, and gender. Fashion illustrates the rising importance of affinity groups and social contest as areas for personal identification and subjectivity. Therefore, commodification is not necessarily depoliticizing or naturalizing gender and beauty norms. To the contrary, commodification can actually be seen as an opening or an opportunity to spread more diversity in affiliations and beauty norms. Commodification of fashion and beauty is a sign of the increasing importance of social identification outside of historical markers such as nation, ethnicity, race, and social class. It also illustrates how some historical markers of group identity, such as nation, ethnicity, race and social class, are becoming less salient to youth in comparison to their music and fashion affinities. For the category of gender, however, fashion illustrates one category of subjectivity and identification that is very resistant to change.

In sum, the increasing commodification of beauty and fashion in the global economy is surprisingly not limiting in terms of ideals for feminine beauty. To the contrary, there are many alternative globalizations that espouse ideals of beauty quite contrary to social convention and history. While on the one hand we see that the global virtual exchange of signs is fostering the naturalization of consumption, consumption remains very political, and consciously so, for subcultural groups. This breaks up the assumption that globalization of the beauty and fashion industries is homogenizing. Indeed, rather than homogenizing, it is actually a diversifying force. In Guadalajara, a culturally conservative Mexican city, ideals for beauty and gender are certainly multiplying.

STRUCTURAL INEQUALITIES

One central problem with the virtual economy is that it is unevenly articulated globally, so that there is unequal access to its resources, and the agenda-setters in the virtual economy are concentrated among a global elite privileged by nation, race, class, and gender. Those privileged by the global virtual economy are those with historically privileged subjectivities, reinforcing historic inequality.

The *Tianguis Cultural* subverts some of these structures of power, but structures of gender difference have proven resistant to change. With regard to structures that privilege the cultural elite, *el Cultural* illustrates ways that young people and counter-cultural elites are privileged in these types of markets. *El Cultural* was developed as a way to circumvent middlemen, and to give artisans more power over setting the prices of their merchandise by selling directly to a large market. *El Cultural* was started in 1996 by a civil association that collected small donations to maintain operations, but overhead costs were cut down through volunteerism and the street market model. Only local artists and artisans were allowed to sell in *el Cultural*; vendors or resellers were expressly prohibited and, if found, removed from the market. Since the city government assumed control of market governance in 2003, the rule that wares must be locally produced has been relaxed, but the vending stalls were already spoken for, and may not officially be sold. Therefore, despite some attrition and some illegal selling of vending space, locally produced goods are still the backbone. The *tianguis* provides young artists and craftspeople cheap access to a large market. The artists that I spoke with did not develop their crafts through schools or specialized training, but rather through learning to sew, paint, and make crafts at home. Usually, as the vendors increase their sales, they hire groups of friends and family to act as manufacturers and salespeople.

To return to the example of the *metaleros*: on the one hand, the bands are the major taste-makers, but on the other, these local designers and producers and their consumers are the taste arbiters locally, and some of them produce for the regional, if not global, fashion markets. These local designers are not particularly privileged in the classical sense of class and ethnicity. There is a section of the market reserved for indigenous artists, who are not charged rent because of their historical hardships and disadvantages. The market itself is an attempt to provide a foothold for artists and artisans without the means or the demeanor to garner market share or solo exhibitions on their own. And yet, despite their supposed disadvantages, vendors at *el Cultural* do very well, much better than they would in an office job, even in government, for some. As the center for various subcultures' weekly public gatherings, the market frames public space as very diverse. As argued above, the structure of *el Cultural* and the subcultures in it are diverse examples of social contestation in everyday life, undermining traditional hierarchies such as race, ethnicity, religion, and nation.

Despite this, however, in the area of gender, there is a lot of sameness. Karmen MacKendrick (1998) argues that subcultural uses of body modifications and adornments such as piercings, tattoos, and corsets are undoing the link between beauty and "nature," undoing the naturalization of beauty as a concept, making beauty heavily constructed, and making the gender components of beauty exaggeratedly visible. MacKendrick therefore sees transgression or subversion in the use of historically gendered and painful modifications such as the use of the corset. It is easy to see the play with corsets, which raise the bust unnaturally high, squeeze the waist, and exaggerate an hourglass figure, as constructing and exaggerating the feminine shape so much as to denaturalize it. Speaking with the youth, however, leads me to conclude that the denaturalization of gender does not make the masculine-feminine dichotomy less salient.

Masculine and feminine gender norms, while rebellious and contesting many mainstream standards, in many ways parallel mainstream gender norms. Mainstream masculine standards of dress and comportment for youth closely resemble the celebrity soccer players and their "*cuerpo de futbolista*," or soccer-player's body. The norm of masculinity for *metaleros* is a clean but grungy look, unathletic, with long, product-free hair usually held in a tie at the nape of the neck. These features contrast with the short, gelled hairdos, athletic bodies, athletic clothing, and bright clean colors favored by mainstream youth.

This masculine look is the *metalero* equivalent of the "unmarked man" (Higgins 1998). The unmarked man, or the belief that men are not wearing gendered fashion but rather just wearing clothes, is the embodiment of the myth that women are gendered and men are not. The myth of the unmarked man perpetuates the idea that masculinity is the default, and that femininity is the aberration. *Metaleros* themselves expressed this myth of the unmarked man within their subculture. Men *metaleros* expressed to me that they rejected using any style or supporting any brand. From my perspective, this seemed absurd given that I had only identified them as a group by their use of black, band t-shirts, jeans, grungy tennis shoes, and long hair in low ponytails. Within their group, however, they identified themselves as not having any style, of being normal, of being the unmarked, default norm. This is where the strongest parallel to mainstream masculinity can be seen. Masculinity is performed, in whichever group, through the posture of having no style, of being the unmarked norm.

Femininity, on the other hand, is highly visible and constructed; it is the marked other. It takes care and investment with time, money, and education. And, it is simultaneously ridiculed for its superficiality and triviality. For example, among the *metaleros* is a subgroup of young women, the *vampiras*, who wear fangs, the shortest mini-skirts, and the tightest corsets. These sexy *metaleras* are also called "*cazagreñas*" (hunts grungy people) because they pursue "*greñudos*," or grungy metalheads. These young women are at one and the same time sexualized and ridiculed for their supposed superficiality and triviality. Still, they are not *poser* or outside of the authentic subculture.

Even non-*vampiras* are slammed for their attention to looks. One young man criticized women for being too interested in their looks, dyeing their hair too red or too blond, wearing too much makeup, and caring too much about the way they look. A few feet from us, three carefully fixed up young women one with her hair bleached blond and another with her hair dyed red, ignored us and pretended not to hear his condemnations. He and others explained the difference in gender styles to me by referring to women's inherent vanity. In sum, while the *Tianguis Cultural* and the subcultures in it espouse counter-hegemonic ideologies and identities, their gender ideologies parallel those of the mainstream.

CONCLUSION

This chapter argues that globalization in the virtual economy is playing an important role in the beauty economy. The global virtual economy enables rapid and extensive communication of images and ideas about beauty. Likewise, the exchange of beauty signs and information are important to the virtual economy. While shaped by structural inequalities in the reproductive and productive economies, the virtual economy is also susceptible to change due to its openness and accessibility, particularly to youth. Youth, as idea and commercial entrepreneurs, are also more interested and invested in the virtual economy of beauty, demonstrating a high level of involvement in the exchange of beauty signs and information about beautification.

The globalization of beauty fashions is important because beauty is a practice of bodily construction and representation that is central to processes of producing subjectivity and social identification and differentiation. The gender politics of beauty fashions are particularly important because beauty is central to constructing gender relations. The politics of beauty and fashion suggest that commodification and the increasingly consumer-based economy is helping to spread diverse subjectivities and group identifications, creating more diversity on the ground through globalization rather than hegemony. Still, while some historical group configurations are less important to youth, gender identification, even as it is denaturalized, remains resistant to change.

Conclusion: Youth, Gender and Fashion Globalization

In the 1980s, a group of feminist scholars proposed a simple yet provocative set of ideas: that beauty products, images, and ideals are powerful socializing agents for women that, rather than illustrating women's vanity and frivolity, are evidence of deep social inequalities, especially in terms of gender, race, and class. This literature, along with frequent references to the globalizing Anglo-American beauty ideals obliterating local beauty norms, informed a curiosity about whether conditions of globalization were transforming the use of beauty products, images, and ideas, and by extension transforming the socialization of femininity and concomitant social inequalities. This research therefore began with a simple set of questions: How do beauty images, products, and ideals circulate globally? Who benefits from the beauty industry? How do adolescents experience and act on the globalizing beauty industry? Are youths' norms of beauty and gender changing in ways that signify changes in gender, race, or national constructions?

Where a feminist theoretical sensibility informed the research questions, a feminist methodological sensibility suggested that people's lived experience of beauty globalization would be more informative than generalizing feminist theories developed in Anglo-American context, or writing off beauty globalization as merely superficial. The *quince años*, an event where typically marginalized subjects—aspiring middle class young people in the developing world—explore and display their beauty ideals and practices could not have been a better point of entry for viewing the globalization of beauty from the ground-up. Upon exploring and analyzing the information that young people and their families in Guadalajara recounted, some patterns emerged that indicated these questions could be answered, if only partially.

ARE NORMS OF BEAUTY AND GENDER CHANGING?

To begin with the last two research questions, socialization of gender through beautification *is* changing, and it *is* related to the global beauty economy. Beautification is so important to the *quince años*, it has replaced the religious service as the most important part of the tradition. Today, the makeover is the rite of passage into adolescence for girls, and the *quince* makeover is just one exaggerated manifestation of it. Globalization in the beauty economy, and the change it effects on the socialization of gender norms, is directly related to adolescents' experience of and interaction with the global beauty economy.

Gender construction through beautification in the *quince*, compared to previous generations, is more important, and it is also more reliant on artifice, dependent on reproductive labor, and diverse. The explosion in beautification is leading to widespread beauty entrepreneurialism. These developments result from a significant investment by young women to achieve a rarely—and usually momentarily—attainable ideal of beauty based broadly on youthfulness, thinness, curviness, and technological improvements. Artifice in beautification is evident through the proliferation of beauty products, services, and practices employed in beautification. Examples are eyelash extensions, use of multiple shades of eye shadow, and alien-esque proportions for hairstyles. The denaturalization of beauty and gender does not, however, indicate an equivalent reduction in the salience of the gender dichotomy to beauty. In order to meet their beauty objectives, girls and their friends and family are making ever more significant commitments of reproductive labor to become beautiful, hence the trend toward increased reproductive labor. Related to the increasing demand on reproductive labor, as well as economic insecurity, aspiring middle class women are also increasingly commodifying and commercializing their beauty products and services to meet demand and earn extra income. The result is a transforming context for gender socialization through beautification, defined by increases in products, practices, and ideas about beauty and, surprisingly, in the case of Mexico, more diversity of beauty norms today than fifty years ago.

Europe and the United States do remain the most revered agenda-setters in beauty and fashion industries. There are, however, contradictory patterns: global flows of media favor Anglo-American images and products, but they are also more multicultural than locally produced images. Global products and images of beauty are significantly more diverse than images and products that were available to the current generations' mothers and grandmothers. The information revolution has enabled local-global subcultures to communicate and grow, contributing to the diversity of beauty cultures on the ground in Guadalajara.

Further, standards for beautification are not easily defined or fixed because they sit at a crux between opposing forces for normalization and particularization, and because adolescents are central actors in setting standards for beauty. On one axis, parents and tradition encourage *quinceañeras* to choose a conservative, standardized approach toward beautification, while they and their peers push to express their uniqueness. On another axis, norms for beautification balance a youth's sense of fixing herself up to fit society's standards with a youth's sense of identity as original and unique. Desires to be normal and to be unique are not incompatible, and most youth pursue both goals at the same time. Fixing oneself up according to social standards of beauty, while also expressing personal uniqueness through color and style, gives boys and girls pleasure and confidence. The push for originality and uniqueness leads to creative, global, searches for new sources of inspiration; paired with unprecedented access to information sharing, youths' drive for originality has become a major engine of beauty image globalization among both *quinceañeras* and subcultural groups.

Social standards for beauty and beautification do still exist, and carry gendered and racialized patterns. In Guadalajara, beautification is gendered primarily through women's overwhelmingly higher degree of investment in beauty products, services, practices, and entrepreneurialism. This is not to say that men do not invest themselves, their time, and their money in looking good, but their efforts are much less visible and their objectives are driven by the desire to produce a powerful, natural, unproduced masculinity. The wish to portray a powerful masculinity has led some boys to try to deracialize their bodies and imitate a tall, broad-shouldered, light-skinned body that projects strength and wealth. Those males who are very open in their desire and efforts to look good, however, usually find their sexuality and masculinity brought into question. These gendered patterns of body adornment and modification indicate one set of processes through which masculinity is constructed as the expression of a natural, unproduced, default sex that does not (need to) consume beauty products. In sum, beautification is more important than ever to youth, it is integral to the construction of gendered adolescence, youth are the primary participants in beautification, and the process perpetuates some structures of inequality but also possesses opportunity for transformation.

HOW DO BEAUTY PRODUCTS, IDEALS, AND IMAGES CIRCULATE?

The process of beautification and the fashions involved touches on just about every aspect of cultural, social, and economic life. The globalization of beauty products, images, and practices is also complex, involving the expansion of local and foreign markets, the revolutions in information and transportation, and an expanded social context for youth. How could the role of globalization, a multifaceted global social and economic process, be understood as it intersects with local beauty practices and ideals, another multifaceted area of social life?

Spike Peterson's RPV framework is a way to interpret the beauty and fashion industries as it takes into account the varied dynamics that inform beauty and fashion as well as globalization. There might not be any political economy that illustrates better the deep and intimate connections among production, finance, marketing, media, and consumption, than the beauty economy. The RPV framework, by conceptually and empirically linking material, social, and economic exchanges, provides an analytical tool through which to understand and interpret the local beauty industries in relation to global flows of goods, practices, and ideas.

The *quince* is to reproductive labor what the *quinceañera* is to beautification: one is an exaggerated, in-your-face illustration of the other. As an exaggeration of reproductive labor and investment in childrearing, education, and socialization, the *quince años* illustrates the centrality of the reproductive economy to the global economy of beauty. The reproductive economy, primarily through mothers, sisters, and friends, shapes the use of beauty products, the consumption of beauty information, and the formation of ideas about what is beautiful in the *quince*. By shaping consumption of products, services, and information, the reproductive economy influences the global productive and virtual economies in beauty. In addition, the explosion in reproductive beauty labor and its commercialization for the *quince*—costumes, cosmetics, and hair styling, for example—is shaped by the global virtual and productive economies. As demands for beautification, beauty products, and beauty services rise, reproductive labor is increasingly called upon, as both a source of income and as free labor. This leads to an observable multiplication of *quince* beauty products, markets and expos for the industry.

The intensification of demands on unpaid reproductive labor, the increasing commercialization of reproductive labor, and the role of the *quince* in the construction of social norms means that *quince* beautification is reproducing social hierarchies, principal among them gender and heterosexuality. There is, however, evidence of changing norms of beauty and gender in the *quince*: the reproductive economy is not static. Adolescent desires to push boundaries and try out new things create tensions within the reproductive sphere, illustrating how the reproductive economy is open to changes and shifts.

In the productive economy, commercialization of beauty, beauty products, and beauty services, and the spread of capitalist entrepreneurialism, are shaping how beauty products, practices, and ideas circulate globally. The major actors in the productive economy of beauty are women. The gendered division of labor makes jobs in cosmetics or personal services an attractive way for women to use skills that they have learned in the private sphere. They can work and earn income without reducing their reproductive workload and earn cultural cachet as beauty experts. Women's overwhelming involvement in the cosmetics industry, rather than a sign of women's superficiality or vanity, is a sign of woman-centric recruitment, employment, selling, advertising, and consumption.

Beauty entrepreneurialism has its biggest impact through the direct sales marketing and personal services booms. The considerable employment of women in direct sales and personal services in beauty is part of the global trend toward flexibilization and feminization of labor markets. Network marketing utilizes a gendered type of employment flexibility through which international companies take advantage of women's supposedly "free time" to sell products for commission or discount only. But women are not victims of the direct sales marketing model. Rather, direct sales complicate women's relationship with the feminization of labor markets. Women are encouraged to be empowered through direct sales by exploiting other women in their "downline." Since it is often more lucrative for a salesperson to dedicate themselves to recruiting other sellers (their downline) rather than selling merchandise, the marketing model shares the downside of a pyramid scheme. These multilevel direct sales techniques exploit women's family and social networks in order to sustain profit, and implicate their saleswomen in a web of exploitation among themselves.

Through the virtual economy and the participation of youth as idea entrepreneurs, globalization of beauty commodification and the increasingly consumer-based economy are helping to spread diverse subjectivities and group identifications. Youths' agency in beauty image globalization can be seen through the media and word-of-mouth trends that *quinceañeras* participate in as well as the alternative subcultures at the *Tianguis Cultural*. Through websites and online exchanges, sharing magazines, and evaluating each other, *quinceañeras* and *metaleros* discover and disseminate their beauty ideals, often in rebellion of their parents or in distinction to other social groups. Alternative sites of cultural commodification like the *Tianguis Cultural*, through the denaturalization of social standards of normal beauty and beautification practices and through the politicization of the cultural economy of beauty, also disseminate diverse beauty cultures. Difference and social contestation, while not necessarily good, do present an opportunity for transformation with respect to challenging long-standing social norms, be they generational, group-based, or simply out of fashion. Still, while some historical axes of power, such as race, are less important to youth, gender differentiation, even as it is denaturalized, remains resistant to change.

In sum, global beauty products, practices, and images flow through the reproductive, productive, and virtual economies. One novel idea here is that the reproductive economy and things as simple as word-of-mouth, motherhood, sisterhood, and friendship are central mediums for the exchange of beauty ideas and practices. This helps explain why network marketing is the major source of beauty product sales in developing countries. Without question one can observe, with the high visibility of global media and marketing, that the global virtual economy of signs plays a large role in the dispersion of images about beauty. In previous literatures, however, too much weight has been attributed to media and marketing in the beauty economy. A situated perspective of Guadalajaran youths' use of media tells us that beauty product marketing and celebrity media are not hegemonic. Revolutions in technology and the importance of music to defining subcultures have facilitated an explosion of diverse group representations and identifications.

Another novel result of applying the RPV framework to the global beauty economy is the importance of women and youth—as consumers, producers, distributors, entrepreneurs, fashionistas, family members, and friends— to building and driving the beauty industry. One potential problem with this is that the global beauty economy has led to increased demands on women's time, earning capacity, and investment in beauty. This could be read as exploitative of women. The RPV framework, however, shows that the tremendous beauty economy is built in large part by and for women and adolescents. The beauty economy is a source of work and agency, not simply consumption and passivity.

WHO BENEFITS?

Using triad analytics of the most valued identities, ideologies, and institutions is a useful starting point to understanding who benefits in the global beauty economy. Tables 7.1 and 7.2 specify the identities, ideologies, and institutions that are privileged specifically in the beauty industries as seen from the perspective of youth in an urban Mexican environment. Despite women's centrality to the beauty industry, they are surprisingly not among the most valued identities. To the extent that women do exercise privilege, it is often momentary and/or at the expense of other older, uglier, or downline femininities.

In the *quince*, the father/breadwinner, godparents/sponsors, and mothers hold places of high value. The celebrant herself holds a place of privilege among her family and community, but possibly only for a day or two, or perhaps for a year. Her preciousness revolves around the illusion and enactment of *sus quince*, which passes all too soon. Girls with few economic resources or friends, or those who are isolated from their families, may not celebrate their *quince* and may never enjoy the privilege of being a princess, even for a day. Youth in Guadalajara value fashionable consumers (fashionistas) and tease others for being fat or ugly or not fixed-up. In the cosmetics industry, metrosexual fashion entrepreneurs are highly valued, as are successful network marketers. The metrosexual beauty salon entrepreneur holds more prestige than the neighborhood beauty salon. But in the broader society, the masculinity of men in cosmetics or beauty services is called into question. Likewise, in the broader context of the global economy, successful network marketers are rewarded little for their effort in comparison to global investors and corporate managers.

Tables 7.1 and 7.2 extract the highly valued and less valued categories from chapters one to five of this book. For comparison, Tables 7.3 and 7.4 (below) summarize the privileged and less privileged identities, ideologies, and institutions in the global political economy in general, based on Peterson's global RPV framework. What is interesting in the tables based on *quince* beautification are the details that emerge from having spent time with youth and gaining their perspective on the valued masculinities and femininities. The RPV framework presents a large and complex map for understanding the global political economy as consisting of intertwining and inextricable productive, reproductive, and virtual economies. Peterson uses empirically based scholarship from all over the globe and throughout the last half of the twentieth century. The empirical basis for the RPV project is extensive, and therefore covers enormous breadth. But the broad mapping, in its breadth, loses some of its specificity. The

Table 7.1 HIGHLY VALUED IDENTITIES, IDEOLOGIES, AND INSTITUTIONS IN THE GLOBAL POLITICAL ECONOMY OF BEAUTY

Highly Valued...	Productive	Reproductive	Virtual
Identities	Investors, professional and producer service providers, functional managers, cosmopolitan managers, network marketers	Masculinities: breadwinner, fashion entrepreneur Femininities: fashionable consumer, beautiful, networker, dressmaker, hair stylist, mother	Investors, advertisers, media makers, celebrities, musicians, fashionista, cool kids (*fresas*)
Ideologies	Neoliberal capitalism, competition, modernity	Patriarchy, religion, commercialization of work	Commodification, Information, Consumption
Institutions	Market, firms, OECD states	Family, church, sisterhood, networking, tradition	Corporate capital, finance institutions, Hollywood, manga/anime, music groups, networks of friends

Table 7.2 LESS VALUED IDENTITIES, IDEOLOGIES, AND INSTITUTIONS IN THE GLOBAL POLITICAL ECONOMY OF BEAUTY

Less Valued...	Productive	Reproductive	Virtual
Identities	Personal and distributive service workers, most flexible workers, Feminized, racialized workers	Masculinities: racially marked, unfit, gay, metrosexual Femininities: ugly, unfixed-up, indigenous, friendless, feminists, poor, uncool, unoriginal	Subsistence consumer, uncool, fat, ugly, posers
Ideologies	Governance, transparency, backwardness	Feminism	Anti-consumption
Institutions	States	Caring work	Church, parents, tradition

CONCLUSION [163]

Table 7.3 HIGHLY VALUED IDENTITIES, IDEOLOGIES, AND INSTITUTIONS IN THE GLOBAL POLITICAL ECONOMY. SOURCE: DEVELOPED BY THIS AUTHOR BASED ON PETERSON 2003, CHAPTERS 3-6

Highly Valued...	Productive	Reproductive	Virtual
Identities	Investors, professional and producer service providers, functional managers	Breadwinners, Northern consumers	Investors, Global elite, advertisers, media makers, conspicuous consumers
Ideologies	Neoliberal capitalism, competition	Patriarchy	Commodification, information, consumption
Institutions	Market, Firms, OECD states	Family	Corporate capital, Financial markets, Financing corporations and financial rating corporations, firms' financial and planning departments

Table 7.4 LESS VALUED IDENTITIES, IDEOLOGIES, AND INSTITUTIONS IN THE GLOBAL POLITICAL ECONOMY. SOURCE: DEVELOPED BY THIS AUTHOR BASED ON PETERSON 2003, CHAPTERS 3-6

Valued...	Productive	Reproductive	Virtual
Identities	Personal and distributive service workers, most flexible workers, feminized, racialized workers	Femininities, Housewives, Southern producers	Political identities, workers, poor, people in the "space of places," subsistence consumers
Ideologies	Governance	Feminism	Governance
Institutions	States, IOs	Caring work	States, IOs

narrow focus on the beauty industries restricts the breadth of empirical analysis, and in doing so makes a single case illustration of the RPV framework. As Peterson points out (2003: 18), the generalizations of the RPV framing leave out some specificity in terms of different masculinities and femininities. By using a ground-up perspective and ethnographic

[164] *The Beauty Trade*

methods, the focus on the beauty economy has highlighted multiple femininities and masculinities, and their degrees of privilege within this context. This one case shows how the three spheres relate as different facets of the very same industry. The narrow empirical focus provides the opportunity to see some details that add specificity to the generalizations of the RPV framework.

One striking difference between Table 7.1 and Table 7.3 is that the privileged identities and institutions in the virtual economy of beauty signs are more open to diversity. Through media like the *Tianguis Cultural*, youth become investors, producers, privileged consumers, and trendsetters. Music groups, subculture, and Japanese cartoons share the media landscape with corporate advertisers and Hollywood. I attribute the more open and diverse virtual economy of beauty to two things. First, information technology has made globally diverse fashions, music, and images increasingly accessible to youth consumers and producers. Second, youth put information technology to use in their search for and creation of novelty.

Familiar patterns of privilege also emerge when looking at the highly valued masculinities and femininities, particularly in the reproductive economy. The global economy of beauty rewards women for achieving certain femininities, like "mother," "beautiful girl," "cosmetics entrepreneur," and "fashionable consumer." The rewards for these identities are reinforcing of each other partly because of the global political economy. Because girls are socialized from a young age to value beautification, brands target them as consumers. In turn, they often develop marketable skills that can be put to use in sales or services, which leads them to market their sales and services to other women and socialize their daughters to appreciate beauty in similar ways. Since these highly valued femininities are so central to the beauty industry, one might think that they should be gaining more. But opportunities for advancement are based on achieving a valued femininity, and none of the highly valued femininities is quite as valued as its masculine counterpart.

Masculinity ends up privileged in the beauty economy because the global economy of beauty also rewards men. As with many industries, the beauty industries generally reward men more than women. For example, the successful feminine network marketer as capitalist entrepreneur still does not compare to the metrosexual fashion expert as capitalist entrepreneur. This familiar pattern illustrates that women in the global economy of beauty, successfully performing a highly valued femininity, are still not as valued as men or women who achieve certain types of masculinity. It is important to note that, while women are expected to behave in a feminine way, those characteristics associated with femininity are less valued and less rewarded in general. For example, *powerful* men earn more than *beautiful* women. In the beauty industry, this hierarchy may be even more pronounced because youthful beauty is temporary. Therefore, one of the categories of privilege is achievable only momentarily, if it is achievable at all.

The industry is also gendered in the sense that the industry itself is feminized, and therefore men's masculinity is criticized or undermined as a result of their participation in it. The feminized nature of the industry leads even the men at top, and especially the young metrosexuals, to be considered less than men, and their heterosexuality to be called into question in a negative way.

A global perspective reveals that there is also an element of national privilege to the highly valued identities. Whereas a fashion entrepreneur in Guadalajara may be at the top of the game in the ZMG, his credentials come from having taken classes or competed for titles in Europe, New York, and Los Angeles. Likewise, young metrosexuals in Guadalajara are highly valued by the girls for their dapper styles. But, at the same time, they are the same boys who are most preoccupied with deracializing their bodies in order to achieve a "cosmopolitan" look that is highly influenced by Western European and US fashion brands and fashion centers.

A final note about patterns of privilege in the global economy of beauty is that the structures of inequality are mutually continuous through the reproductive, productive, and virtual economies. In all three economies, the horizontal segregation of women and men into "women's" and "men's" work is still prevalent. This means that women are employed in network marketing much more than in professional management, accounting for some of the inequalities. In addition, as discussed above, when men do adopt feminized work, they generally rise to the top in a pattern called vertical segregation. This means that, in the reproductive economy of commercialized beauty services or in the productive economy of global cosmetics distribution, one is likely to see men in positions of power, prestige, and high earnings. The "network marketer" as capitalist entrepreneur does not compare favorably to the highly valued masculinities in the productive economy.

This analysis of gendered privilege is not to suggest that women should pursue privileged masculine identities and work in non-feminized employment. Rather, femininities, including fashionista, ugly or old woman, and feminist, need to be revalued in order to undermine gendered hierarchies. In addition, feminized labor and women's work in production, distribution, consumption, and trendsetting needs to be valued as an important part of the global economy of beauty.

Despite persistent gender hierarchies, even in woman- and girl-centric industries like beauty, there is reason to hope that they can be unsettled, because these structural hierarchies are not stable. I attribute the instability of structural hierarchies to the fact that people are the engines behind the global economy of beauty. As shown by the overwhelming entrance of women into the productive economy of beauty, the commercialization of beauty services, and the commodification of beauty products in Guadalajara in the last half of the twentieth century, people construct industries. Women and youth construct the beauty industries. Beauty and gender socialization are not natural, but taught in the reproductive economy. Women's integration into all three economies is transformative, and some femininities and metrosexual masculinity have become significantly more important with the explosion of commodification and commercialization in the beauty industries. The virtual economy looks especially unstable, open as it is to new technology and quick and easy communication. Youth, in particular, promise to be a tremendous source of transformation of traditional social norms, as their knowledge of and interest in new communication technologies intersects with their desire for newness and change.

CONCLUSION

There are too many unexplored references to beauty globalization as evidence of globalization, evidence of homogenization, and evidence of global racism and sexism. Underexplored, the global beauty industries have served as an easy reference or evidence of global cultural homogenization. Trivialized, the beauty industries and women's participation in them continue to be underappreciated for their importance to the global economy, for incorporating women into the productive sphere, for reproducing gendered norms, and as an arena for social and cultural transformation.

Upon closer inspection, this study of globalization of beauty products, ideas, and images from the ground-up reveals that there is a global political economy of beauty wherein the beauty industry and women's and youth's lives are mutually shaped. Beauty globalization is neither omnipotent nor irrelevant to everyday lives in Mexico. What the analysis of *quinceañera* and subcultural beautification do show are some persistent structural inequalities, and some ongoing transformations in socialization of gender and race. These transformations illustrate trends toward increasing importance of beauty signs, commodification, sexualization, and artifice in beautification. They show the boom in beauty commodification and personal services commercialization. And finally and perhaps most importantly, they show the crucial roles that women and youth play in this important industry.

As a manner of closing, I would like to suggest some avenues for further research. This study has only begun to indicate what a global political economy of beauty looks like; there are at least four major directions for further research. First, global comparative research would be useful in order to further explore the proposition that the global political economy of beauty is responsible for shaping gendered and racialized identities, and vice versa. What this study gains in specificity, it loses in breadth and in parsimony. It would be particularly interesting to compare the Mexican case to cases where the culture of beauty is either more or less obsessive. By my estimation, Mexico has a middle-to-high degree of cultural obsession with looking good. Countries like Venezuela and India have reputations for cultivating particularly strong national obsessions with beauty. In parts of the Middle East and North Africa, on the other hand, there is some resistance to feminine beautification and the beauty industry. One question to ask in other local contexts is whether the makeover has indeed become a universal rite of passage. Data from a broader regional and global footprint may bring into relief stronger patterns of social transformation and ultimately lead to more parsimony.

Furthermore, the proposition that the global virtual economy of signs is both increasing heterogeneity and open to transformation merits further inquiry. Of particular interest is the role of subcultural group affiliation in spreading diversity and affinity globally and its potential to undermine historical gender, racial, or other norms. This study has presented an admittedly optimistic view of the potential of subcultures to undermine historic structural inequality, but there is not much evidence that they present truly visionary or alternative ideas. Either way, the evidence from Mexico suggests that subcultural groups and alternative cultural commodification will be of growing importance to the global political economy of beauty. The increase in beauty diversity will be interesting to watch and evaluate for its meaning and impact.

Second, there is room for more detailed investigation of the Mexican case. Further research could explore how the beauty industries are or are not transforming racialized identities in Mexico. This study suggests that beauty ideals are indeed racialized in Mexico, but that the context for and attitudes toward racialization are changing. Still, information was difficult to gather and is inconclusive. A study aimed specifically at uncovering the intersections between race and beauty in Mexico could shed light on why some youth experience racialization deeply and others state that they do not, and on how the experience of racialization is changing due to the transformations in the beauty industry.

In addition, the ground-up view from Mexico would be complemented by more analysis at the top. That is, this study has highlighted the perspectives of aspiring middle class youth in an emerging market economy, and has therefore looked at structural hierarchies as they are experienced, or not, by less privileged identities. It would therefore be informative to accompany these perspectives with data on the lives and perspectives of those with the more privileged identities in the beauty industry. A view from the top down could lend more insight into how power functions in the beauty industry.

A third area for further study, in Mexico and elsewhere, is the political economy of network marketing. This study of the beauty industry has drawn attention to the network marketing industry and its particularly gendered organization. Network marketing is of growing importance in the developing world not only for cosmetics but also for health, nutrition, and household products. Advocates are promoting network marketing as a path toward development and toward women's empowerment. The success and importance of network marketing, coupled with its gendered nature, raises questions for feminist international relations and global political economy. For one, the success of network marketing is owed in large part to gendered divisions of labor and the flexibilization of production, distribution, and consumption. In addition, the industry is almost entirely feminized. This raises the question of whether and how network marketing reinforces or undermines gendered hierarchies. At the same time, feminists should evaluate the claims that the industry is an empowering model of development for women and developing countries, especially using empirical data.

Finally, this study highlights the importance of youth as engines of globalization and social innovation. Specifically related to their age and developmental process, youth have an exciting degree of interest and involvement with global imaginaries and entrepreneurialism. In this study, youth seek and disseminate information; contest generational assumptions; and commodify, commercialize, and purchase at a high rate, at the very least as seen through this research on the beauty industry. What other ways might youth be interacting with global ideas, images, and products? When youth seek to connect globally, what is available to them and what are their options? How do structures of inequality shape their opportunities to seek connection with and differentiate themselves from each other? The questions of how youth interact with the global economy merit more scholarly attention, and may even be the future of global political economy.

ACKNOWLEDGMENTS

These pages would be empty if not for the participants of this study who were so generous with their time and their candor. I am grateful to them for teaching me so much about their culture and their lives. Even more, I am grateful to them for instilling in me a deep respect for adolescents and adolescence. Not only did they provide the orientation, knowledge, and experience that forms the backbone of this book, but they also provided the best reason in the world to follow through with it: to honor their generosity and optimism. I am also deeply grateful for the help of many in Guadalajara who were not participants but made my research possible by providing care, friendship, shared meals, directions, Spanish lessons, invitations, introductions, and everything else. In Mexico City, thank you to María Dolores Pérez Quiroz of CANIPEC for help accessing their library.

Without the professional, academic, and financial support of many individuals and institutions, all of my best intentions and great material would have been lost and misdirected. To the members of my dissertation committee, I am humbly grateful for sharing their wisdom and encouragement. J. Ann Tickner, has been a visionary in the field of International Relations, and I am so fortunate and grateful to have had the opportunity to work with her. Both demanding and kind, I can't think of a better guide through this intellectual challenge. Carol Wise's expertise in Mexico and political economy, and her guidance in professionalization, is saving me from considerable embarrassment, and made it possible for me to research and write in the field. Alexander Moore shares credit in these respects as well, and for contributing his expertise in ethnography.

I am also indebted to all of my teachers, who have taught so well and made learning so fun. I am particularly indebted to the guidance and encouragement of Hayward Alker, a great teacher, graduate advisor, and co-founder with Ann Tickner of the Culture, Gender and Global Society (CGGS) specialization at the USC School of International Relations. The

CGGS specialization brought my colleagues and me to the School, and provided a truly exceptional intellectual community that was not bound by institutions or disciplines. Dr. Alker's instruction, enthusiasm, and encouragement helped get this project off the ground, and his visionary thinking remains an inspiration. Ronnie D. Lipschutz also deserves special thanks for being an exceptional, critical, and generous teacher, introducing me to feminism in international relations, and helping me formulate the very first kernel of this book. I am also indebted to Pierrette Hondagneu-Sotelo for teaching me ethnographic methods and helping me formulate these research questions.

From inception and through final drafts, colleagues Christina Gray, Abigail Ruane, Guilherme de Araujo Silva, Catia Confortini, Laura Sjoberg, and Eric Blanchard read sections, listened to presentations, asked questions, and encouraged me through the rough patches. Jenny McCracken read my first and final drafts, offering careful comments and editorial suggestions. Her fresh eyes, undergraduate perspective, thoughtful consideration, and honesty were invaluable to this project at several junctures.

Financial support from the USC School of International Relations, the USC Center for International Studies, the USC College of Letters, Arts and Sciences, and the Center for International Business Education and Research made the research possible. In addition, I am indebted to Arturo Santa-Cruz, the Centro de Estudios de America del Norte and the Departamento de Estudios de Pacifico at the University of Guadalajara for hosting me and making a year of writing comfortable and productive.

Several forums were especially important to the development of this manuscript. Colleagues and participants at the 2010 workshop *Twenty Years of Feminist International Relations: A Conversation About the Past, Present, and Future*, at the University of Southern California's Center for International Studies, offered the very best forum, audience, editorial guidance, and accompaniment that a junior scholar in Feminist International Relations could hope for. Thank you in particular to its organizers and book editors Ann Tickner, Laura Sjoberg, and Jane Jaquette, and my senior scholar dialoguer V. Spike Peterson. The International Studies Association, in particular the Feminist Theory and Gender Studies section, has been helpful host and audience to presentations of several chapters.

Originally a dissertation, this manuscript's transformation into a book was greatly aided by a great deal of editorial support. I am grateful to series editors J. Ann Tickner and Laura Sjoberg for including this book in their vision and for their patience, and to the whole OUP editorial team. OUP editor Angela Chnapko has been a knowledgeable and kind guide to the process, and her keen editing, enthusiasm, and patience were invaluable.

Two anonymous reviewers shared several sets of comments on the whole manuscript. These comments and questions were insightful, challenging, useful, and demanding. These reviewers' expertise and generosity contributed enormously to the improvement of this text. Elina Carmona made excellent observations and revisions, improving the text substantially and saving me from many errors. One would like to live up to the greatness of one's teachers, mentors, and colleagues. But despite our joint efforts it is not easy. There will inevitably be errors, for which I take full responsibility. Finally and with all my heart, I am grateful to my family and friends for their companionship and tolerance. Not least, they have done more than their share of food preparation, cleaning, healthcare, eldercare, phone calls, visits, and acceptance, all of which has sustained and nourished me through this journey.

NOTES

INTRODUCTION
1. Politics in this book is about power and where it is concentrated. I rely on a feminist Foucaultian conception of power as immanent: no one "has" power to wield over another but rather power is produced and reproduced through social and self-surveillance that leads to self-disciplining practices (Foucault 1977, 1978) and self-creating practices (Mahmood 2001).
2. This analysis requires a specific understanding of the term *gender*. *Gender* is a category of analysis based on the social construction of sex differences. Gender is not the biological categories of male and female sexes, but rather a social construction of difference between men and women, and the social relationships and significations of power associated with those categories (Scott 1988). Marchand and Runyan identify at least three dimensions on which gender hierarchy operates: "(1) ideologically, especially in terms of gendered representations and valorizations of social processes and practices; (2) at the level of social relations; and (3) physically through the social construction of male and female bodies" (2000: 8).
3. *Gendered* relations are hierarchical social relations that reward masculinity over femininity.
4. Globalization in this book is understood as a multisectoral process involving increased volume and speed of political, economic, and cultural interaction across borders (see Held et al. 1999, Castells 2000). The processes and effects of this globalization are understood, following Lipschutz (2003), to be material, ideological, and cognitive. Globalization is a material process because it increases the movement of people, products, and images. It is ideological because it is rationalized by the ideologies of liberal capitalism, democratic imperialism, and modernization, and it is cognitive in that it changes cognitive perceptions of the boundaries of our social, economic, and, to some extent, political, worlds.
5. E.g., Altman 2002: 58-61; Enloe 2004 chapter 3; Hammond and Prahalad 2004; Seager 2003. McGrew states that "globalization as 'simply the intensification of global interconnectedness' and stresses the multiplicity of linkages it implies: 'Nowadays, goods, capital, people, knowledge, images, crime, pollutants, drugs, fashions and beliefs all readily flow across territorial boundaries. Transnational networks, social movements and relationships are extensive in virtually all areas from the academic to the sexual'" (McGrew 1992: 65, 67, qtd in Tomlinson 1999: 2).

6. Gender lenses (Peterson and Runyan 1993) is an analytical approach that brings into focus gender and gender relations, while also necessarily leaving some things out.

CHAPTER 1

1. Feminists during this time also garnered the infamy of being ugly, either as explanation for their rejection of beautification or as a result of it.
2. Following Hayward Alker, I use the uppercase International Relations (IR) and International Political Economy (IPE) to refer to the academic disciplines and lowercase international relations and international political economy to refer to the subject matters of the respective disciplines.
3. In the tradition of feminist IR, I use Global Political Economy (GPE) instead of International Political Economy (IPE). This reformulation signifies the conceptual shift away from state-centricity and away from privileging the public sphere to gender and the axes of power that conventional approaches disregard. For an overview of feminist reformulations of global political economy, particularly the shift away from privileging the state and the public sphere, see McCracken 2010.
4. This book employs Peterson's (2003) definition of economy as a social system that produces social institutions through the exchange of material, cultural, and symbolic capital (174).
5. It is common to use the word *quinceañera* to refer to both the *fiesta de quince años* and the celebrant. In this book, following custom in Guadalajara, I use *quinceañera* to refer to the celebrant and her fifteen-year-old peers, and I use *fiesta de quince años* or *quince* to refer to the celebration.
6. The following historical survey relies heavily on Joseph and Henderson 2002 and González 1974.
7. I use Anderson's (1983: 6) conceptualization of national identity as the identification with an "imagined political community" and therefore as socially constructed through mass communication and discourses about the nation as a community.
8. I use Wade's (1997) conceptualization of race as a social categorization built on phenotypical cues that are themselves historical constructions. Thus, race does not refer to objective reality of biological differences or phenotypes, but rather social categories of difference, as well as bodily modifications such as clothing, that have emerged as racial signifiers.

CHAPTER 2

1. There are signs that the ritual celebration of the fifteenth birthday is being celebrated by some (very few) boys (this research, Salcedo 1997, Alvarez 2007). However, the definition in the popular press, academic press, and on the street continues to reference a girl's birthday.
2. There are documented variations in dress and style among and between Mexicans in Chicago (Davalos 1996, Stewart 2004), Latinos in the borderlands of Texas and Northern Mexico (Cantú 1999), Mexicans in Guadalajara (Napolitano 1997), and Mexican, Central American, and Caribbean celebrants all over the US and in their sending countries (Alvarez 2007). For example, Cantú described a color divide between Mexicans and Central Americans in Texas during the 1990s: Mexican *quinceañeras* preferred to wear a white dress, whereas Central Americans preferred a pastel color, usually rose pink. In Guadalajara in the 2000s, one would not witness a white dress on a *quinceañera*, because white is reserved for weddings, and brighter, darker, and contrasting colors are more fashionable every year.

3. Not all *quinceañeras* celebrate their *quince* with a Mass and a big party. Celebrations are limited by money, family circumstances, and the *quinceañera's* wishes. Also, budgets permitting, some *quinceañeras* are offered a big gift, like a car, or a trip to a foreign country or another city in Mexico to celebrate their new degree of maturity.
4. *Marianismo* (Stevens 1973) is a norm of femininity within which feminine virtue is measured in self-denial, commitment to the family, and spirituality.
5. Participant quotes are based on the author's translations. Interviews were transcribed verbatim or according to detailed notes taken during and after interviews.
6. It is worth noting that at the end of my research period, the "emo" style was increasingly popularized. In March 2008, while I was visiting friends in Guadalajara, I had the opportunity to witness a street demonstration of emos asking to be treated with respect and protected from discrimination. During this month, fighting between emos and other subcultures reached a crescendo and filled the national news as emos were attacked, some physically, for having poor taste or for being unauthentic "posers." Emo boys do make use of the hair straightener in order to make their hair fall in their face. During 2008 and 2009, the emo style became common almost to the point of normalization.
7. This discursive separation of "Mexicans" from "indigenous" is also material. In the twenty-nine months I have lived in Guadalajara, my only interaction with ethnically identifiable minority groups has been in markets. Despite my efforts to know Guadalajarans from diverse backgrounds, I never was introduced to anyone of an ethnic minority for the purposes of this study.
8. Some *fiestas de quince años* are even bigger than this, but this researcher did not have the privilege to see one firsthand.
9. While virtually all young women have pierced ears, it is a ritual they endure as infants. See also Gutmann 2007.
10. 90-60-90 centimeters refers to bust, waist, and hip measurements, respectively, and converts roughly to 36-24-36 inches.

CHAPTER 4
1. Madrina, feminine for padrino, means godmother.
2. Thank you to Wendy Alker for sharing her insights on the momentary nature of wedding and *quince* princess status.

CHAPTER 5
1. Flexibilization involves several ways in which companies seek more flexibility in sourcing and changing labor pools. An old example in Mexico is the maquiladora sector, which takes advantage of Mexico's cheapened labor and NAFTA by sourcing low-skilled assembly line production for US multinationals near the US/Mexico border (Fernández-Kelly 1983; Tiano 1994; Salzinger 2003).
2. This survey is not a representative sample. The CANIPEC conducted a survey of its members, but does not report its response rate, only that thirty-four companies responded, and twenty-four included sales data. Still, it is the only national data, and is useful for a starting point.
3. Subcontracted or "outsourcing" employees are contracted through an employment placement agency, and therefore they hold a contract with the employment agency rather than the employer. This arrangement is exemplary of the global trend toward flexibilization, which gives businesses more flexibility and less responsibility vis-à-vis its workers.

4. This assertion is supported by the demographics of direct sellers, as well. The Ernst and Young report on Mexican direct selling reported that 77 percent of sellers are married or live with a partner, and 79 percent of sellers have three or more dependents (AMVD 2008).
5. These supposedly privileged identities, however, have a built-in contradiction considering that the model of empowerment as fashionable consumer is dubiously empowering.
6. AMVD reports that 25 percent of direct sales representatives make purchases for themselves. A high rate of auto-consumption is also echoed in my field data.

CHAPTER 6
1. Ethnic ambiguity is a trend in modern advertising (LaFerla 2003).
2. One exception to this trend stood out: a picture of the Black American model and host of "America's Next Top Model" Tyra Banks.
3. Post-colonial refers to the period of time after place experienced a colonial phase, rather than the philosophical term *postcolonial*.
4. A macho refers to an animal of the male sex, as opposed to an hembra.

APPENDIX A

A Note about Methods

Ethnographic inquiry began with the *quince años* in Guadalajara, and focused specifically on the construction of ideals of feminine beauty and fashion through the *fiesta*. In order to understand beauty ideals in the *quince*, I conducted semi-structured interviews with youth about their experiences and ideas of beauty. In order to understand ideals in the *quince*, as well as general opinions and opinions of those who don't practice the *quince*, I asked questions about beautification both especially for the *quince años* and in everyday life, among youth who did and did not practice the *quince* tradition. In order to understand beauty ideals across gender, I spoke with youth regardless of their gender, but made an effort to speak to as many young men as I could recruit, and asked all about both feminine and masculine beauty ideals. Therefore, the research began with semi-structured interviews with forty adolescents between fourteen and sixteen years of age about the *fiesta* and their ideals of feminine and masculine beauty and fashion in the *fiesta* and in everyday life. Having participated or planning to participate in a *quince* was not a requirement for study participation.

Potential participants were initially approached in the street with informational sheets, but the response rate was zero, and the recruiting method had to be revised. Because interviews were to be conducted with minors, I had more formal requirements for recruiting and asking for consent, and later conversations with participants led me to believe that I made it too difficult for a busy adolescent to become a participant and that the formal information sheet and requirement for parental permission intimidated them. In the end, all participants were recruited through personal introductions via my social and extended social networks and through snowball recruitment. While most of my initial introductions came through friends and friends of friends at a centrally located dance school, participants' profiles are varied, and they lived in almost every area of the city. I interviewed twenty-three girls and seventeen boys. Interviews ranged between twenty-two minutes and one hour and forty-five minutes, but most often lasted within ten minutes of an hour.

Interviewees were also asked to allow me to spend participant observation time with them. Participant observation allowed me to understand more personally the lives and priorities of youth in Guadalajara, put their interviews in context, and interact with participants in an unstructured way. This participant observation time proved to be very informative for two main reasons. First, interviewees knew that I was interested in beauty and *quince años*, so they offered much more commentary and information when we hung out. Second, interviewees often presented their best selves and their best behavior to me during interviews, but relaxed, joked and teased while we were just "hanging out." It was during this time that I learned of many of the contradictions between what youth will say in an interview and how they will act in an informal environment, especially with friends around. During interviews, they were much more open about their personal insecurities about friendships and romantic relationships. They were also less likely to reveal negative attitudes toward their peers. During unstructured time, they were much more likely to present themselves as confident (especially when peers were around) and also more likely to make negative comments about other people's looks, including their stature, their body size, their skin color, or their clothing (again, particularly when their peers were around).

When we just hung out, we did household chores, went to the movies, went to malls, bought ice cream, watched television, exercised, danced, worked, watched soccer, watched boys, went to family events, attended *fiestas*, went to school, went to coffee, put on makeup, styled hair, went to a beauty pageant, and cooked. In all, I spent time with thirty-three participants outside of interviews. Usually, I spent an afternoon or a morning with a participant, depending on whether they went to school or worked during the day or during the afternoon. With a number of participants, I spent several half-days as they opened their lives more to me, introduced me to their social networks and their families, and showed me around.

In addition, I spent fourteen months, between June 2006 and January 2007 and June 2008 and January 2009, immersed in youth beauty and fashion culture in Guadalajara. I tried every beauty procedure that a participant reported trying, except hair bleaching or highlighting or dyeing.

I took dance, beauty, hairstyling, and etiquette classes, and I spent my afternoons and weekends at the malls, plazas, and centers of youth attraction throughout the city. I took buses and walked in almost every *colonia* in the city, looking for beauty salons, signs, fashion shops, *quince* services, and observing the public lives of Guadalajara, particularly its youth.

The extended case method also requires that the researcher extend out from the local site of research, into sociohistorical context. Aside from using established scholarship on beauty ideals and the *quince* in Guadalajara (see chapters two and six), this research places the participants' lived experience within its sociohistorical context in two ways. First, in order to give an historical perspective on beauty norms in the *quince años*, interviews were conducted with older family members. Seventeen parents, grandparents, or other older relatives of sixteen participants were recruited and interviewed formally. By interviewing adult relatives of participants about their lives and beauty ideals during their own adolescence, this case study compares the lived experiences of beauty ideals over a period of about fifty years. Informal conversations about their views on the *quince* were also conducted with another six older adult family members, in addition to countless conversations with everyone from taxi drivers, party revelers, classmates, and friends. These added perspectives also lent historical and broader social perspective.

Second, in order to extend out from the interviews into the global networks that influence the production of beauty in the *quince*, I explored the origins of beauty information sources and beauty products cited by participants. To do this, I asked interviewees about their idols, their favorite places to shop, and their sources of information. Research proceeded to extend out from the experiences of youth into the networks of information and product distribution that youth cited in interviews. In this stage, I collected magazines, watched popular television shows, went to outdoor markets, malls, expos, dress shops, and commercial plazas. I also gathered statistical information on the global cosmetic industry.

Interviews were transcribed verbatim or according to detailed notes taken during interviews. I then read the interview transcriptions for patterns, made a preliminary list of codes, and read through the transcriptions again, together with fieldnotes, coding them for topics and themes such as hair, cell phones, color combining, beauty services, originality/uniqueness, insecurities, and emotional support. I also made a database of participant information, including age, sociodemographic information, and particulars about their *quince* participation. I combined notes and quotes into theme-based memos that essentially summarized the ideas of participants as they were expressed to me and the related observations that I made while hanging out with them or while on personal participant observation excursions. These memos form the basis for chapters one and two and the starting points for chapters three, four, and five. Some themes made it into the analyses, and some did not.

APPENDIX B

Youth Interview Questions

Cluster 1:
The current significance of beauty-making in youths' everyday life (desire, strategy, techniques, appropriateness).

1) When, if ever, is it important to you to look your best? How important?
   all the time?
   certain occasions
      work?
      date?
      special occasion?
      formal? (e.g. funeral, graduation, wedding)
      informal? (e.g. a party)
2) Why is it important to you to look good (in these venues)?
   to what extent is it a matter of personal satisfaction?
   to what extent are you doing it to be socially appropriate?
3) Is it ever preferable for you not to look your best?
   do you ever feel that you have to "dress down"?
4) Do you do anything special to make yourself look your best?
      special attention to clothes?
      makeup?
      hair?
      jewelry/adornments?
      skin treatments/resurfacing?
         smoothing

            lightening
            tanning
      body treatments?
          Exercise—what type?
          Diet—what type?
          Surgery—what type?
      face treatments?
          Surgery?

5) What in your beauty regime is most important? How important is it?
6) What about your looks do you spend the most time trying to "fix" or "improve"? Why?
7) What about your looks most satisfies you? Why?

Cluster 2:
How she is preparing for the quince.

8) Are you going to have/ have you considered/are you going to have a quince años?
     How did you decide?
Tell me about it—what did you do, what are you going to do?

9) What are you going to wear? Why?
10) Are you going to do anything else special to get your look ready?
11) What do you think is the significance of your presentation?

Cluster 3:
The significance of beauty images and beauty products in her life, how she responds to "global beauty ideals," how her ideals change over time (ideas, information, other "looks," change) Pay special attention to the fiesta with follow-up questions.

12) Where do you get your inspiration for ways to look your best?
    Celebrities—who are your favorites, who you think are the most beautiful? What do you like about their looks? Do you emulate them?
    Friends—tell me about them (race, gender, age, social class). And how do they inspire you?
    Magazines—are they beauty magazines or other types of magazines? What do you get out of them?
    Internet—what kind of inspiration do you get there?
    Art—what kind of inspiration do you get there?

13) Where do or did you get your information about products and services?
do you seek it out, or just pick up information?
magazines
TV ads
internet
beauty salon
friends
14) Do you see many images of beauty or "how to look" from people not like you in terms of race, age?
15) Are you particularly attracted to "looks" from other cultures (e.g. Indian, Chinese, Flamenco, Middle Eastern, European, African, US)?
16) Do you incorporate looks, in whole or part, from other places?
If yes, have you always?
If no, did you in the past?
17) How has your idea of how you would like to look changed over time? (each can define her own time period, e.g. middle-age, 45-55, or when I was raising kids).
kid
teen
young adult
18) How has your idea of how you think you should look changed over time? (each can define her own time period, e.g. middle-age, 45-55, or when I was raising kids).
kid
teen
young adult

Cluster 3:

To what degree she considers personal beauty standards universal.

19) Do you and your friends share ideas about what looks good?
20) Do you think the same standards you have for your own beauty also apply for other people?
your friends?
your family?
the women in your community?
women of your race/ethnicity/age group
women in your country?
all women?

21) How do you judge another woman's beauty?
22) Do you have different measures for women outside your culture?
23) Do you think there is or will emerge one standard type of beauty for all women? What would it look like, in your opinion?

APPENDIX C

Adult Interview Questions

Cluster 1:
Quinceañeras in history

1) Were you ever in/ did you consider being in or having a quince años?
    Tell me about it
    How did you decide?
    What did you do?
        Do you have any pictures, memorabilia to show? Was it a special day?

Cluster 2:
The significance of the ceremony and the fiesta. Very open-ended.

2) What is the general significance of the ceremony? The fiesta? What did it mean to you?
    Religious
    Social
    Familial
    Fun
    Tradition
    Other

3) Has the meaning changed between then and now?
4) Is there something equivalent to the quince for a man? If there isn't, do you think there should be? If there is, what is it? Tell me more about what it means to become a man

**Cluster 3 (if there was a quinceañera):
Beauty regime.**

5) What did you wear? Why?
6) Where did you get your information?
    Celebrities
    Friends
    Magazines
    Movies
    Internet
    Art
    TV
    Beauty salon
7) Where did you get the dress made? Tiara? Ring? Other accessories?
8) Did you do anything else special to get your look ready?
    makeup?
    hair?
    jewelry/adornments?
    skin treatments/resurfacing?
        smoothing
        lightening
        tanning
    body treatments?
        Exercise—what type?
        Diet—what type?
        Surgery—what type?
    face treatments?
        Surgery?
9) What about your appearance was most important? How important was it?
10) What about your looks did you spend the most time trying to "fix" or "improve"? Why?
11) What about your looks most satisfied you? Why?
12) What do you think was the significance of your presentation at the fiesta?

BIBLIOGRAPHY

Adrian, Bonnie. 2003. *Framing the Bride: Globalizing Beauty and Romance in Taiwan's Bridal Industry*. Berkeley: University of California Press.
Agathangelou, Anna M. 2004. *The Global Political Economy of Sex: Desire, Violence and Insecurity in Mediterranean Nation States*. New York: Palgrave Macmillan.
Aitken, Rob. 2007. *Performing Capital: Toward a Cultural Economy of Popular and Global Finance*. New York: Palgrave Macmillan.
Alcoff, Linda. 1997. "Cultural Feminism versus Post Structuralism: The Identity Crisis in Feminist Theory." In *The Second Wave*, edited by Linda Nicholson, 330–355. New York: Routledge.
Altman, Dennis. 2002. *Global Sex*. Chicago: University of Chicago Press.
Alonso, Jorge. 2003. "Votar en Guadalajara." *Espiral* 9(27): 123–151.
Alvarez, Julia. 2007. *Once Upon a Quinceañera: Coming of Age in the USA*. New York: Viking.
AMVD. 2008. "Ventas Directas en Números." *Associación Mexicana de Ventas Directas*. Accessed August 28 http://www.amvd.org.mx/amvd_ventadirecta_numeros.php.
Anastasakos, Kiki. 2002. "Structural Adjustment Policies in Mexico and Costa Rica." In *Women in Developing Countries: Assessing Strategies for Empowerment*. Edited by Rekha Datta and Judith Kornberg, 113–128. Boulder, CO: Lynne Rienner.
Anderson, Benedict. 1983. *Imagined Communities: Reflections on the Origin and Spread of Nationalism*. New York, NY: Verso.
Arrizón, Alicia. 1999. *Latina Performance: Traversing the Stage*. Bloomington, IN: Indiana University Press.
Avon. 2008. Website. http://www.avoncompany.com/ (accessed June, 2008).
Bakker, Isabella, ed. 1994. *The Strategic Silence: Gender and Economic Policy*. London: Zed.
Balsamo, Anne. 1995. "On the Cutting Edge: Cosmetic Surgery and New Imaging Technologies." In *Technologies of the Gendered Body*, by Anne Balsamo, 56–79. Durham, NC: Duke University Press.
Banet-Weiser, Sarah. 1999. *The Most Beautiful Girl in the World: Beauty Pageants and National Identity*. Berkeley: University of California Press.
Banner, Lois W. 1983. *American Beauty*. New York: Alfred Knopf.
Barba Solano, Carlos and Fernando Pozos Ponce. 2001. "El Mercado de Trabajo de los Trabajadores no Manuales de la Industria Electrónica de la Zona Metropolitana de Guadalajara: Un Estudio de Caso." *Espiral* 8(22): 197–221.
Barker, Drucilla K. 2005. "Beyond Women and Economics: Rereading Women's Work." *Signs: Journal of Women in Culture and Society* 30(4): 2189–2209.

Barthes, Roland. 1983. *The Fashion System*. Translated by Matthew Ward and Richard Howard. New York: Hill and Wang.

Bartky, Sandra L. 1990. *Femininity and Domination: Studies in the Phenomenology of Oppression*. New York: Routledge.

Bartlett, Richard C. 1997. "Microenterprise and the Empowerment of the Poor. State of the World Forum." Microenterprise and the Empowerment of the Poor Plenary Session November 6, 1997. www.wfdsa.org, accessed August 2008.

Basyouny, Iman Farid. 1998. *Just a Gaze: Female Clientele of Diet Clinics in Cairo: An Ethnomedical Study*. Cairo: American University in Cairo Press.

Bellón, Araceli Ibarra. 1994. "Epistemología, Moral y Maternidad: Consecuencias del Trastocamiento de Valores en las mujeres de Jalisco," In *La Condicion de la Mujer en Jalisco*, edited by Rosa Rojas and María Rodríguez Batista, 157-168. Guadalajara: Universidad de Guadalajara.

Benería, Lourdes, ed. 1982. *Women and Development: The Sexual Division of Labor in Rural Societies*. Westport, CT: Praeger.

Benería, Lourdes, and Martha Roldán. 1987. *The Crossroads of Class and Gender: Industrial Homework, Subcontracting, and Household Dynamics in Mexico City*. Chicago: University of Chicago Press.

Benería, Lourdes. 1991. "Structural Adjustment, the Labour Market and the Household: The Case of Mexico." In *Towards Social Adjustment, Labour Market Issues in Structural Adjustment*, edited by G. Standing and V. Tokman, 161-83. Geneva: International Labour Organisation.

Bergeron, Suzanne. 2001. "Political Economy Discourses of Globalization and Feminist Politics." *Signs: Journal of Women in Culture and Society* 26(4): 985–1006.

Biggart, Nicole Woolsey. 1989. *Charismatic Capitalism: Direct Selling Organizations in America*. Chicago: University of Chicago Press.

Bordo, Susan. 1993. *Unbearable Weight: Feminism, Western Culture, and the Body*. Berkeley: University of California Press.

Borland, Katherine. 1996. "The India Bonita of Monimbó: The Politics of Ethnic Identity in the New Nicaragua." In *Beauty Queens on the Global Stage: Gender, Contests, and Power*, edited by Colleen Ballerino Cohen, Richard Wilk and Beverly Stoeltje, 75–88. New York: Routledge.

Brandes, Stanley. 1990. "Ritual Eating and Drinking in Tzintzuntzan: A Contribution to the Study of Mexican Foodways." *Western Folklore* 49(2) April 1990:163–175.

Burawoy, Michael. 1991. *Ethnography Unbound: Power and Resistance in the Modern Metropolis*. Berkeley: University of California Press.

Butler, J. 1999 (1990). *Gender Trouble: Feminism and the Subversion of Identity*. New York: Routledge.

Cahill, Ann J. 2003. "Feminist Pleasure and Feminine Beautification." *Hypatia* 18(4): 42–64.

Cahn, Peter S. 2006. "Building Down and Dreaming Up: Finding Faith in a Mexican Multilevel Marketer." *American Ethnologist* 33(1): 126–142.

CANIPEC. 2006. *Memoria Estadística, Cámara Nacional de la Industría de Perfumería, Cosméticos, Articulos de Tocador e Higiene*. Mexico City: CANIPEC.

CANIPEC. 2008. Website. Cámara Nacional de la Industría de Perfumeria, Cosméticos, Articulos de Tocador e Higiene. http://www.canipec.org.mx/ accessed July 11, 2008.

Cannon, Aubrey. 1998. "The Cultural and Historical Contexts of Fashion." In *Consuming Fashion: Adorning the Transnational Body*. Edited by Sandra Niessen and Anne Brydon, 23–38. Oxford: Berg.

Cantú, Norma E. 1999. "La Quinceañera: Towards an Ethnographic Analysis of a Life-Cycle Ritual." *Southern Folklore* 56(1): 73–101.

Carrillo, Hector. 2002. *The Night Is Young: Sexuality in Mexico in the Time of AIDS*. Chicago: University of Chicago Press.

Cassidy, C. 1991. "The Thin Body: When Big is Better." *Medical Anthropology* 13: 181–213.

Castells, Manuel. 2000. *The Rise of the Network Society, The Information Age: Economy, Society and Culture Vol. II*. 2nd edition. Blackwell: Oxford.

Castellanos, M. Bianet. 2007. "Adolescent Migration to Cancún: Reconfiguring Maya Households and Gender Relations." *Frontiers* 28(3): 1–27.

Chang, Kimberly, and L. H. M. Ling. 2000. "Globalization and Its Intimate Other: Filipina Domestic Workers in Hong Kong." In *Gender and Global Restructuring*, edited by Marrianne Marchand and Anne Sisson Runyan, 27–43. New York: Routledge.

Chant, Sylvia. 1991. *Women and Survival in Mexican Cities: Perspectives on Gender, Labour Markets and Low-Income Households*. Manchester: Manchester University Press.

Chant, Sylvia and Nikki Craske. 2003. *Gender in Latin America*. New Brunswick, NJ: Rutgers.

Chapkis, Wendy. 1986. *Beauty Secrets: Women and the Politics of Appearance*. Boston, MA: South End Press.

Chin, Christine. 1998. *In Service and Servitude*. New York: Columbia University Press.

Cohen, Colleen Ballerino, Richard Wilk and Beverly Stoeltje, eds. 1996. *Beauty Queens on the Global Stage: Gender, Contests, and Power*. New York: Routledge.

Collins, Jane. 2003 *Threads: Gender, Labor and Power in the Global Apparel Industry*. Chicago: University of Chicago Press.

Collins, Patricia Hill. 1990. *Black Feminist Thought: Knowledge, Consciousness, and the Politics of Empowerment*. New York: Routledge, 1990; 2nd edition 2000.

Craske, Nikki. 1999. *Women and Politics in Latin America*. New Brunswick, NJ: Rutgers University Press.

Crenshaw, Kimberle. 1991. "Mapping the Margins: Intersectionality, Identity Politics and Violence Against Women of Color." *Stanford Law Review* 43: 1241–1279.

Cudd, Ann E. 2005. "Missionary Positions." *Hypatia*; Fall 2005; 20(4): p 164.

Cunningham, Patricia A. 2003. *Reforming Women's Fashion, 1850-1920: Politics, Health, and Art*. Ohio: Kent State University Press.

Davalos, Karen Mary. 1996. "La Quinceañera: Making Gender and Ethnic Identities." *Frontiers: A Journal of Women Studies* 16(2/3): 101–127.

Davalos, Karen Mary. 1997. "La Quinceañera and the Keen-say-an-YAIR-uh: The Politics of Gender and Ethnic Identity," *Voces: A Journal of Chicana/Latina Studies* 1:1 (1997): 57–68.

Davis, Kathy. 1995. *Reshaping the Female Body: The Dilemma of Cosmetic Surgery*. London: Routledge.

Dickerson, Marla and Daniel Yi. 2007. "Living Large on Diet Aids; Finding a Way to Sell Costly Herbalife Products to Mexico's Poor has Made One Couple Rich. Their 30,000 Helpers Have the Same Dream." *Los Angeles Times*. Oct 13, 2007. sec. A.

Dow, James. 2005. "The Expansion of Protestantism in Mexico: An Anthropological View." *Anthropological Quarterly* 78(4): 827–851.

Duran, Juan Manuel and Fernando Pozos Ponce. 1995. "Reestructuración Sectorial y Cambios en el Empleo: El Caso de la Zona Metropolitana de Guadalajara," *Espiral* 2(4): 81–100.

Dussel-Peters, Enrique. 1998. "Mexico's Liberalization Strategy, 10 Years On: Results and Alternatives." *Journal of Economic Issues* 32(2): 351–363.

Dussel-Peters, Enrique. 2000. *Polarizing Mexico: The Impact of Liberalization Strategy*. Boulder, CO: Lynne Rienner Publishers.

Elias, Juanita. 2004. *Fashioning Inequality: The MNC and Gendered Employment in a Globalising World*. Aldershot: Ashgate.

Elson, Diane, and Ruth Pearson. 1981. "Nimble Fingers Make Cheap Workers: An Analysis of Women's Employment in Third World Export Manufacturing." *Feminist Review* 8(Spring): 87–107.

Elson, Diane, ed. 1991. *Male Bias in the Development Process*. Manchester: Manchester University Press.

Enloe, Cynthia. 1989. *Bananas, Beaches and Bases: Making Feminist Sense of International Relations*. Berkeley: University of California Press.

Enloe, Cynthia. 1995. "The Globetrotting Sneaker." *Ms. Magazine* March, April 1995.

Enloe, Cynthia. 1996. "Margins, Silences, and Bottom Rungs: How to Overcome the Underestimation of Power in the Study of International Relations." In *International Theory: Positivism and Beyond*, edited by Steve Smith, Ken Booth, and Marysia Zalewski, 186–202. New York: Cambridge University Press.

Enloe, Cynthia. 2004 (2000). "Daughters and Generals in the Politics of the Globalized Sneaker." In *The Curious Feminist*, Cynthia Enloe, 57–68. Berkeley: University of California Press.

Enloe, Cynthia. 2004. *The Curious Feminist: Searching for Women in a New Age of Empire*. Berkeley: University of California Press.

Entwistle, Joanne. 2000. *The Fashioned Body: Fashion, Dress and Modern Social Theory*. Cambridge, UK: Polity Press.

Erevia, Angela. 1996. *Quince Años: Celebrating a Tradition: A Handbook for Parish Teams*. San Antonio: Missionary Catechists of Divine Providence.

Escobar Latapí, Agustín. 1988. "The Rise and Fall of an Urban Labour Market: Economic Crisis and the Fate of Small Workshops in Guadalajara, Mexico." *Bulletin of Latin American Research* 7(2): 183–205.

Etcoff, Nancy. 2000. *Survival of the Prettiest*. New York: Anchor Books.

Etcoff N. L., Stock S., Haley L. E., Vickery S. A., House D. M. (2011) "Cosmetics as a Feature of the Extended Human Phenotype: Modulation of the Perception of Biologically Important Facial Signals." *PLoS ONE* 6(10): e25656. doi:10.1371/journal.pone.0025656.

Euromonitor GMID Database. 2008. "Cosmetics and Toiletries: Euromonitor from Trade Sources/National Statistics." Date Exported (GMT/BST): 02/09/2008 19:23:38.

Fadzillah, Ida. 2005. "The Amway Connection: How Transnational Ideas of Beauty and Money Affect Northern Thai Girls' Perceptions of Their Future Options." In *Youthscapes: The Popular, the National the Global*, edited by Maria Sunaina and Elisabeth Soep, 85–102. Philadelphia, PA: University of Pennsylvania Press.

Fernandez-Kelly, Maria Patricia. 1983. *For We Are Sold, I and My People: Women and Industry in Mexico's Frontier*. Albany, NY: SUNY Press.

Financial Times (FT). 2008. "Andrew Taylor Downturn Sees Upturn in Direct Sellers." [London 1st Edition] Financial Times. London (UK): Feb 29, 2008. p. 4.

Financial Times (FT). 2009. Aidin Beatrice. "Avon Calling the Shots; Direct Sales Companies are Enjoying Unprecedented Success in the Recession." London (UK): Jul 4, 2009. p. 7.

Freeman, Carla. 2000. *High Tech and High Heels in the Global Economy: Women, Work, and Pink-Collar Identities in the Caribbean*. Durham, NC: Duke University Press.

Freeman, Carla. 2001. "Is Local: Global as Feminine: Masculine? Rethinking the Gender of Globalization." *Signs* 26(4): 1007–39.

Freeman, Carla. 2010. "Introduction," *Spirits of Resistance and Capitalist Discipline*. By Aihwa Ong, xv-xx. Albany: State University of New York Press.

Frieden, Jeffry. 1981. "Third World Indebted Industrialization." *International Organization* 35(3): 407–31.

Foucault, Michel. 1995 (1977). *Discipline and Punish: The Birth of the Prison*. Translated by Alan Sheridan. Second Vintage Books Edition. New York: Random House.

Foucault, Michel. 1990 (1978). *History of Sexuality: An Introduction*. Vintage Books Edition. New York: Random House.

Gallagher, Kevin and Lyuba Zarsky. 2007. *The Enclave Economy: Foreign Investment and Sustainable Development in Mexico's Silicon Valley*. Cambridge, MA: MIT Press.

Gavenas, Lisa. 2002. *Color Stories: Behind the Scenes of America's Billion-Dollar Beauty Industry*. New York: Simon & Schuster.

Gibson-Graham, J. K. 1996. *The End of Capitalism (as we knew it): A Feminist Critique of Political Economy*. Oxford: Blackwell.

GMID (Global Market Information Database). 2008. Euromonitor International.

González, Luis. 1974. *San José de Gracia: Mexican Village in Transition*. Translated by John Upton. Austin: University of Texas Press.

González de la Rocha, Mercedes. 1994. *The Resources of Poverty: Women and Survival in a Mexican City*. Oxford: Blackwell.

Gray, Mark M., Miki Caul Kittilson, and Wayne Sandholtz. 2006. "Women and Globalization: A Study of 180 Countries, 1975—2000." *International Organization* 60: 293–333.

Gremillion, Helen. 2005. "The Cultural Politics of Body Size." *Annual Review of Anthropology* 34: 13–32.

Grewal, Inderpal, and Caren Kaplan, eds. 1994. *Scattered Hegemonies: Postcolonial and Transnational Feminist Practices*. Minneapolis and London: University of Minnesota Press.

Gutmann, Matthew C. 2007 (2nd ed). *The Meanings of Macho: Being a Man in Mexico City*. Berkeley: University of California Press.

Halberstam, Judith. 1994. "F2M: The Making of Female Masculinity." In *The Lesbian Postmodern*, edited by Laura Doan, 210–228. New York: Columbia University Press.

Hamermesh, Daniel S and Jeff E Biddle. 1994. "Beauty and the Labor Market." *American Economic Review* 84(5): 1174-94.

Hamermesh, Daniel S., 2011. *Beauty Pays: Why Attractive People Are More Successful*. New Jersey: Princeton University Press.

Hammond, Allen L. and C. K. Prahalad. 2004. "Selling to the Poor." *Foreign Policy* 30(May/June): 30–37.

Harris, Ron. 1994. "Avon Is Calling, and It's a Jungle Out There: Brazil: Women Find Independence Doing Big Business in the Amazon." *Los Angeles Times*. August 29.

Harvey, David. 1989. *The Condition of Postmodernity: An Inquiry into the Origins of Cultural Change*. Cambridge, MA: Blackwell.

Held, David, Anthony McGrew, David Goldblatt and Jonathan Perraton. 1999. *Global Transformations: Politics, Economics and Culture*. California: Stanford University Press.

Hellman, Judith Adler. 1988. *Mexico in Crisis*. New York: Holmes and Meier.

Hennessy-Fiske. 2008. "Climbing a Ladder Made of Lipstick; Altagracia Valdez and Other Latinas are Changing the Face of Cosmetics Giant Mary Kay. They Seek a Path to the Middle Class." *Los Angeles Times*. Jan 15, 2008. sec. A.

Hernández Águila, Elena de la Paz. 2006. "Retos y Perspectives de la Industria Mexicana del Calzado ante la Apertura Comercial. El Impacto de la Competencia con China." *Espiral* 14(40): 95–121.

Higgins, Ross. 1998. "Á la mode: Fashioning Gay Community in Montreal." In *Consuming Fashion: Adorning the Transnational Body*, edited by Sandra Niessen and Anne Brydon, 129–61. Oxford: Berg.

Hilsenrath, Jon E. 1996. "Is Tupperware Dated? Not in the Global Market." *New York Times*, May 26: C3.

Hochschild, Arlie Russell. 1997. *The Time Bind: When Work Becomes Home and Home Becomes Work*. New York: Metropolitan Books.

Holt, Douglas B. 2004. *How Brands Become Icons*. Boston, MA: Harvard Business School Press.

Hondagneu-Sotelo, Pierette. 2001. *Domestica: Immigrant Workers Cleaning and Caring in the Shadows of Affluence*. Berkeley, CA: University of California Press.

Hooper, Charlotte. 2000. "Masculinities in Transition: The Case of Globalization." In *Gender and Global Restructuring*, edited by Marianne Marchand and Anne Sisson Runyan, 59–73. New York: Routledge.

Hoskyns, Catherine and Shirin M. Rai. 2007. "Recasting the. Global Political Economy: Counting Women's Unpaid Work." *New Political Economy* 12(3): 297–317.

Hull, Gloria T., Patricia Bell Scott, and Barbara Smith, eds. 1982. *All the Women Are White, All the Blacks Are Men, But Some of Us Are Brave: Black Women's Studies*. New York: The Feminist Press at The City University of New York.

Huntington, Samuel. 1968. *Political Order is Changing Societies*. New Haven: Yale University Press.

INEGI. 2004. Instituto Nacional de Estadística, Geografía e Informática-Secretaría del Trabajo y Previsión Social. www.inegi.org.mx, accessed June 2009.

INEGI. 2007. Síntesis de Resultados. II Conteo de Polacion y Vivienda 2005. México: Estados Unidos Mexicanos. www.inegi.org.mx, accessed June 2009.

Jones, Geoffrey. 2008. "Blonde and Blue-Eyed? Globalizing beauty, c.1945–c.1980." *Economic History Review* 61(1): 125–154.

Jones, Geoffrey. 2010. *Beauty Imagined: A History of the Global Beauty Industry*. New York: Oxford University Press.

Joseph, Gilbert M. and Timothy J. Henderson, eds. 2002. *The Mexico Reader: History, Culture, Politics*. Durham, NC: Duke University Press.

Keck, Margaret and Kathryn Sikkink. 1998. *Activists Beyond Borders*. Ithaca: Cornell University Press.

Klein, Naomi. 2000. *No Logo: Taking Aim at the Brand Bullies*. New York: Picador.

Kumar, Sameer, Cindy Massie and Michelle D. Dumonceaux. 2006. "Comparative Innovative Business Strategies of Major Players in Cosmetic Industry." *Industrial Management & Data Systems* 106(3): 285–306.

LaFerla, Ruth. 2003. "Generation E.A.: Ethnically Ambiguous." *The New York Times*. December 28, 2003. Section 9, p. 1.

Leal, Luis. 1983. "Female Archetypes in Mexican Literature." In *Women in Hispanic Literature: Icons and Fallen Idols*, edited by Beth Miller, 227–242. Berkeley: University of California Press.

Leeds-Craig, Maxine. 2002. *Ain't I a Beauty Queen? Black Women, Beauty, and the Politics of Race*. New York: Oxford University Press.

Li, Xiaoping. 1998. "Fashioning the Body in Post-Mao China." In *Consuming Fashion: Adorning the Transnational Body*, edited by Sandra Niessen and Anne Brydon, 71–89. Oxford: Berg.

Lipschutz, Ronnie D. 2003. "Regulation for the Rest of Us? Global Social Activism, Corporate Citizenship, and the Disappearance of the Political." UC Santa Cruz: Center for Global, International and Regional Studies. Retrieved from: http://escholarship.org/uc/item/64q087vp.

Lozano Ochoa, Aurelio. 2008. Author Biography. *Clase, Porte, y Estilo*. 11/28/2008, Milenio.com.

Lukose, Ricky. 2005. "Consuming Globalization: Youth and Gender in Kerala, India." *Journal of Social History* 38 (Summer): 915–35.

MacKendrick, Karmen. 1998. "Technoflesh, or 'Didn't that hurt'?" *Fashion Theory* 2(1): 3–24.

Mahmood, Saba. 2001. "Feminist Theory, Embodiment and the Docile Agent: Some Reflections on the Egyptian Islamic Revival." *Cultural Anthropology* 16(2): 202–236.

Marchand, Marianne and Ann Sisson Runyon, eds. 2000. *Gender and Global Restructuring*. London and New York: Routledge/RIPE Series in Global Political Economy.

Martínez Casas, Regina and Guillermo De La Peña. 2004. "Migrantes Y Comunidades Morales: Resignificación, Etnicidad Y Redes Sociales En Guadalajara." *Revista De Antropología Social*, t/v 13, España, p. 38.

McCracken, Angela. 2010. "Globalization Through Feminist Lenses." *The International Studies Encyclopedia*, edited by Robert A. Denemark, doi: 10.1111/b.978144433 6597.2010.x.

McGrow, Andrew. 1992. "A Global Society?" In *Modernity and its Futures*, edited by Stuart Hall, David Held and Tony McGrew, 61-102. Cambridge: Polity Press.

Mendoza, Jorge, Fernando Pozos Ponce and David Spener. 2002. "Fragmented Markets, Elaborate Chains: The Retail Distribution of Imported Clothing in Mexico." In *Free Trade and Uneven Development*, edited by Gereffi G., Spener, D. and Bair J., 266–286. Philadelphia: Temple University Press.

Mies, Maria. 1986. *Patriarchy and Accumulation on a World Scale*. London: Zed Books.

Mobius, Markus M. and Tanya S. Rosenblat. 2006. "Why Beauty Matters." *The American Economic Review* 96(1): 222–235.

Mohanty, Chandra Talpade. 1988. "Under Western Eyes: Feminist Scholarship and Colonial Discourses," *Feminist Review* 30, Autumn 1988: 61–88.

Montero Recoder, Cyntia. 2008. "'Vieja a los Treinta Años': El Proceso de Envejecimineto Sgún Algunas Revistas Mexicanas de Fines de Siglo XIX." In *Enjaular Los Cuerpos: Normativas Decimónicas y Femininidad en México*, edited by Julia Tuñon, 281–326. Mexico City: El Colegio de Mexico.

Moon, Katherine. 1997. *Sex Among Allies: Military Prostitution in U.S.-Korea Relations*. New York: Columbia University Press.

Moraga, Cherrie, and Gloria Anzaldua, eds. 1983. *This Bridge Called my Back: Radical Writings by Women of Color*. New York: Kitchen Table.

Morgan, Robin. 1970. "No More Miss America! Ten Points of Protest." In *Sisterhood Is Powerful: An Anthology of Writing from the Women's Liberation Movement*, edited by Robin Morgan, 521–523. New York: Vintage Books.

Moskalenko, Lena. 1996. "Beauty, Women, and Competition: Moscow Beauty 1989." In *Beauty Queens on the Global Stage: Gender, Contests, and Power*, edited by Colleen Ballerino Cohen, Richard Wilk and Beverly Stoeltje, 61–74. New York: Routledge.

Napolitano, Valentina. 1997. "Becoming a Mujercita: Rituals, Fiestas and Religious Discourses." *The Journal of the Royal Anthropological Institute* 3(2): 279–296.

Napolitano, Valentina. 2002. *Migration, Mujercitas and Medicine Men: Living in Urban Mexico*. Berkeley and Los Angeles: University of California Press.

Nash, June and María Patricia Fernández-Kelly, eds. 1983. *Women, Men and the International Division of Labor*. New York: State University of New York Press.

Niessen, Sandra, Ann Marie Leshkowich, and Carla Jones. 2003. *Re-Orienting Fashion: The Globalization of Asian dress*. Oxford/New York: Berg.

Niessen, Sandra and Anne Brydon, eds. 1998. *Consuming Fashion: Adorning the Transnational Body*. Oxford: Berg.

Newell, Roberto G. and Luis F. Rubio. 1984. *Mexico's Dilemma: The Political Origins of Economic Crisis*. Boulder: Westview Press.

Ong, Aihwa. 2010. *Spirits of Resistance and Capitalist Discipline: Factory Women in Malaysia*. Albany, NY: State University of New York Press.

Ossman, Susan. 2002. *Three Faces of Beauty: Casablanca, Paris, Cairo*. Durham, NC: Duke University Press.

Parrado, Emilio A. and René M. Zenteno. 2001. "Economic Restructuring, Financial Crises, and Women's Work in Mexico." *Social Problems* 48(4) Special Issue on Globalization and Social Problems: 456–477.

Pastor, Manuel. 1998. "Why the Surprise, and Why the Recovery?" In *The Post NAFTA Political Economy*, edited by Carol Wise, 119-147. Pennsylvania: University of Pennsylvania Press.

Pastor, Manuel and Carol Wise. 1998. "Mexican Style Neoliberalism: State Policy and Distributional Stress." In *The Post-NAFTA Political Economy*, edited by Carol Wise, 41–81. Pennsylvania: University of Pennsylvania Press.

Paz, Octavio. 2002 [1950]. "The sons of La Malinche." In *The Mexico Reader: History, Culture, Politics*, edited by Gilbert Joseph & Timothy Henderson, 20–27. North Carolina: Duke University Press.

Pedrero Nieto, Mercedes. 1990. "Evolucion de la Participacion Economica Femenina en los Ochenta." *Revista Mexicana de Sociología* 52(1): 133–149.

Peiss, Kathy. 1998. *Hope in a Jar: The Making of America's Beauty Culture*. New York: Henry Holt and Company.

Peiss, Kathy. 2002. "Educating the Eye of the Beholder—American Cosmetics Abroad." *Daedalus* 131(4): 101–9.

Peterson, V. Spike. 2003. *A Critical Rewriting of Global Political Economy: Integrating Reproductive, Productive and Virtual Economics*. New York: Routledge.

Peterson, V. Spike and Anne Sisson Runyan. 1999. *Global Gender Issues*. Second edition. Boulder, CO: Westview Press.

Peterson, V. Spike. 2009. "Interactive and Intersectional Analytics of Globalization," *Frontiers*; 30(1) Research Library Core p. 31.

Pettman, Jan Jindy. 1996. "An International Political Economy of Sex?" In *Globalization: Theory and Practice*, edited by Eleanore Kofman and Gillian Youngs, 191–208. London: Pinter.

Pettman, Jan Jindy. 1996. *Worlding Women: A Feminist International Politics*. London & New York: Routledge.

Pozos Ponce, Fernando, 2004. "Guadalajara: En Busqueda de una Nueva Function Urbana?" *Espiral,* Enero/Abril, ano/vol.X, numero 029. Universidad de Gualdalajara. Guadalajara, Mexico. pp. 135–160.
Prahalad, C. K., 1996. *The Fortune at the Bottom of the Pyramid.* Philadelphia: Pearson Prentice Hall.
Prahalad, C. K. 2006. *The Fortune at the Bottom of the Pyramid: Eradicating Poverty through Profits.* New Jersey: Wharton School Publishing.
Prügl, Elisabeth. 1999. *The Global Construction of Gender: Home-Based Work in the Political Economy of the 20th Century.* New York: Columbia University Press.
Prügl, Elisabeth. 2010. "Toward a Feminist Political Economics." *International Feminist Journal of Politics* 4(1)2002: 31–36. doi: 10.1080/14616740110116164. 31–36.
Randall, Kimberly. 2005. "The Traveler's Eye: Chinas Poblanas and European-Inspired Costume in Postcolonial Mexico." In *The Latin American Fashion Reader,* edited by Regina Root, 44–75. Oxford: Berg.
Rénique, Gerardo. 2003. "Race, Region, and Nation: Sonora's Anti-Chinese Racism and Mexico's Postrevolutionary Nationalism, 1920s-1930s." In *Race and Nation in Modern Latin America,* edited by Nancy P. Appelbaum, Anne S. McPherson, and Karin Alejandra Rosemblatt, 211–236. Chapel Hill: University of North Carolina Press.
Rhode, Deborah L., 2011. *The Beauty Bias: The Injustice of Appearance in Life and Law.* New York: Oxford University Press.
Root, Regina. ed. 2005. *The Latin American Fashion Reader.* Oxford: Berg.
Rubenstein, Anne. 2002. "El Santo's Strange Career." In *The Mexico reader: History, Culture, Politics,* edited by Joseph Gilbert M. and Timothy J. Henderson, 570–578. Durham, NC: Duke University Press.
Rugh, Andrea. 1986. *Reveal and Conceal: Dress in Contemporary Egypt.* Syracuse, NY: Syracuse University Press.
Safa, Helen. 1981. "Runaway Shops and Female Employment: The Search for Cheap Labor." *Signs: Journal of Women in Culture and Society* 7(2): 418–33.
Salcedo, Michele. 1997. *Quinceañera!: The Essential Guide to Planning the Perfect Sweet Fifteen Celebration.* New York: Henry Holt.
Salzinger, Leslie. 2003. *Genders in Production: Making Workers in Mexico's Global Factories.* Berkeley: University of California Press.
Santamaria Gomez, Arturo. 1997. *El Culto a las Reinas de Sinaloa y el Poder de la Belleza.* Mexico: Universidad Autónoma de Sinaloa, Comisión de Promoción y Desarrollo Tuístico de Mazátlan, Colegio de Bachilleres del Estado de Sinalóa.
Scott, Joan Wallach. 1988. *Gender and the Politics of History.* New York: Columbia University Press.
Seager, Joni. 2003. *The Penguin Atlas of Women in the World.* New York: Penguin.
Secretaría de Desarollo Social (SEDESOL), Consejo Nacional de Población (CONAPO), and Instituto Nacional de Estadística, Geografía e Informática (INEGI). 2007. Delimitación de las zonas metropolitanas de México 2005. Mexico: SEDESOL, CONAPO, and INEGI.
Skoggard, Ian. 1998. Transnational Commodity Flows and the Global Phenomenon of the Brand. In *Consuming Fashion: Adorning the Transnational Body,* edited by Sandra Niessen and Anne Brydon, 57–70. Oxford: Berg.
Standing, Guy. 1989. Global Feminization Through Flexible Labor. *World Development* 17(7): 1077–1095.

Stern, Alezandra Minna. 2003. "From Mestizophilia to Biotypology: Racialization and Science in Mexico, 1920-1960." In *Race and Nation in Modern Latin America*, edited by Nancy P. Appelbaum, Anne S. McPherson, and Karin Alejandra Rosemblatt, 187–210. Chapel Hill: University of North Carolina Press.

Stevens, Evelyn P. 1973. "*Marianismo*: The Other Face of Machismo in Latin America." In *Female and Male in Latin America: Essays*, edited by Ann Pescatello, 89–101. Pittsburg: University of Pittsburg Press.

Stewart, Heather. 2004. *Senoritas and Princesses: The Quinceñeara as a Context for Female Development*. Unpublished Book.

Tiano, Susan. 1994. *Patriarchy on the Line: Labor, Gender and Ideology in the Mexican Maquila Industry*. Philadelphia, PA: Temple University Press.

Tickner, J. Ann. 1992. *Gender in International Relations: Feminist Perspectives on Achieving National Security*. New York: Columbia University Press.

Tickner, J. Ann. 1996. "Identity in International Relations Theory: Feminist Perspectives." In *The Return of Culture and Identity in IR Theory*, edited by Yosef Lapid and Friedrich Kratochwil, 147–162. Boulder, CO: Lynne Rienner.

Tickner, J. Ann. 2001. *Gendering World Politics: Issues and Approaches in the Post-Cold War Era*. New York: Columbia University Press.

Tomlinson, John. 1999. *Globalization and Culture*. Chicago, IL: The University of Chicago Press.

Tong, R. 1998. *Feminist Thought: A More Comprehensive Introduction*. 2ed. Boulder, CO: Westview Press.

True, Jacqui. 2000. "Gendering Post-Socialist Transitions," In *Gender and Global Restructuring*, edited by Marianne Marchand and Anne Sisson Runyan, 74–94. New York: Routledge.

True, Jacqui. 2003. *Gender, Globalization, and Postsocialism*. New York: Columbia University Press.

Van Gennep, Arnold. 2004. *The Rites of Passage*. Translated by Monika B. Vizedon & Gabrielle L. Caffee. London: Routledge.

Vasconcelos, Jose. 2002 (1925). "The Cosmic Race." Translated by Didier T. Jaén. In *The Mexico Reader: History, Culture, Politics*, edited by Gilbert Joseph & Timothy Henderson, 15–19. Durham, NC: Duke University Press.

Veblen, Thortstein. 1945 (1899). *The Theory of the Leisure Class: An Economic Study of Institutions*. New York: Viking.

Wade, Peter. 1997. *Race and Ethnicity in Latin America*. London: Pluto Press.

Wallerstein, Immanuel. 1995. *Historical Capitalism with Capitalist Civilization*. 2nd Edition London: Verso.

Waring, Marilyn. 1988. *If Women Counted: A New Feminist Economics*. San Francisco: Harper and Row.

Weldon, Laurel S. 2006. "The Structure of Intersectionality: A Comparative Politics of Gender." *Politics & Gender*. 2(2)June 2006: 235–248. DOI: http://dx.doi.org/10.1017/S1743923X06231040 (About DOI), Published online: August 30, 2006.

Wilson, Ara. 1999. "The Empire of Direct Sales and the Making of Thai Entrepreneurs." *Critique of Anthropology* 19(4): 401–422.

Wilson, Ara. 2004. *The Intimate Economies of Bangkok: Tomboys, Tycoons, and Avon Ladies in the Global City*. Berkeley, CA: University of California Press.

Wilson, Elizabeth. 2003. *Adorned in Dreams*. New York: Rutgers.

Wilson, Fiona. 2007. "Mestizaje and Clothing: Interpreting Mexican-US transnational social space." In *Living Across Worlds: Diaspora, Development, and Transnational*

Engagement, edited by Ninna Nyberg Sørensen, 37–59. Geneva: International Organization for Migration.

Wilkinson, Timothy J. and Anna McAlister and Scott Widmier. 2007. "Reaching the International Consumer: An Assessment of the International Direct Marketing Environment." *Direct Marketing: An International Journal* 1(1): 17–37.

Winders, Jamie and John Paul Jones and Michael James Higgins. 2005. "Making Güeras: Selling White Identities on Late-Night Mexican Television." *Gender, Place and Culture* 12(1): 71–93.

Wise, Carol. 1998. "The Trade Scenario for Other Latin Reformers." In *The Post NAFTA Political Economy*, edited by Carol Wise, 259-301. University Park, PA: University of Pennsylvania Press.

Wolf, Naomi. 1991. *The Beauty Myth*. New York: Doubleday.

World Federation of Direct Selling Associations. (WFDSA). 2009d. *2009 Direct Selling Worldwide Corporate Philanthropy Report* online at www.wfdsa.org, last accessed January 23, 2010.

Young, Iris Marion. 2005. *On Female Body Experience: "Throwing Like a Girl" and Other Essays*. New York: Oxford University Press.

Youngs, Gillian. 1996. "Dangers of Discourse: The Case of Globalization." In *Globalization: Theory and Practice*, edited by Eleanore Kofman and Gillian Youngs, 58–71. London: Pinter.

Youngs, Gillian. 2000. "Breaking Patriarchal Bonds: Demythologizing the Public/Private." In *Gender and Global Restructuring*, edited by Marianne Marchand and Ann Sisson Runyan, 44–58. London and New York: Routledge/RIPE Series in Global Political Economy.

Yuval-Davis, Nira. 1997. *Gender and Nation*. London: Sage Publications.

Zolov, Eric. 1999. *Refried Elvis: The Rise of the Mexican Counterculture*. Berkeley: University of California Press.

INDEX

Note: Material in figures or tables is indicated by italic page numbers. Endnotes are indicated by n after the page number.

adolescence
   beauty entrepreneurialism by adolescents, 77, 137, 148
   changing male–female relationships, 47
   fun of, 46–47
   gendered, and global economy of beauty, 92, 139
   gendered, and racialized beautification, 69–73
   gendered, construction through beautification, 76, 78, 158
   global economy of beauty and construction of gendered adolescence, 76, 78, 92, 158
   global economy of beauty driven by youth, 34, 77
   globalization, shaping and generation by youth, 3–4, 13, 34–35, 76–77, 161, 167
   increased liberties, 47
   makeovers and construction of gendered adolescence, 8, 36, 49–50, 76, 85–86, 157
   as privileged identity, 109–111
   quince años and, 45–46, 48, 76
adornments, 14
anti-footbinding movement, 17
arreglandose, 52, 59
   See also beautification, process of

Baywatch, 2
beautification, process of
   adornments, 14
   agency in, 16
   as analytical entry point, 12, 14–18
   artifice in, 76, 90, 91, 157, 167
   comportment, 55–59
   connection to global political economy of beauty, 89–90
   conventional beautification, 50–52
   corsets and body shape, 62, 88, 153
   cosmetics and makeup, 10, 52–53, 72
   dancing, learning, 59–62, 70
   diets, exercise, and body shape, 62–64
   fashion as social process, 68, 138–139, 144, 148
   feminist view as universally oppressive of women, 14–15
   gendered and racialized adolescent beautification, 69–73, 158
   and gender identification and differentiation, 14
   generational tension, 65–66, 109, 158
   global economy of beauty and construction of gendered adolescence, 76, 78, 92, 157–158
   hairstyles, 54–55, 72
   importance of looking good, 50–52, 107–108, 158
   lens of beautification and centrality of bodies, 17
   lens of beautification and social relations, 16–17
   modifications, 14
   overview, 8, 14–18
   productive economy of, 116

beautification (*Cont.*)
   quinceañera dress, 55–59
   racialized beauty consumption and production, 73–76
   and reproductive economy, 94, 97–100
   sources of media and marketing to young people, 73
   tension of originality *vs.* social identification, 66–68
   tension of tradition *vs.* individual taste, 65, 110–111, 158
   usefulness in finding employment, 107–108
   word-of-mouth and friends-and family approach, 98–100, 161
   youth normalization *vs.* particularization and globalization, 64–69
   See also beauty standards; makeovers; *quince años*
beauty industries
   gendered production, reproduction, and consumption, 9, 78
beauty makeovers. *See* makeovers
Beauty Myth, The, 15
beauty pageants, 2, 15–16, 16, 55, 68, 99
beauty premium theory, 16
beauty products
   in cosmetics makeovers, description, 118–119
   direct sales among *quinceañeras*, 10, 85–86, 100–101, 117, 119–120
   See also cosmetics
beauty services
   beauty salon signs and advertisements, 142–143, 178n1–2
   commodification and commercialization of, 10, 105, 159
   employment patterns in personal services, 122–124
   and gendered cultural expectations of labor market, 85
   and global economy of beauty, 85–86
   home-based beauty salons, 85, *91*, 123, *124*
   national hierarchy in beauty services, 109, *110*
   and network-based direct sales of beauty products, 85–86, 100–101
   prestigious beauty salons, 108–109
   privileged status of men, 108–109
   service sector, importance in productive economy of beauty, 10, 121–122
beauty standards
   and biological universals, 16
   changing norms, 157–159, 160
   and color combining, 59
   fashion as social process, 68, 138–139, 144, 148
   feminist rejection of, 15, 176n1(Ch1)
   fresa beauty standards, 57, 139
   general beauty ideals, 52, 63–64
   generational tension, 65–66, 109, 158
   globalization, 4–5
   historical ideals of beauty in Mexico, 150
   and power, 16
   quinceañera beauty standards, 51–52, 59
   racialized aspects of beauty ideals, 73–76
   scholarly focus on hegemonic standards, 140
   tension of originality *vs.* social identification, 66–68
   tension of tradition *vs.* individual taste, 65, 110–111, 158
   variation by culture, 16
   youth normalization *vs.* particularization and globalization, 64–69
   See also beautification, process of
bloomers and early feminists, 15
boys
   clothing, 55, 69–70, 71
   gendered adolescent beautification in Guadalajara, 69–71, 158
   general beauty ideals, 52, 75
   hairstyles, 55, 70, 72
   makeup as outside the masculine norm, 53, 72
   participation in makeover experience, 50
   racialized aspects of beauty ideals, 73–76
   sources of media and marketing of beauty information, 73, 101
bra-burners, 16

CANIPEC survey, 122, *123, 126,* 127, 177n2(Ch5)
caring labor, 18, 32, 132
Carlota, Empress, 41
Catholic Church
   ecclesial base communities (CEBs), 41
   and Mexican colonization process, 30–31
   as privileged institution, 110, 113
   and *quince años* ceremonies, 37–38, 41–42, 113
cell phones, 173, 193
chambelan-de-honor
   Quinceañera (movie), 36, 37
   symbolic relationship with *quinceañera*, 44
   waltz with *quinceañera,* 37, 60, 86
   See also *quince años*
chambelanes (chamberlains)
   beautification processes, 51, 52–64, 61
   clothing, 55, 69–70
   color combining, 55
   dancing, 37, 60–61, 86–88
   as Prince Charming, 48, 69, 98, 112
   professional *chambelanes,* 59, 60, 61, 87, 97
   Quinceañera (movie), 36, 37
   reasons for participating, 47
   and reproductive economy, 98
   socialization of boys, 48
   tuxedos/dinner jackets *(smokings),* 51, 59
   See also *quince años*
color combining, 55, 57, 59, 72–73
commodification of culture
   commodification of beauty signs, 139
   and diversity in consumer markets, 140, 148
   structural hierarchies of access to global economy, 144
   Tianguis Cultural, 136–137, 140, 145, 147–148, 161
cosmetics
   acquisition by *quinceañeras,* 117, 119
   beauty industry consolidation, 121
   CANIPEC survey, 122, *123, 126,* 127, 177n2(Ch5)
   circulation of, 116–117
   cosmetics and toiletries companies, market share, 120–121
   cosmetics makeover, description, 118–119
   direct sales of, 117, 119–120
   employment patterns in cosmetics industry, 122–124, 126
   flexibilization of production, 121–122, 177n1(Ch5)
   global distribution channels, 128–129
   globalizing productive economy of cosmetics, 118–124
   high- and low-valued identities, ideologies, and institutions in cosmetics industry, *125*
   short product life cycle, 121
   structural inequalities in the cosmetics industry, 124–134
   undefined boundary between public and private exchange, 117
   use by *quinceañeras,* 10, 52–53, 118–119
   See also direct sales industry
counter- *macho,* 150
criollos or Creoles, 29

damas (maids-in-waiting)
   beautification processes, 51, 52–64
   dancing, 37, 60
   number of, 37, 41
   Quinceañera (movie), 36, 37
   See also *quince años*
dancing
   commodification and commercialization of, 105
   connection to global political economy of beauty, 87–89
   productive economy, 87
   reproductive economy, 87
   surprise dance, 38, 47, 59–62, 86, 88–89
   toast *(brindis),* 37, 38, 60, 86
   virtual economy, 87, 88, 89
   waltz, learning, 61, 70, 86–87
   waltz music, 87–88
   waltz with father or escort, 36–38, 59–60, 86–87
delgada, definition, 2
Díaz, Porfirio, 30

direct sales industry
  auto-consumption by sales representatives, 135, 178n6
  avenues for further research, 169
  beauty products sales among *quinceañeras*, 10, 85–86, 100–101, 117, 119–120
  employment, 122, *123*, 126, 160
  and empowerment of women, 132, 133–134, 160
  expansion in developing economies, 128–129, 161
  flexibilization of labor markets, 85, 130, 131, 160, 169
  gendered model of labor, 10, 130–132, 134, 178n4(Ch5)
  and globalization, 129
  history, 130–131
  importance in beauty product distribution channels, 117, 126, 127, 161
  low levels of remuneration, 130
  makeovers and network distributors of beauty products, 85–86
  multilevel direct sales marketing, 120, 130–131, 133, 160
  risks and lack of benefits for workers, 133
  sales by product category, 126–127
  as source of entrepreneurialism, 10, 129–130
  and stress of economic pressures, 132–133

economy, definition, 176n5
edecanes (product demonstration models), 107
emos, 147, 177n6
emotional support, coding in field notes, 193
ethnocentric universalization, 24
ethnographic inquiry
  adult interview questions, 198–199
  as analytical entry point, 12, 23–24
  avenues for further research, 168–169
  comparison to RPV framework, 162–165
  direct sales industry, 129
  extended case method, 23–24, 193
  findings, summary, 33–35
  focus on local experience of body politics, 24
  importance of ground-up view, 24, 164–165, 168
  informant demographics, 31–33
  and marginalized subjectivities, 24
  methods, 191–194
  research setting and historical context, 25–31
  youth interview questions, 195–198
etiquette learning through reproductive economy, 93
Euromonitor, 141
Expo Quinceañera, 39, 56, 59, 68, 83, 86–87, 99

fashion
  commodification of, 139, 151
  globalization of, 5–6, 139, 140
  Northern consumers and women's fashion consumption, 6, 20, 106, *164*
  production of increased consumer desire, 139, 141
  as social process, 68, 138–139, 144, 148
Fashionista (James), 1, 2–3, 116
feminist activism
  arguments against categorizing women, 15–16
  beautification viewed as universally oppressive of women, 14–15
  early history, 15
  essentializing of women's experience and interests, criticism of, 21–22
  rejection of mainstream beauty standards, 15, 176n1(Ch1)
  second wave, 15
feminist global political economy
  as analytical entry point, 12, 18–23, 156–157, 176n3
  challenge to public-private divide in politics, 23
  gender lenses, 8, 176n6(Intro)
  reproductive, productive, and virtual (RPV) framing, 18–23
feminization of export-processing labor, 17
fiestas as family events, 50
fiestas de quince años
  costs, 13

importance of looking good, 50–52, 106
overview, 12, 36–37
transition to being a *señorita*, 48
variations, 38
waltzing, 36–38, 59–60, 86–87
See also quince años
fresas (privileged, adolescents), 57–58, 67, 73, 139, 143
Frontier Industrialization Program, 26

gendered division of labor, 89, 111, 117–118, 132, 134, 160
See also specific topics
gendered relations, definition, 175n3
gender hierarchies
among youth subcultures, 35
body and identity dimension, 22–23, 175n2
ideology dimension, 22, 175n2
masculinities valued over femininities, 20, 162–165
social relations dimension, 22, 175n2
structural inequalities in the cosmetics industry, 10, 124–134, 166–167
in youth subcultures, 35, 151, 152, 153–154, 161
gender lenses, 8, 176n6(Intro)
gender socialization
changing norms, 140, 157–159, 167
importance for youth, 150
socialization of boys, 48, 150
socialization of girls, 47–49, 79, 156, 165, 167
General Agreement on Tariff s and Trade (GATT), 27
genital mutilation, 17
girls
awareness of healthy body image, 64, 75–76
color combining, 55, 57, 59, 72–73
cosmetics and makeup, 52–53, 72
diets, exercise, and body shape, 62–64
general beauty ideals, 52, 63–64
hairstyles, 54, 72
quinceañera beauty standards, 51–52
racialized aspects of beauty ideals, 75–76
sources of media and marketing of beauty information, 73, 99–101

See also damas (maids-in-waiting); quinceañeras
globalization
beauty imperialism and corruption of women, 2
of beauty industry, 137–138, 144, 154–155, 169
of beauty products, 4–5, 159–161
of beauty standards, 4–5
competing, parallel beautification globalizations, 144
contribution to diversity, 11, 35, 90, 140, 151, 157–158
creation of a universal beauty ideal, 2
definition, 4, 175nn4–5
and direct sales industry, 129
of fashion, 5–6, 139, 140
and gendered production, reproduction, and consumption, 9, 78–79
globalizing productive economy of cosmetics, 118–124, 129
ground-up view, 24–25, 33, 90
as homogenization, 140, 144, 151, 167
and production of feminine beauty, 8–9, 17–18, 34–35, 78–79, 90–92
and the reproduction of beauty, 94–95
shaping and generation by young people, 3–4, 13, 34–35
of subcultures, 11, 140
transforming global beauty context, 144–145
youth normalization *vs.* particularization and globalization, 64–69
Global Political Economy (GPE), 18, 23, 176n3
See also feminist global political economy; International Political Economy (IPE)
god's-eye-view analyses, 24
Guadalajara
conservative Mexican national identity, 30–31
and export-oriented growth, 26
Guadalajara Metropolitan Zone (ZMG), 25, 29, 141, 143, 166
historical context, 25–31

Index [205]

Guadalajara (*Cont.*)
  import substitution industrialization (ISI) model, 26–27, 28
  industrialization, 26
  migration, 25–26
  plazas (commercial malls and plazas), 28, *40*, 136
  population, 25
  quinceañera and bridal shopping district, *40*, 82, 98
  second-largest metropolitan area in Mexico, 2, 25
  stereotype of beautiful women, 31
  structural adjustments in 1980s and 1990s, 27–28
  tianguis (street markets), 28, 119, 136, 143, 152
  transition from manufacturing to distribution and sales, 28

hair
  boys' hairstyles, 55, 70, 72
  coding in field notes, 193
  emo hairstyles, 177n6
  fauxhawk, 54, 55
  quinceañera hairstyles, 54
historical gender ideals in Mexico, 148–151

import substitution industrialization (ISI) economic growth model, 26–27, 28
"indebted industrialization," 26
indigenous groups, prejudices against, 58–59, 75
informalization in the global economy, 104
insecurities, coding in field notes, 193
International Monetary Fund (IMF), 27
International Political Economy (IPE), 18–19, 20, 23, 176nn2–3(Ch1)
  See also Global Political Economy (GPE)
International Relations (IR), 17, 20, 23, 171–172, 176n2(Ch1)
intersectional feminist analysis, 21–22, 162
intersectionality, 22, 139

James, Jimmy, 1, 2, 116

lipstick and early feminists, 15
L'Occoco, Alejandro, 109
Lozano, Aurelio, 108

machismo, 149–150
macho ideal of masculinity, 150, 178n4(Ch4)
Madrid, Miguel de la, 27
madrinas and *padrinos* (godparents), 42, 45, 79, 96–97, 177n1(Ch4)
makeovers
  avenues for further research, 168
  beauty salons, 85, 99
  and construction of gendered adolescence, 76, 157
  cosmetics makeovers, description, 118–119
  and global economy of beauty, 85–86, 88–92
  importance in *quince años*, 12, 36, 76, 157
  and network distributors of beauty products, 85–86
  participation of boys, 50
  as universal rite of passage, 8, 45, 49–50, 118, 157, 168
  See also beautification, process of; cosmetics
Malinche, la, 149
Malone, Annie Turnbo, 130
maquiladoras (in-bond factories), 26, 122, 177n1(Ch5)
marianismo, 44, 149, 177n4
mestizaje, 30
mestizos, 29, 30
metaleros (metalheads)
  band t-shirts, 145–146, 152
  color coordination, 59, 147
  fashion signals, 145–147
  masculine and feminine gender norms, 153–154
  posers, 145, 146, 154, 177n6
  sense of exclusivity, 144–145, 146–147
  values, or way of life, 145, 146
  vampiras, 145, 154
metropolitan areas in Mexico, 2, 25
metrosexual masculinity, 107, 110, 162, 165–166, 167
Mexico, historical background
  colonial period, 29

Cristero Wars, 30–31
export-oriented growth, 26
Frontier Industrialization Program, 26
historical gender ideals in Mexico, 148–151
import substitution industrialization (ISI) economic growth model, 26–27, 28
"indebted industrialization," 26
integration into global economy, 28
and International Monetary Fund (IMF), 27
metropolitan areas in Mexico, 2, 25
national identity, 29–30, 176n7
North American Free Trade Agreement (NAFTA), 27, 177n1(Ch5)
race and racism, 30, 176n8
state-led modernization and nationalization, 28, 29
structural adjustment program (SAP), 27
structural adjustments in 1980s and 1990s, 27–28
transition from manufacturing to distribution and sales, 28
middle class in Mexico, characteristics, 31–33, 38, 96, 101, 105, 109, 120, 141, 157
Mier de Varela, Graciela, 120
Miss America contest, 15–16
Miss Universe, 2

naca(o), 58
network marketing. *See* direct sales industry
North American Free Trade Agreement (NAFTA), 27, 177n1(Ch5)
Northern consumers and women's fashion consumption, 6, 20, 106, *164*

padrinos and *madrinas* (godparents), 42, 45, 79, 96–97, 177n1(Ch4)
peninsulares, 29
piercings, 71, 147, 153, 177n9
plazas (commercial malls and plazas), 28, 40, 136
posers, 145, 146, 154, 177n6
productive economy, overview, 18–19

productive economy of beauty
beauty industry consolidation, 121
CANIPEC survey, 122, *123, 126*, 127, 177n2(Ch5)
cosmetics and toiletries companies, market share, 120–121
dancing, 87
definition, 116
direct sales of cosmetics, 117, 119–120
distribution channels, market share, 117, 126, 127
flexibilization of labor markets, 85, 114, 131, 160, 169, 177n1(Ch5)
flexibilization of production, 121–122, 129, 169, 177n1(Ch5)
gendered division of labor, 117–118, 160
globalizing productive economy of cosmetics, 118–124
opportunities for some women, 10, 117–118
privileged identities, 134–135, *163–164*
in the *quince años*, 79
service sector, importance of, 10, 121–122
short product life cycle in beauty industry, 121
as source of entrepreneurialism, 4, 10, 129–130
structural inequalities, 124–134, 166–167
undefined boundary between public and private exchange, 4, 117
See also cosmetics; direct sales industry
punk culture, 59, 144, 147

quinceañera dresses
color combination, 57–59
copying, 82
designers, 82–83
desire for uniqueness, 56, 82, 84
global virtual economy of signs and dress design, 84
and process of beautification, 55–59
production of, 84
shopping districts, *40*, 81, 82
shopping for and selecting, 81–84
Quinceañera (movie), 36–37

Index [207]

quinceañeras
- becoming *señoritas* or "Misses," 8, 46, 48
- color combining, 55, 57, 59
- comportment, 59–62
- cosmetics and makeup, 52–53
- cosmetics makeover, description, 118–119
- dance classes, 47, 86–87
- definition, 36, 176n1(Ch2)
- diets, exercise, and body shape, 62–64
- dresses, color combination, 57–59
- dresses, copying, 82
- dresses, desire for uniqueness, 56, 82, 84
- dresses, shopping districts, *40*, 81, 82
- dresses, shopping for and selecting, 81–84
- dresses and process of beautification, 55–59
- hairstyles, 54
- makeovers, importance of, 12, 36, 76
- in marketing and advertising, 80–81
- surprise dance, 38, 47, 59–62, 86, 88–89
- toast (*brindis*), 37, 38, 60, 86
- waltz, learning, 61, 70, 86–87
- waltz with father or escort, 36–38, 59–60, 86–87

quince años
- adolescence and, 45–46
- as analytical entry point, 12–13
- beauty globalization and, 13–14
- for boys, 48–49, 176n1(Ch2)
- Catholic Mass, 37–38
- as coming-of-age rite of passage, 8, 37, 43–44
- comparison to Western-style weddings, 8, 13, 38, 39, 111
- connection to global political economy of beauty, 8–9, 78–79, 88–92
- costs, 13, 96–97
- family as privileged institution, 112
- format and main elements, in Guadalajara, 36–39
- gender difference as privileged institution, 111, 112
- heterosexual marriage as privileged institution, 113
- history and changes, 12–13, 39–40, 41, 102–104, 110
- list of preparation activities, 38–39
- as living tradition, 44–50
- as Mass attendance and a family meal in 1960s, 103
- meaning, questions about, 40–44
- overview, 8, 12–13, 36–37, 76–77
- *padrinos* and *madrinas* (godparents or sponsors), 42, 45, 79, 96–97, 177n1(Ch4)
- as party in the streets, 102–103
- as path to courtship and marriage, 42–43
- privileged identities in, *106*, 107–108, 109–111, 162, *163*
- privileged ideologies, *106*, 111–112, *163*
- religions nature of, questions about, 40–42
- reproducing gender in, 95–101
- reproductive labor, increasing role of, 103–104, 115, 157, 159
- as social debut, 102, 103
- and socialization skills, 47–48
- and social networks, 47–48, 79–80
- symbolic rituals, 38
- variations, 37, 176n2(Ch2), 177n3(Ch2)
- *See also* beautification, process of; *fiestas de quince años*

rape as act of war, 17
reproductive, productive, and virtual (RPV) framework
- and beauty industry, 134–135, 159, 161
- categorization of three types of global virtual exchange, 138
- comparison to ethnographic inquiry, 162–165
- convenience for analysis of global beauty politics, 20, 34, 91–92
- feminism as important feature, 20–21
- gendered globalization and, 9, 78–79
- gender hierarchies, 21–23, 166–167
- high- and low-valued identities, ideologies, and institutions in cosmetics industry, *125*
- overview, 18–20

privileged identities in global
  economy, 106, 134–135,
  162–167, 178n5
triad analytics of identities, social
  institutions, and ideologies
  categories, 21–23, 162, *163*
See also productive economy;
  reproductive economy; virtual
  economy
reproductive, productive, and virtual
  (RPV) framing
  feminist global political economy, 18–23
reproductive economy
  in beautification of the *quinceañera*,
    94, 97–100, 159
  in beauty information, 99–101
  caring labor, 18, 32, 132
  changing role of, 102–105
  commercialization and
    commodification of labor, 10,
    104–105, 115, 157
  and dancing, 87
  definition, 94
  gendered division of labor, 111
  and global economy of beauty,
    113–115, 159–160
  globalization and the reproduction of
    beauty, 94–95
  increased role of reproductive labor,
    103–104, 115, 157, 159–160
  overview, 18, 19, 93–95
  privileged identities, 106–111
  privileged ideologies, *106*, 111–112,
    165–166
  privileged institutions, *106*, 112–113
  in the *quince años*, 9, 79–80, 95–115,
    159
  reproducing gender in the *quince años*,
    95–101
  reproductive labor viewed as
    unimportant and infinite, 19
  social etiquette, 93
  and social networks, 79–80, 95–96
  as source of entrepreneurialism by
    women, 105, 107, 114, 135
  See also reproductive, productive, and
    virtual (RPV) framework
rites of passage
  beauty makeover, 8, 45, 49–50, 118,
    157, 168

criteria, 49
Mayan and Aztec traditions, 41
quince años as coming-of-age rite of
  passage, 8, 37, 43–44
rituals of incorporation, 43–44
rituals of separation, 43, 44, 50
rituals of transition, 43, 44, 45, 50

Salinas de Gortari, Carlos, 27
sex industry, 16, 17
skateboarders or *skate* style, 147
Social Darwinism, 30
social etiquette, learning through
  reproductive economy, 93
Southern women's labor in apparel
  industry, 6, 20, *164*
structural adjustment program (SAP), 27
subcultures
  color coordination, 59
  commodification of beauty ideal, 137,
    151
  commodification of culture, 136–137,
    140
  diverse range of fashion and beauty
    ideals, 137
  emos, 147, 177n6
  gender hierarchies in, 35, 151, 152,
    153–154, 161
  globalization of, 11, 140
  increasing diversity, 11, 140, 151
  posers, 145, 146, 154, 177n6
  psychos, 59, 147
  punks, 59, 144, 147
  resistance to change in structures
    of gender difference, 151, 152,
    153–154, 161
  skateboarders or *skate* style, 147
  vampiras, 145, 154
  See also metaleros (metalheads)

Tianguis Cultural
  for artisans and wholesalers, 141,
    145, 152
  commodification of culture, 136–137,
    145, 147–148, 161
  history and background, 145, 152
  sale of alternate and locally designed
    clothing, 144, 147, 152
  as weekly social event, 136, 147–148
  weekly street market description, 136

Index [209]

tianguis (street markets), 28, 119, 136, 143, 152
triad analytics
    identities, social institutions, and ideologies as categories, 21–23, 162, *163*
    intersectional feminist analysis, 21–22

ugly, 1, 3, 58, 162, *163*
universalization, 24
unmarked man, 153

vampiras, 145, 154
Varela, Enrique, 120
Vasconcelos, Jose, 30
Vergara, Jorge, 120
vertical segregation, 109, 134, 166
virgen, la, 149
virtual economy
    avenues for further research, 168
    beauty salon signs and advertisements, 142–143, 178nn1–2
    commodification of beauty ideal, 137, 139, 160–161
    competing, parallel beautification globalizations, 144
    and dancing, 87, 88, 89
    dress design and global virtual economy of signs, 84
    exchange of beauty signs and information, 84, 138–139, 141–145, 154
    exchange of symbols, 137, 141–145
    finance, information, and cultural modes, 137–138
    globalization of beauty industry, 137–138, 144, 154–155, 169
    globalization of fashion, 5–6, 139, 140
    naturalization of consumption, 141
    overview, 18, 137–140
    privileged identities, 139–140, *163–164*, 165
    production of increased consumer desire, 139, 141
    promotion of white, Anglo-American beauty ideals, 137, 139, 141, 142–143
    in the *quince años*, 18, 79, 80–81
    RPV categorization of three types of global virtual exchange, 138
    sources of media and marketing of beauty information, 73, 99–101, 139–140
    structural inequalities, 152–154, 166–167
    surprise dances and global virtual economy of signs, 84
    transforming global beauty context, 144–145
    See also reproductive, productive, and virtual (RPV) framework

Walker, C. J., 130
war, gendered nature of, 17

Printed in the USA/Agawam, MA
February 22, 2019